Eurykleia and Her Successors

Greek Studies: Interdisciplinary Approaches
General Editor: Gregory Nagy, Harvard University
Assistant Editor: Timothy Power, Harvard University

On the front cover: A calendar frieze representing the Athenian months, reused in the Byzantine Church of the Little Metropolis in Athens. The cross is superimposed, obliterating Taurus of the Zodiac. The choice of this frieze for books in *Greek Studies: Interdisciplinary Approaches* reflects this series' emphasis on the blending of the diverse heritages—Near Eastern, Classical, and Christian—in the Greek tradition. Drawing by Laurie Kain Hart, based on a photograph. Recent titles in the series are:

The Shield of Achilles and the Poetics of Ekphrasis, Andrew Sprague Becker, Virginia Polytechnic Institute

The Blinded Eye: Thucydides and the New Written Word, Gregory Crane, Tufts University

The Wrath of Athena: Gods and Men in the Odyssey, Jenny Strauss Clay, University of Virginia

Talking Trojan: Speech and Community in the Iliad, Hilary Mackie, Rice University

Poet and Audience in the Argonautica *of Apollonius*, Robert V. Albis, The Hotchkiss School

Theatrical Space and Historical Place in Sophocles' Oedipus at Colonus, Lowell Edmunds, Rutgers University

Choruses of Young Women in Ancient Greece: Their Morphology, Religious Role, and Social Function, Claude Calame, University of Lausanne, Switzerland; translated by Derek Collins and Jane Orion

Eurykleia and Her Successors: Female Figures of Authority in Greek Poetics, Helen Pournara Karydas, Boston Latin School and Harvard University

Speech in Speech: Studies in Incorporated Oratio Recta *in Attic Drama and Oratory*, Victor Bers, Yale University

Aegean Strategies: Studies of Culture and Environment on the European Fringe, P. Nick Kardulias, College of Wooster and Mark T. Shutes, Youngstown State University

Aglaia: The Poetry of Alcman, Sappho, Pindar, Bacchylides, and Corinna, Charles Segal, Harvard University

ROWMAN & LITTLEFIELD PUBLISHERS, INC.

Published in the United States of America
by Rowman & Littlefield Publishers, Inc.
4720 Boston Way, Lanham, Maryland 20706

12 Hid's Copse Road
Cummor Hill, Oxford OX2 9JJ, England

Copyright © 1998 by Rowman & Littlefield Publishers, Inc.

All rights reserved. No part of this publication may be reproduced, stored in a retrieval system, or transmitted in any form or by any means, electronic, mechanical, photocopying, recording, or otherwise, without the prior permission of the publisher.

British Library Cataloguing in Publication Information Available

Library of Congress Cataloging-in-Publication Data

Karydas, Helen Pournara, 1946–
  Eurykleia and her successors : female figures of authority in Greek poetics / Helen Pournara Karydas.
    p.   cm. — (Greek studies)
  Includes index.
  ISBN 0–8226–3066–4 (cloth : alk. paper). — ISBN 0–8226–3067–2 (pbk. : alk. paper)
  1. Greek literature—History and criticism. 2. Women and literature—Greece—History. 3. Eurycleia (Greek mythology) in literature. 4. Euripides—Characters—Nurses. 5. Sophocles—Characters—Nurses. 6. Aeschylus—Characters—Nurses. 7. Homer—Characters—Eurycleia. 8. Aged women in literature. 9. Authority in literature. 10. Nurses in literature. I. Title. II. Series.
PA3015.W65k37   1998
880.9'352613—dc21   98-448
Printed in the United States of America   CIP

☉™ The paper used in this publication meets the minimum requirements of American National Standard for Information Sciences—Permanence of Paper for Printed Library Materials, ANSI Z39.48–1984.

Eurykleia and Her Successors

*Female Figures of Authority
in Greek Poetics*

HELEN POURNARA KARYDAS

ROWMAN & LITTLEFIELD PUBLISHERS, INC.
Lanham • New York • Boulder • Oxford

Contents

Foreword by Gregory Nagy	vii
Acknowledgements	ix
Introduction	1
1 Eurykleia, the Predecessor	8
1. Introduction	8
2. Eurykleia, the Nurse of Telemakhos	11
2.1. Eurykleia and Telemakhos	11
2.2. Eurykleia and Penelope	18
2.3. The Return of Telemakhos	20
3. The Recognition of the Old Master	22
3.1. Eurykleia and the Stranger	22
3.2. The Recognition	25
3.3. The Competition for Authority	28
4. Eurykleia in Full Authority	32
4.1. Eurykleia defends Penelope	32
4.2. In Charge of the Maids	34
4.3. The 'Old Woman' as Odysseus' Accomplice	36
5. Eurykleia and the Reunion of the Couple	43
5.1. The Persuasion of Penelope	43
5.2. Tricking Odysseus	48
5.3. Eurykleia and the Reunion of the Couple	50
5.4. Eurynome, Another Nurse	51
6. Conclusions	53
7. Table I: Eurykleia's Interaction with the Other Characters	59
8. Table II: Summary of the Epithets of Eurykleia	60
9. Table III: Summary of the Terms 'Nurse' and 'Old Woman'	62
2 Nurse Characters in Aeschylus, Sophocles, and Euripides	64
1. Introduction	64
2. Kilissa and the Change of Klytaimnestra's Orders in Aeschylus' *Libation-Bearers*	64
3. The Nurse Triggers the Action in Sophocles' *Women of Trachis*	76
4. Nurse and Handmaid in Euripides' *Andromache*	83
5. The Nurse in Euripides' *Medea*: The Nurse who Foreshadows her Mistress	93

3 The Nurse in Euripides' *Hippolytus*	115
1. Introduction	115
2. The Nurse Among the *Sophoi*	119
3. The Nurse as the Advocate of Speech	131
4. The *Agôn* or the 'Contest of Words'	140
5. The Nurse as the Advocate of Action	162
6. Phaedra in Charge of Speech and Action	168
7. Conclusions	176
Bibliography	181
Index	191
About the Author	199

Greek Studies: Interdisciplinary Approaches

Foreword

by Gregory Nagy, General Editor

Building on the foundations of scholarship within the disciplines of philology, philosophy, history, and archaeology, this series spans the continuum of Greek traditions extending from the second millennium BCE to the present, not just the Archaic and Classical periods. The aim is to enhance perspectives by applying various disciplines to problems that have in the past been treated as the exclusive concern of a single given discipline. Besides the crossing-over of the older disciplines, as in the case of historical and literary studies, the series encourages the application of such newer ones as linguistics, sociology, anthropology, and comparative literature. It also encourages encounters with current trends in methodology, especially in the realm of literary theory.

Eurykleia and Her Successors: Female Figures of Authority in Greek Poetics, by Helen Karydas, examines the role of the "Nurse" in epic and tragedy from the historical standpoint of early Greek traditions of education, especially women's education. Karydas proves that the role of the Nurse in the upbringing of young boys and girls is not just a literary construct: it is an educational reality, at least in the aristocratic traditions of early Greek society. This reality comes to life in the portrayal of the nurse Eurykleia in the Homeric *Odyssey*.

Moreover, Karydas shows that the educational role of the Nurse as a model of authority is closely related to another role, that of the *khorêgos* or "chorus-leader." Moving beyond the innovative contexts of classical Athenian society, where the word *khorêgos* designates a prominent citizen who undertakes the costs of producing dramas for the State Theater, Karydas investigates the more archaic contexts of conservative Dorian societies like that of Sparta, where *khorêgos* refers to the premier performer in a traditional *khoros* or "chorus," which is an ensemble of singing *and* dancing performers. According to early Greek customs, choral performances were centerpieces of festive occasions involving the whole community. On those occasions where the *khoros* was comprised of females, the *khorêgos* could be male *or* female. As the premier performer, the *khorêgos* was a model of authority for members of the *khoros*.

More important for now, the *female* chorus-leader was a model of *female* authority for members of the chorus. Here Karydas builds on the discoveries of Claude Calame, whose exhaustive historical survey of female choruses in early Greece has revealed a basic principle in the "educating" of girls and women in ancient Greece: the hierarchy implicit in the *khorêgos* interacts with the egalitarianism implicit in the rank-and-file membership of the *khoros*, and this interaction becomes symbolic of the community or even of society writ large. The educational symbolism of this relationship between *khorêgos* and *khoros*, Karydas finds, is replicated in the highly evolved choral conventions of Athenian drama: in tragedies like the *Hippolytus* of Euripides, we see the archaic patterns of interaction between *khorêgos* and *khoros* replayed in the novel form of dramatic tensions between the authoritative (but fallible) old Nurse and the vulnerable (but determined) young woman placed under her care. The sentimental education of a tragic young woman like Phaedra is a far cry, we discover, from the choral "formation" of the archaic Kore.

Acknowledgements

I wish to express my thanks to all who helped in the completion of this book. To Michael Halleran, for his continuous support and his constructive criticism from the early stages, and to Mary Whitlock Blundell for her challenging insight. To Mary Lefkowitz, Peter Reid, and Jeffrey Henderson for their support and our stimulating discussions, and for giving me the opportunity to present parts of this research at Wellesley College, Tufts, and Boston University; I also want to extend my thanks to the members of the Classics Departments of these colleges for their useful comments. My warmest thanks to Nicole Loraux, and to Sheila Murnaghan, who, by sharing with me their valuable insight, helped me crystallize many of my ideas.

I am indebted to Harvard University and especially to the Department of the Classics for their generous fellowship that provided me with a stimulating and congenial environment in which to complete this project. I wish to thank all the members of the Department of the Classics at Harvard who shared with me their insight and their comments during the presentations of various parts of this book. My sincere thanks to Richard Tarrant for his interest and support. Special thanks to Margaret Alexiou and to Richard Thomas for their helpful suggestions. I am deeply indebted to Charles Segal for reviewing my book and for offering his invaluable comments, suggestions, and criticism. My very special thanks and deepest gratitude to Gregory Nagy for his generous encouragement and support and for his inspirational insight and guidance. Without him this book would not have been accomplished.

Thanks also to Brenda Sens for her help and support and to Timothy Power for his careful proofreading. Special thanks to Costas Mermengis for his technical assistance.

Finally, I wish to thank with all my heart my husband, Dimitrios, my daughters, Melissa and Daphne, and my mother, Eva, for their help, their patience, and their support. This book is dedicated to them and to the memory of my father.

Introduction

This book discusses the Nurse figures in Greek poetics from Homer to Euripides as figures of female authority. Among the secondary roles in Greek tragedy, the role of the Nurse, the *trophos*, is of special importance and interest. It is a role whose earliest attested extant example is found in the character of Eurykleia in Homer's *Odyssey*. The character of the Nurse appears in the works of all three tragedians—Aeschylus, Sophocles, and Euripides—but it is fully developed by Euripides, to such an extent that it became the model for later tragedians (Seneca, Racine, Shakespeare).

Both in the *Odyssey* and in several Greek tragedies that are centered around women (Aeschylus' *Libation-Bearers*, Sophocles' *Women of Trachis*, Euripides' *Medea*, *Andromache*, and *Hippolytus*), the Nurse plays an important role as a figure of female authority. She displays her authority through her comments of approval or disapproval, her advice, and sometimes her orders. In particular, *Hippolytus* provides the most fully developed Nurse figure, unparalleled in extant drama. Here Phaedra's old Nurse displays an older woman's wisdom, common sense, and reasoning, which she tries to transmit to her younger mistress. Moreover, she appears to have an authority that allows her not only to advise, praise, or blame, but even to direct her mistress.

Despite the importance of the *trophos*, both in epic and in tragedy, no comprehensive study of this influential female figure has yet been undertaken. Modern scholarship refers to the character of the Nurse only *passim* in general works on Greek epic and tragedy or in studies on the *Odyssey* or on particular tragedies.

This book attempts a comprehensive and systematic study of all the extant Nurse figures in Greek literature from Homer to Euripides. It examines all the Nurses in extant tragedy—Aeschylus' *Libation-Bearers*, Sophocles' *Women of Trachis*, Euripides' *Medea*, *Andromache*, and *Hippolytus*—starting with the earliest attested example and predecessor, Eurykleia, the Nurse in Homer's *Odyssey*.

Although this book discusses the Nurse as a literary figure, a few remarks regarding her position in the household will provide a better understanding of her role.

A *trophos* is, as a rule, an older woman, implicitly or explicitly a slave or servant in the household. She is an essential member in the household of noble and wealthy Greek families since the earliest attestations.[1] She is an old and trustful servant regarded as part of the family. The Homeric *Hymn to Demeter* (101-104) provides the oldest and best definition of a Nurse. As Demeter prepares to wander abroad, she is disguised, "looking like an old woman born of old, who has been cut off from childbirth and the gifts of garland-loving Aphrodite, such as are the nurses [*trophoi*] of children of law-giving kings and the stewards [*tamiai*] in their echoing homes." A perfect example of an old woman who is both nurse and steward-housekeeper is Eurykleia.[2]

As the Nurse is typically a servant in the household (cf. Plato *Laws* VII, 790a), she is comparable to other older female or male servants, especially her male counterpart, the Tutor, the *paidagogos*. In addition to rearing children, the role of the Nurse also involved educational duties. As Plato remarks, a child's education started at home where, along with the mother and the father, the *trophos* and the *paidagogos* were the first teachers in the child's ethical formation (*Protagoras* 325c-d). A girl's education [*paideia*] was in the hands of her *trophos*, as the boy's was in the hands of his *paidagogos*. Just as the oldest fully developed figure of the *paidagogos* is found in the *Iliad* in the character of Phoenix, Achilles' teacher, so the oldest fully developed figure of the *trophos* is found in the *Odyssey* in the character of Eurykleia, the Nurse of Odysseus and Telemakhos, advisor of Penelope, and steward of the household. The influence of both *trophos* and *paidagogos* becomes all the more important and respected as these figures are characterized by old age. Old age was connected

---

[1] The institution of the Nurse has much broader synchronic and diachronic applications, but we will restrict our discussion to the extant examples in Greek epic and tragedy.

[2] Eurykleia's role as both nurse and housekeeper matches perfectly the description of Demeter in the *Hymn to Demeter* 101-104, and further 140-144, where Demeter explains in more details the tasks that she can perform as nurse and housekeeper. For a complete discussion see chapter 1.

Acknowledgements

I wish to express my thanks to all who helped in the completion of this book. To Michael Halleran, for his continuous support and his constructive criticism from the early stages, and to Mary Whitlock Blundell for her challenging insight. To Mary Lefkowitz, Peter Reid, and Jeffrey Henderson for their support and our stimulating discussions, and for giving me the opportunity to present parts of this research at Wellesley College, Tufts, and Boston University; I also want to extend my thanks to the members of the Classics Departments of these colleges for their useful comments. My warmest thanks to Nicole Loraux, and to Sheila Murnaghan, who, by sharing with me their valuable insight, helped me crystallize many of my ideas.

I am indebted to Harvard University and especially to the Department of the Classics for their generous fellowship that provided me with a stimulating and congenial environment in which to complete this project. I wish to thank all the members of the Department of the Classics at Harvard who shared with me their insight and their comments during the presentations of various parts of this book. My sincere thanks to Richard Tarrant for his interest and support. Special thanks to Margaret Alexiou and to Richard Thomas for their helpful suggestions. I am deeply indebted to Charles Segal for reviewing my book and for offering his invaluable comments, suggestions, and criticism. My very special thanks and deepest gratitude to Gregory Nagy for his generous encouragement and support and for his inspirational insight and guidance. Without him this book would not have been accomplished.

Thanks also to Brenda Sens for her help and support and to Timothy Power for his careful proofreading. Special thanks to Costas Mermengis for his technical assistance.

Finally, I wish to thank with all my heart my husband, Dimitrios, my daughters, Melissa and Daphne, and my mother, Eva, for their help, their patience, and their support. This book is dedicated to them and to the memory of my father.

with experience and wisdom, and it invited respect and attention. For women, especially, age conferred authority and power.[3]

The Nurse, through her function as an essential character in the education of children, especially of young girls, had special power and influence. As our discussion of the examples in Greek epic and tragedy will show, she has the authority to advise her mistress and express her approval or disapproval, and so exercise her influence on her. Her influence on her male masters is just as important, as the case of Odysseus will show. (Unfortunately, we have no instance of a nurse/master relationship in tragedy.)

Since this book focuses on the Nurse's authority, a working definition of authority, as the term is used in my discussion, is necessary. This authority is manifested through the Nurse's advice, approval or disapproval (praise or blame), directions and orders, and also through the respect, influence, and effectiveness that they inspire in the different characters to whom they are addressed. The authority of a Nurse may be determined from her speech, and from its effectiveness. Therefore, the focus of this study is on the verbal manifestations of a Nurse's authority—advice, approval, disapproval, directions, orders—and their effectiveness on her master and mistress, or on the other characters with whom she interacts.

The speech of a Nurse is also examined in regard to the message it conveys and the tone with which it is delivered (verbal moods, especially the imperative, will be important clues); special emphasis is also given to key words which in traditional poetic language are registered as speech of authority.[4] In the discussion of the epic figure Eurykleia, her epithets will be examined carefully, since they represent the narrator's voice, the narrator's perception and presentation of her character.[5] In the discussion of the Nurse figures in tragedy, since the narrator's voice is missing, comments and characterization provided by other characters, and especially by the chorus, will be examined instead.

In addition, an attempt is made to trace back the Nurse's authority to models of female hierarchy in early choral lyric performances; this book examines how the poetics of female *paideia* in early choral performances are appropriated and reshaped in the poetics of epic

---

[3] On the elderly in Greek literature see M. I. Finley 1981.156-71; on the portrayal of older women in Attic Old Comedy see Henderson 1987.105-129.

[4] On the traditional language of poetic authority see Nagy 1989.1-77, especially 8-11.

[5] On the meaningful use of the epithet by Homer, see introduction to chapter 1.

4 *Introduction*

and tragedy. It discusses the possible development of the Nurse figure from a model of fundamental hierarchy embodied in the figure of the lyric *khorêgos*, the female leader of a *khoros* (a song and dance circle) of early choral performances (e.g., in Alcman's maiden song PMG 1). In pursuing this goal, I follow the interpretation of Claude Calame, further developed and supported by Gregory Nagy.[6] I suggest that a 'contest of words' like that between Phaedra and her Nurse in *Hippolytus* 373-524 (as each presents a course of action after Phaedra's love for Hippolytus is revealed), is an agonistic performance that also resembles the choral contest between two 'leading' lyric personalities like Agido and Hagesikhora in Alcman PMG 1.[7] These resemblances pertain to diction, dramatized occasion, and constructs of hierarchy.[8]

Moreover, following Calame and Nagy in their interpretation of early lyric compositions and their survival in Athenian drama, I further investigate the survival of the female *khorêgos* of lyric songs and dances in drama in the differentiated form of the *trophos*. As Nagy has suggested, the early lyric persona of the *khorêgos* survived in Athenian drama in an undifferentiated form as the chorus-leader and in a differentiated form as one of the main actors.[9]

This book discusses first the most developed predecessor, the Homeric Nurse Eurykleia. Then it looks at the other Nurse characters in Aeschylus, Sophocles, and Euripides, with special attention to the

---

[6] Calame 1977.437-439 [=Calame 1997.255-258], and Nagy 1990a.344ff. Calame has suggested that the *khoros* is a microcosm of society and consequently a microcosm of social hierarchy within which a majority of younger members act out a pattern of subordination to a minority of older leaders. The concept of older leaders, within the hierarchy of the *khoros*, is, in most instances, embodied in the central persona of the female *khorêgos* the 'leader of the *khoros*'; the superiority of the *khorêgos* vs. the egalitarian choral aggregate is a fundamental model of hierarchy.

[7] An example of the choral form as a hierarchical construct is the Spartan song sung and danced by the chorus of Spartan girls, as dramatized in Alcman PMG 1. In this composition Hagesikhora, the 'leader of the *khoros*', competes with another 'leading' personality, Agido, dramatized as the choral rival of Hagesikhora. See Calame 1977.437-439 [=Calame 1997.255-258].

[8] A possible similarity with a figure like Sappho, who, as Nagy notes, stepped out of the *khoros* circle into monody, is also considered. "The voice of the *khorêgos* can also be found in the 'I' of a personality like Sappho, whose persona speaks as a *khorêgos* both to and about members of an aggregate of female characters who are bound together by ties that correspond to the ties that bind a *khoros* together.... A figure like Sappho speaks in a monodic form, as a choral personality, even when the element of dancing and even the presence of a choral group are missing" (Nagy 1990a.370, 344-347).

[9] Nagy 1990a.377-379.

Introduction 5

most developed Nurse, in Euripides' *Hippolytus*. My discussion is based on a close examination of the Greek text with focus on the verbal manifestations of authority—advice, approval, disapproval, directions, orders—and their effectiveness on the different characters that are addressed, such as master or mistress, other servants, and the members of the chorus.

Chapter 1 centers on Eurykleia, the old Nurse in the *Odyssey*, and her authority over the characters with whom she interacts: Odysseus, Telemakhos, Penelope, and the maids. Eurykleia is the Nurse and the confidante of both Odysseus and Telemakhos, as also the confidante of Penelope. She expresses her approval or disapproval and offers suggestions and advice to Telemakhos, Odysseus, and Penelope; and she instructs and gives orders to the maids. She helps her three masters by keeping their crucial secrets. She is the only person in Ithaca who recognizes Odysseus—who on all other occasions chooses when to reveal himself—despite his calculations, and so she defeats his intelligence. Outwitting her master encourages her constant and steady effort to direct him with suggestions, which he always follows, despite his initial resistance. The encounters between Eurykleia and Odysseus in *Odyssey* xix, just as those between Eurykleia and Penelope in xxiii 1-84, are viewed as agonistic performances of "speech-acts" and suggest a background of choral tradition.

Chapter 2 looks closely at the Nurse characters in Aeschylus, Sophocles, and Euripides (except *Hippolytus*). The first part considers the role of the Nurse in Aeschylus' *Libation-Bearers*. The Nurse here has an important part and a multiple function; she even has a name, Kilissa—a unique example in Greek tragedy, where all the other nurses are referred to by the anonymous and generic term *trophos*. The second part of chapter 2 considers the Nurse of Deianeira in Sophocles' *Women of Trachis*, who, despite her short part, sets the action of the play in motion through her advice. The third part examines both the Nurse of Hermione and the Handmaid of Andromache in Euripides' *Andromache*, and compares these two similar characters in order to observe their differences and similarities. Finally, the fourth part discusses the Nurse of Medea in Euripides' *Medea*, who understands her mistress and foreshadows her reactions.

Chapter 3 looks closely at the Nurse scenes in Euripides' *Hippolytus*, concentrating on the language, in particular the language of persuasion and the language of authority, and compares it with that of women-centered poetry.[10] In my discussion of *Hippolytus*, I also entertain the question of a possible development of the figure of the Nurse from a model of fundamental hierarchy embodied in the figure of the lyric *khorêgos* of early choral lyric. I suggest that the encounter between Phaedra and the Nurse in *Hippolytus* 373-524, like the encounter between Eurykleia and Penelope in *Odyssey* xxiii 1-84, is an agonistic performance and suggests a background of choral tradition. It resembles the choral contest between two leading lyric personalities, Agido and Hagesikhora, in Alcman PMG 1.

This interpretation supports the argument that the persona of the early lyric female *khorêgos* survived in Athenian drama in an undifferentiated form as the chorus-leader and in a differentiated form as one of the actors. It also explores the self-referential qualities of the ending of the play, which presents itself as a commentary on the play's origins.

The book concludes that all the Nurses have authority over their mistresses or have special importance in the plot. The most influential Nurses are Eurykleia in the *Odyssey* and Phaedra's Nurse in *Hippolytus*. Eurykleia exercises her authority not only over young Telemakhos and Penelope, but, surprisingly, mainly over Odysseus, the king of Ithaca. Phaedra's Nurse not only advises, but directs her mistress, undertakes the initiative of action, and directs the action. As Austin has argued, there is inversion of order in the house of Odysseus before the hero's arrival: Eurykleia and Eumaios have more power than they would have in his presence.[11] This view explains partly what I see as Eurykleia's competition with Odysseus for authority: she wants to preserve the prerogatives she had acquired in his absence. I further suggest, however, that she had exercised her authority over him even before his absence, when Odysseus was younger, as his first Teacher, in charge of his *paideia*. So too, in Euripides' *Hippolytus*, the Nurse has more power and influence than what might be expected: beyond her advisory role, she exceeds the limitations of her traditional authority, directs her mistress, and undertakes the initiative of action. Again, this pattern can be explained partly because of the absence of Theseus, the *kurios*, the

---

[10] An attempt is also made to establish the relation between the utterances of the Nurse and those of the chorus-leader. Elaborating on Nagy's suggestion (cf. above), I investigate whether both these characters evolved from the same archetypal role, that of the lyric *khorêgos*, and, if so, whether this relation is complementary or antithetical.

[11] Austin 1975.165-156.

Introduction 7

master of the house, but also as part of Euripides' intention to shock his audience.[12] Furthermore, Phaedra, distraught and unable to function, is more easily influenced and guided by her Nurse, who, as Phaedra admits, is superior in the art of persuasion, in cleverness and wisdom, in *sophia*. In the end, however, Phaedra is ready to assume the responsibility for action, and directs the action herself, proving a worthy student of her Nurse and Teacher.

---

[12] On Euripides' reception in fifth-century Athenian society cf. Michelini 1987.70-71.

1

Eurykleia, the Predecessor

1. Introduction

This chapter examines how the poetics of female *paideia* in the *khoros* 'song and dance' ensemble are appropriated and reshaped by the poetics of epic. The *khoros* is an old and conservative institution, and Homeric poetry, our oldest form today of Greek (pre-)literature, already presupposes the existence of the *khoros*. In this light, Eurykleia can be seen as the leader of a *khoros* of younger women and in charge of their *paideia*—as we see her when she gives orders to the maids in *Odyssey* xx 147-156. But even in the absence of younger women, she can still be seen as the crystallization of a *khorêgos* 'leader of the *khoros*' figure. Although we see her in a role that has become separated from the ensemble of *khoros*-members, she nevertheless maintains the characteristics of authority derived from the hierarchical relationship between leader and members of the archaic Greek *khoros*. Her involvement in the *paideia* of her younger mistress or masters—even in the absence of the context of the archaic *khoros*— endows her with the same kind of hierarchical authority such as that defined in the archaic Greek choral constructs.

In this chapter we will trace Eurykleia's hierarchical authority over the maids, but also over Penelope, a younger female figure, and, even more important, over two younger male figures, Odysseus and Telemakhos. As I suggested above, it is her role in the *paideia* of her masters that endows her with authority and influence over them. This chapter discusses the manifestations of such authority, as the story in the *Odyssey* unfolds.

Central in my discussion is Eurykleia's speech—advice, directions, orders, comments of approval or disapproval, or merely expressions of fondness, sympathy, and understanding—and the effect of her speech on the different characters to whom it is addressed—Odysseus, Telemakhos, Penelope, and the maids. It is important to keep in mind that Eurykleia is a *dmôiê*, a 'house servant' (see *Odyssey* i 435), and as such she will also take orders and perform certain duties. Special emphasis is also given to the terms for 'nurse' and 'old woman', as well as to her name and to the epithets accompanying her name.[1]

The discussion of the epic figure of Eurykleia is based on three working assumptions: 1) in epic poetry "the diction is a most accurate expression of the theme"; 2) the application of an epithet is both traditional and "thematically appropriate"; 3) "the entire formula is an accurate response to the requirements of traditional theme."[2] These assumptions by no means contradict Milman Parry's established theory of the formulaic heritage of the *Iliad* and the *Odyssey*, nor his definition of the formula as "a group of words which is regularly employed under the same metrical conditions to express a given essential idea."[3] Rather, they stress "the freedom of the poet to say accurately what he means," although "what he means is strictly regulated by tradition."[4] These assumptions are fundamental to my discussion of Eurykleia's epithets, her speech, and its effects.[5]

Furthermore, following the theories of J. L. Austin, J. R. Searle, and Richard Martin, I have applied the notion of "speech-act" to Eurykleia's discourse.[6] A "speech-act," according to Austin and Searle, entails a situation in which the word is the action. Martin has applied the notion of "speech-act" to the oral performance of Homeric poetry. He treats "speech-acts" as "poetic" performances "in the sense that they require verbal artistry on the part of the speaker and a

---

[1] The use of these epithets varies in narrative and in dialogue. A study of such differences in the epithets of Eurykleia will reinforce Austin's findings on the different employment of name formulas in dialogue and in narrative. Austin 1975.11-80 studied the epithets used of Odysseus, Penelope, and Telemakhos "to determine distinctions between one character and another in formula usage or between the characters and the poet speaking through his own persona" (40). On the use of the Homeric formula, in general, see the illuminating discussion in Nagy 1990b.18-35.

[2] Nagy 1979.1-4. For more arguments, see also Nagy 1990b.18-35.

[3] Parry 1971.272.

[4] Nagy 1979.3. On the meaningful use of the Homeric epithet see also Austin 1975.11-80, and Nagy 1992.17-60.

[5] Simultaneously, such an examination will reinforce these working assumptions, especially the meaningful use of the Homeric epithet.

[6] Austin 1962, Searle 1976, and Martin 1989.

commitment to an audience, which in turn, judges the performance."[7] Martin defines performance as "authoritative self-presentation to an audience."[8] Moreover, Martin treats the speech-acts of Iliadic heroes, and especially those of Achilles, as "poetic performances with *agonistic* character." Martin argues that the heroic discourse of the *Iliad* is competitive, as heroes speak to win. I find that, in the same way, women's speech in the *Odyssey* is also often competitive. The study of Eurykleia's speech, in particular, reveals similarities with the speech of Homeric heroes, especially the speech of Odysseus, and her "speech-acts" can be viewed and treated as "agonistic poetic performances." Furthermore, as Eurykleia's speech contains praise and blame, boasts and commands, she can be characterized as a performer of these genres within the poem.[9]

This chapter is divided into four parts. The first discusses Eurykleia's role as the Nurse of Telemakhos through her interaction with Telemakhos and his mother, Penelope. The second part centers around the recognition of Odysseus by Eurykleia: it discusses her confrontation with Odysseus first as a beggar and then as her master, and concentrates on Eurykleia's effort to exercise her authority over him, in what I see as an "agonistic poetic performance." The third part observes the authority of the 'old woman' as she defends Penelope against Telemakhos' blame, as she gives orders to the maids, and as she offers her assistance to Odysseus in overthrowing the suitors. Finally, the fourth part views Eurykleia's role in the reunion of Odysseus and Penelope, first as she skillfully persuades Penelope to accept the truth of Odysseus' return—one more example of an "agonistic poetic performance"—and then as she helps Penelope in tricking Odysseus; this section also briefly discusses the role of another Nurse figure, Eurynome, who also serves as an advisor to Penelope, and it outlines a comparison of the two similar characters.

---

[7] Martin 1989.89 and 231.

[8] See also Lord 1960.78. Lord maintains that "an oral poem is composed not *for* but *in* performance."

[9] On the poetry of praise and blame see Nagy 1979.222-242; see also further Nagy 1990a.146-198 for a discussion of the interrelation of Pindar's praise poetry with Homeric epic. Martin 1989.94 notes, "the very act of composing boasts, commands, insults... characterizes the speaker within the poem as a particular type of performer, since these discourse types constitute poetic 'genres' outside epic and are subject to audience evaluation.... The system of praise and blame that operates within Homeric society conceivably might have remained implicit in the *Iliad*"—and in the *Odyssey*, I should add.

2. Eurykleia, the Nurse of Telemakhos

2.1. Eurykleia and Telemakhos

Eurykleia is introduced in the *Odyssey* as the Nurse of Telemakhos (i 428 ff.). She is accompanying him to his chamber with blazing torches:[10]

τῷ δ' ἄρ' ἅμ' αἰθομένας δαΐδας φέρε <u>κεδνὰ ἰδυῖα</u>
Εὐρύκλει' Ὤπος θυγάτηρ Πεισηνορίδαο,

Odyssey i 428-429

With him came and carried the flaring torches devoted <u>[kedna iduia]</u> Eurykleia, the daughter of Ops, son of Peisenor.[11]

She is described as *kedna iduia* (κεδνὰ ἰδυῖα from κεδνός, a derivative of κήδομαι, and εἴδω, οἶδα), 'knowing caring feelings', 'with affectionate feelings', 'devoted'.[12] The description continues with important biographical information starting with her father's and grandfather's names.[13] This is quite unique for a servant.[14] Laertes bought her when she was young, he continues, for the price

---

[10] Stanford 1965 I.233 notes the quiet entrance of a character who plays an important part later (xix 386ff.). West 1988.126 suggests that the detailed description of Telemakhos going to bed reminds us that, in the eyes of those around him, he is still a child; but its main purpose is to introduce Eurykleia.

[11] The name 'Eurykleia' suggests 'the one with the wide fame' (*euru kleos*). Dimock 1989.24 sees a connection between Eurykleia's torches and the *kleos* that she plans for Telemakhos. Telemakhos is also going to "acquire *kleos* for himself after his father, Odysseus." Eurykleia nursed both these men: her *kleos*, I suggest, is possibly due partly to being their Nurse, and partly to her noble past (see i 428-429); most likely, however, it is also due to her influential representation in the story.

[12] This epithet is used only of Eurykleia and Penelope. Cf. xix 346, also on Eurykleia; and xx 57, xxiii 182, 232 on Penelope.

[13] I agree with Scott 1921.168 that the fact that both her father and grandfather are named shows that she is of good family, though a servant, and emphasizes her importance. West 1988.126 remarks, "the poet of the *Odyssey* is sparing with patronymics and the archaistic hybrid *Peisenoridês* (Πεισηνορίδης) is markedly honorific. Her father's name is not otherwise attested, and its derivation is mysterious; this is most unusual in the case of a character of no importance whom we should suppose to be the poet's own invention." I would add to West's observations that this impressive introduction of Eurykleia indicates that although we might otherwise consider her "a character of no importance," we should expect just the opposite.

[14] The only other case where a servant's father and grandfather are named is Eumaios, the old loyal swineherd, a father figure for Telemakhos (see xv 413-414). On the importance and noble birth of both Eumaios and Eurykleia, cf. Austin 1975.165ff.

of twenty oxen.[15] He honored her in his house "like his own noble wife" (ἶσα...κεδνῇ ἀλόχῳ, i 432).[16] Still, he never lay with her in love, for he feared the anger of his wife (χόλον δ' ἀλέεινε γυναικός). Notice that the wording refers to Laertes' wife in general terms as *alokhos* (i 432) and *gunê* (i 434), both meaning 'wife', without mentioning her name, Antikleia. This is perhaps an indication of Eurykleia's greater importance than that of Antikleia in the story. The etymology of both women's names supports this view: Eurykleia (Εὐρύκλεια, from εὐρύ and κλέος, a derivative of κλύω 'hear'), 'the one widely heard of', 'the one with the broad fame', and Antikleia (Ἀντίκλεια, from ἀντί and κλέος), 'the one with matching fame' (rather than 'against fame' or 'equal to fame'). And as the narrative continues, two very important clues are added: she among the handmaids loved Telemakhos the most, and she is the one who nursed him when he was a baby (i 434-435):

τήν ποτε Λαέρτης πρίατο κτεάτεσσιν ἑοῖσι,
πρωθήβην ἔτ' ἐοῦσαν, ἐεικοσάβοια δ' ἔδωκεν,
ἶσα δέ μιν κεδνῇ ἀλόχῳ τίεν ἐν μεγάροισιν,
εὐνῇ δ' οὔ ποτ' ἔμικτο, χόλον δ' ἀλέεινε γυναικός·
ἥ οἱ ἅμ' αἰθομένας δαΐδας φέρε, καί ἑ μάλιστα
δμωάων φιλέεσκε, καὶ ἔτρεφε τυτθὸν ἐόντα.

Odyssey i 430-435

Laertes bought her long ago with his own possessions
when she was in her first youth, and gave for her twenty oxen,
and he honored her in his halls as much as his own noble wife;
still, he never lay in love with her for fear of his wife's anger.
She carried the flaring torches for him. She among the maids
loved him the most, and she nursed him when he was little.

The narrative continues with two additional important details. Telemakhos opens the door, sits on the bed, and, taking off his tunic, lays it in the hands of the "clever old woman" (γραίης πυκιμηδέος, i 438).[17] She is described as old and characterized with the epithet

---

[15] This is a high price, compared to four oxen, the price of a skilled woman slave, as in XXIII 237; see Stanford 1965 I.233.

[16] Note here the use of the same epithet *kednê* for both Laertes' wife and Eurykleia, which stresses even more the equal honor they shared. See also Table II with the epithets of Eurykleia at the end of the chapter.

[17] Eurykleia is often referred to as 'old woman', γρηῦς/γρηΰς, cf. ii 377, especially xix 346 and 353, when she recognizes Odysseus, and thereafter xix 361, 386, 467, 503, xxii 433, 495, xxiii 1, 33, 292; she is also addressed as γρηῦς/γρηΰς (xix 383, xxii 395, 411,

pukimêdês (πυκιμηδής, from πυκά and μήδεα), 'with dense thoughts', 'shrewd in counsel', a characterization she shares only with her master, Odysseus.[18] This episode ends as she folds and smoothes the tunic and hangs it on a peg beside the bedstead, and then, fastening the door behind her, she leaves the chamber (i 436-442).

The role of Eurykleia in relation to Telemakhos is now established. She is his Nurse, his *trophos*, the woman who 'nursed' him (*trephein*, i 435) as a baby.[19] She, among the handmaids, loved him the most. We should note that Eurykleia is mentioned here as one of the handmaids (i 435). This is the only occasion that Eurykleia is referred to as a *dmôiê* (δμῳή) 'handmaid', 'house servant'. Still, as I suggested before, this characterization explains why she performs certain duties and, more important, why she has to obey the orders of her masters.

From this brief but carefully detailed introduction of Eurykleia we learn about her background and her position in the household. Her age and her cleverness are also established with her characterization as a 'shrewd old woman'. This is Eurykleia 'of the wide fame', the woman who nursed Telemakhos as a baby and still takes care of him. From this introduction, we may expect Eurykleia to be an influential character in the story.

The occasion of Eurykleia's introduction is not trivial, as J. H. Finley remarks. Telemakhos goes to bed after meeting with Athena/Mentes and pondering over her advice to call an assembly and undertake a trip to Pylos and Sparta in quest for information about his father.[20] And as we will see next (ii 345ff.), Eurykleia will be more involved in the process of Telemakhos' passage from boyhood to adulthood.

In ii 345 we hear of Eurykleia again, this time as the *tamiê* (ταμίη), the housekeeper and stewardess of Odysseus' storeroom, watchful night and day:[21]

---

481). A detailed discussion on the use of this term in connection with her cleverness and power follows below (see also Table III at the end of the chapter).

[18] The epithet *pukimêdês* (πυκιμηδής) is used only here in the *Odyssey* of Eurykleia. Cf. similar epithets in xix 346 = xix 353 of Eurykleia, and ix 445 and III 202 of Odysseus. See also Table II with the epithets of Eurykleia at the end of the chapter.

[19] This passage (i 435) defines Eurykleia's role as Telemakhos' Nurse, and it explains etymologically the term *trophos* 'Nurse', which is used hereafter in the *Odyssey*.

[20] Finley 1978.156ff.

[21] The expression 'night and day' is a common hyperbole suggesting her continuous alertness; it does not mean that she spent all her time in the storeroom, but that she was frequently there, as West 1988.151 comments. She has other duties too, as we have seen

14 Chapter 1

>...ἐν δὲ γυνὴ <u>ταμίη</u> νύκτας τε καὶ ἦμαρ
>ἔσχ', ἣ πάντ' ἐφύλασσε <u>νόου πολυϊδρείῃσιν</u>,
>Εὐρύκλει', Ὦπος θυγάτηρ Πεισηνορίδαο.
>
> Odyssey ii 345-347
>
>...and there by night and day a <u>housekeeper [*tamiê*]</u> was in charge,
>who, <u>with the many skills of her mind [*noou poluïdreiêisin*]</u>
>   watched over all these,
>Eurykleia, the daughter of Ops, son of Peisenor.

Her role as a housekeeper is accompanied by an attribute reflecting again her cleverness: *noou poluïdreiêisin* (νόου πολυϊδρείῃσιν, from πολύς and οἶδα), 'with a mind which knows many things', 'of many skills of the mind', similar to *pukimêdês* 'with dense thoughts', 'shrewd in council' (i 438). The emphasis on the cleverness of her mind is conveyed by an epithet not used of any other housekeeper or stewardess.[22] This unique epithet is used later of Odysseus only (xxiii 77).[23] Further on, following her name, in a formulaic pattern, we are told for the second time of her father's and grandfather's names.[24] The repetition of her patronymics emphasizes once more her importance as well as her additional role: she is both Telemakhos' nurse and the *tamiê* 'housekeeper' of the household.

Telemakhos calls her to the storage room and asks her to prepare provisions for him, which he will fetch in the evening when his mother goes to bed. He asks Eurykleia to keep this secret, explaining the reason for his request: he will go to Sparta and to Pylos to seek information about his father's return (ii 349-360).

Telemakhos relies on Eurykleia's help with the supplies for his crucial trip, but also on her confidentiality, as he plans to leave secretly from his mother. Furthermore, he provides details about his trip and an explanation of its purpose. Not only does he rely on and trust Eurykleia, but he also shares with her his plans and the

---

already (i 428ff.) and we will see further. Besides, there is another *tamiê* in the household, Eurynome (see xvii 495, xviii 169, xix 96, xxiii 154).

[22] The only epithets used with other housekeepers or stewardesses are *philê* (φίλη) 'dear' (i 207), and *aidoiê* (αἰδοίη) 'modest' in the formula used on the serving of food (σῖτον δ' αἰδοίη ταμίη παρέθηκε φέρουσα, i 139, iv 55, vii 175, x 371, xv 138, xvii 94, 259).

[23] Cf. also a similar form of the same epithet used of Eurykleia in xxiii 82. For more details, see discussion and comments below. Cf. also the summary of her epithets in Table II at the end of the chapter.

[24] Her father's and grandfather's names are later repeated for the third time in xx 147 as a new role and a new attribute of her character are introduced. See below.

Eurykleia, the Predecessor   15

reasoning behind them. We should also note here the form of his address of her as *maia* 'nurse' or 'nanny' (μαῖα, ii 349), in contrast to the form 'old woman', which he uses later in the story (xxii 395). [25]

Eurykleia responds to Telemakhos' request with an emotional reaction that reveals a motherly affection and concern for what she considers an unnecessary danger. At Telemakhos' words, she gives a shrill cry and in tears she speaks to him, in an effort to prevent him from his trip: "Ah, dear child, how has this thing come into your mind?" (ii 363-364). She enumerates the risks to his safety of such a dangerous trip. Does he want to perish like his father?, she implies. She warns him that the suitors, as soon as he is gone, will plot against his life and divide all his possessions. Therefore, she advises, he should stay at home in charge of his property; there is no need to suffer ills and wander over the barren seas (ii 364-370).

Telemakhos is not convinced he should cancel his trip.[26] Still, he tries to dismiss her worries by telling her to take heart, "for this plan is not without a god's will" (οὔ τοι ἄνευ θεοῦ ἥδε γε βουλή, ii 372). He further asks her to swear that she will not tell his mother "until the eleventh or twelfth day comes," or until she misses him and hears that he is gone and worries for him (ii 373-376).[27] The old woman swears to say nothing and prepares his supplies (ii 377-380).

In this episode we can observe the trust, the affection, and the concern between Eurykleia and Telemakhos. Telemakhos confides in Eurykleia rather than in his own mother, whose emotional reaction—as we see later when she discovers his absence (in iv 697ff.)—could prevent him from his trip. They address each other with affection.

---

[25] The term *maia* (μαῖα, a hypocoristic formed by adding the suffix -ya to the root μα- and cognate with μήτηρ 'mother') is used in the *Odyssey* always in the vocative case, as a form of address to Eurykleia (by Telemakhos, Odysseus, and Penelope), and to Eurynome, another nurse-like figure (by Penelope). The implicit tone of familiarity contained in the term *maia* is generally translated as 'nanny' or 'nurse'. Cf. also the same form of address to Demeter in the *Hymn to Demeter* 147.

[26] Telemakhos does not follow Eurykleia's advice, as he will not follow Eumaios' advice of xvi 137-145. (On Telemakhos' reaction to his loyal servant's suggestions, see Olson 1992.219-227, especially 221). Also compare Telemakhos' dismissal of Eurykleia's objections and fears here (ii 361-376) and his brisk dismissal of his mother's concerns for him at xvii 36-51. Olson 1992.226n20 suggests that the two women's efforts may be seen as part of the regular role of Homeric women, "to try to restrain men from doing their duty." (Cf. also Kakridis 1971.70-74). For a different interpretation see below.

[27] Telemakhos deliberately refers to an approximate number of days and leaves it to Eurykleia to find the right moment to tell Penelope, when she misses him and discovers that he is gone.

16 Chapter 1

Eurykleia calls him *phile teknon* 'dear child' (φίλε τέκνον, ii 363), and he calls her *maia* 'nanny/nurse' (μαῖα, ii 349, 372). Eurykleia tries to prevent him from his trip, and Telemakhos tries to reassure her that she does not need to worry.

It is important to note that Eurykleia does not hesitate to advise Telemakhos and that her judgement in evaluating his risks is very accurate. Indeed, the suitors plot against Telemakhos' life as soon as they find out that he is gone (see iv 663-673). The fact that Telemakhos does not follow her advice is not an indication that Eurykleia's fears are unreasonable or unrealistic, nor should it be seen as a sign of Eurykleia's lack of influence and authority over him; it is primarily an indication of his own growth. And let us not forget that this is according to the divine plan and direct influence of Athena.[28] Therefore, if this is the will of the gods, she will not have any further objections; instead, 'the old woman' swears not to say a word and prepares the supplies.[29] She becomes Telemakhos' confidante and accomplice in the trip that will be his passage from boyhood to adulthood. She, who nursed and raised him, will now help him to gain his independence and so to become a man. Her diminishing authority is an essential and necessary condition of his coming of age, and she readily accepts it and yields. She offers to him both her help with the supplies for his trip, and the confidentiality of her silence, while later, when the time comes, she will fulfill her promise to tell Penelope.

Eurykleia's role as both nurse and housekeeper matches the description of Demeter in the *Hymn to Demeter* (101-104) as the goddess prepares to wander abroad, disguised as an old woman:[30]

γρηῒ παλαιγενέϊ ἐναλίγκιος, ἥ τε τόκοιο
εἴργηται δώρων τε φιλοστεφάνου Ἀφροδίτης,
οἷαί τε τροφοί εἰσι θεμιστοπόλων βασιλήων

---

[28] Telemakhos invokes the divine will in ii 372, as discussed above. In fact, Athena visits Telemakhos twice and helps him prove his manhood by way of her visits. In the first visit, she assumes the form of Mentes (i 105ff.), in the second, that of Mentor (ii 68). As Nagy 1974.266-267 explains, both names morphologically mean 'he who reminds' and are connected with the noun *menos* 'power'. Hence, *menos* is actually being infused by Athena as *Mentês*. Later she encourages Telemakhos in the form of *Mentôr*, and again she reminds him of his father's *menos*.

[29] Note her characterization as 'old woman' at this crucial point, as she undertakes the important task of keeping Telemakhos' venture secret.

[30] On the *Hymn to Demeter*, see Foley 1994. On the similarities between Eurykleia and Demeter in disguise, see also Introduction.

παίδων καὶ <u>ταμίαι</u> κατὰ δώματα ἠχήεντα.

Hymn to Demeter 101-104

looking like an <u>old woman born of old</u>, who has been cut off
from childbirth and the gifts of garland-loving Aphrodite,
such as are the <u>nurses</u> of law-giving kings'
children and the <u>stewards</u> in their echoing homes.

Further on, as Demeter speaks to the daughters of Keleos, the ruler of Eleusis, she asks for a house where she can perform such tasks as those of elderly women:

...οἷα <u>γυναικὸς ἀφήλικος</u> ἔργα τέτυκται·
καί κεν παῖδα νεογνὸν ἐν ἀγκοίνῃσιν ἔχουσα
καλὰ <u>τιθηνοίμην</u> καὶ <u>δώματα τηρήσαιμι</u>
καί κε λέχος στορέσαιμι μυχῷ θαλάμων ἐϋπήκτων
δεσπόσυνον καί κ' ἔργα <u>διδασκήσαιμι γυναῖκας</u>.

Hymn to Demeter 140-144

...such tasks as are done by an <u>elderly woman</u>;
I could <u>nurse</u> well a newborn child holding it
in my arms, and I could <u>watch over a house</u>;
and I could make a master's bed in the recess of a
well-built house, and I could <u>teach women</u> their work.

There are, indeed, many similarities between Eurykleia and Demeter in disguise. In addition to their duties, which we will consider further, Eurykleia, like Demeter, is also called *grêüs palaigenês* (γρηῢς παλαιγενής) 'old woman born of old', when she is addressed by Telemakhos after the destruction of the suitors (xxii 395). In addition, two of the epithets of Eurykleia refer to her *mêdea* 'thoughts', *pukimêdês*, 'with dense thoughts' (i 438), and *pukina mêdea ekhousa* 'having dense thoughts' (xix 353), both following her characterization as 'old woman'. The same word *mêdea* (μήδεα) 'thoughts', derived from the verb *mêdomai* (μήδομαι) 'think/plan/devise', is used to describe Demeter's cosmic potency (*Hymn to Demeter* 351ff. and again 452ff.).[31] It is interesting to note that Demeter's cosmic devices, her *mêdea*, are here, as she assumes the

---

[31] On the connotations of the word *mêdea* see Nagy 1974.265-278. As Nagy explains, the word *mêdea* is also connected with the word 'genitals'; the notions of generative and mental power are both inherent in the ambivalent word *mêdea*, as we see in the example of 'Zeus of imperishable *mêdea*' in XXIV 88 (Ζεὺς ἄφθιτα μήδεα εἰδώς). Zeus, Nagy notes, has supreme power because he has supreme knowledge.

form of a nurse, connected with her qualities as a nurse. In addition to physically nursing a child, a nurse nurses a child mentally (cf. Plato's notion, in *Protagoras* 325cd, of the nurse as the first Teacher of the child); therefore, her power is double.[32] Both Demeter and Eurykleia share this power.

2.2. Eurykleia and Penelope

Indeed, in iv 697ff. Penelope learns from the herald Medon of her son's trip and of the suitors' plans to kill him upon his return. She is very upset and wants to send her servant Dolios to Laertes, in the hope that he can think of a plan to prevent Telemakhos' destruction (iv 722-741). At this point, we can observe briefly how Eurykleia interacts with her mistress, Penelope, whom, interestingly, she addresses as 'dear bride' (νύμφα φίλη, iv 743). This may seem an odd way to address a married woman, but to Eurykleia, who had been a member of Odysseus' household since Odysseus was born, Penelope is still a young bride. As a result, as we will observe in the continuation of her speech, she faces Penelope not only as an older and more experienced woman, but also from the standpoint of her established privileges and authority in the household before Penelope's arrival as the young bride of Odysseus.

Eurykleia boldly tells Penelope that "whether she slays her or spares her," she will not hide the truth (iv 743-744).[33] She tells her that she knew about Telemakhos' trip, but she had taken an oath not to inform her before now (iv 745-749). She even advises Penelope to wash herself, put on clean clothes, and go up with her maids to her room to pray to Athena for the safety of Telemakhos:

ἀλλ' ὑδρυναμένη, καθαρὰ χροῒ εἵμαθ' ἑλοῦσα,
εἰς ὑπερῷ' ἀναβᾶσα σὺν ἀμφιπόλοισι γυναιξὶν

---

[32] Let us also consider here Nagy's observations on the double meaning of the noun *mêdea* referring to both mental and physical qualities (see above note).

[33] Eurykleia's confidence is appropriate to her position as senior house-servant (cf. West 1988.239); moreover, it derives from her authority as the old Nurse of the master of the house. Beyond her equanimity, as she accepts Penelope's power of life and death "with no fear at all that it might be used unfairly" (cf. Dimock 1989.311), I also see here her cleverness in anticipating Penelope's anger and rendering it weaker by this statement, which, exaggerated as it may be, still reveals her status as a servant, and her mistress' power over her. On the power of masters over their servants see among others Olson 1992.219. On the social and legal status of Homeric servants, see M. I. Finley 1978, Garland 1988, and Beringer 1982.13-32. On ancient slavery in general see Brockmeyer 1979.

εὖχε' Ἀθηναίῃ κούρῃ Διὸς αἰγιόχοιο·
ἡ γάρ κέν μιν ἔπειτα καὶ ἐκ θανάτοιο σαώσαι.

Odyssey iv 750-753

> But wash up and put clean clothes on your body,
> and go on to the upper floor with your attendants
> to pray to Athena, daughter of Zeus of the aegis,
> for she can save him then even from death.

Furthermore, she disapproves of her decision and advises her to refrain from telling old Laertes, while at the same time she hints at her son's coming of age and assuming responsibility:

μηδὲ γέροντα κάκου κεκακωμένον· οὐ γὰρ ὀίω
πάγχυ θεοῖς μακάρεσσι γονὴν Ἀρκεισιάδαο
ἔχθεσθ', ἀλλ' ἔτι πού τις ἐπέσσεται ὅς κεν ἔχῃσι
δώματά θ' ὑψερεφέα καὶ ἀπόπροθι πίονας ἀγρούς.

Odyssey iv 754-757

> And don't trouble the troubled man. For I do not think
> that the seed of Arkeisios is altogether hated by the
> blessed gods, but there will still be one left who will inherit
> the high-roofed halls and the rich fields that lie at a distance.

With this statement Eurykleia shows her accurate evaluation of Telemakhos' growth. She knows that very soon—after his trip—he will be the man in the house, and take charge of his property; and she has helped him to make the first step—to undertake this trip—both by providing him with supplies and by keeping his departure secret.

From her first encounter with Penelope we see that Eurykleia respects but does not fear her mistress. Although Penelope has the institutional authority over her as a master over a slave/servant, still, Eurykleia also has her own authority over Penelope, which is certainly very different but still very important: as an older and experienced female member of the household holding two responsible roles, as the housekeeper and, more important, the Nurse of both the older and the younger master, she can advise her younger mistress, as if she were her own Nurse. She has the cleverness, the skill, and, more important, the power to persuade her what to do (wash, change, and pray) and what not to do (tell Laertes). At the same time, she prepares Penelope to accept the fact that her son has grown up. In advising Penelope, Eurykleia uses the hierarchical authority inherent in Greek poetics in the education of younger female figures by an older experienced woman. As a result of her short but successful "speech-act," to use Martin's term, Penelope listens to her and follows her advice without objection (iv 758-761).[34]

It is interesting, at this point, to note that when Telemakhos returns and Penelope welcomes back her son, Telemakhos advises his mother to do exactly the same things that Eurykleia advised her to do, when Penelope discovered her son's absence (iv 750-753)—namely, to wash herself, to put on clean clothes, and then, going up with her handmaids to her room, to pray—to Zeus this time (xvii 48-51); and Penelope obeys his directions (xvii 57-60) just as she obeyed Eurykleia's (iv 758-761).[35] Although in oral composition formulaic similarities are a pattern in a "typical scene," the similarities in this scene still reveal that Penelope obeys Telemakhos, just as she obeys Eurykleia; the close similarities of these passages, apart from the restrictions of formulaic composition, show that the old Nurse, Eurykleia, has no less influence in advising and directing Penelope than does Telemakhos.[36]

2.3. The Return of Telemakhos

In xvii 31ff. Eurykleia is the first person to see Telemakhos, as soon as he crosses the threshold of his home, after his return from his trip. In a geometric pattern typical of Homeric composition it is fitting that, since she was the last person in the house to see him off (ii 349-380), she should be the first person to welcome him back to the palace.[37]

---

[34] By contrast, Penelope does not follow the suggestions of her old serving woman, Eurynome, when she later advises her to wash and anoint herself (xviii 172-174). Penelope's acquiescence can be explained better if it is seen as deriving from Eurykleia's role as the Nurse and her involvement in Penelope's *paideia* in the context of Greek poetics. For further discussion see also below (section 5.4).

[35] In fact, iv 750-751 and xvii 48-49 are identical formulas, while iv 752-753 and xvii 50-1 refer respectively to a prayer to Athena and a prayer to Zeus. Again, xvii 57-60 and iv 758-761 are similar lines, while iv 759 and xvii 58 are identical.

[36] Consequently, I do not quite agree with the comment of Stanford 1965 II.228, on xvii 46-51, that "the cold and superior tone of Telemakhos implies that men must act, women must pray." For a comprehensive classification of the "typical scenes" in Homer, see the classic work of Arend 1933.

[37] Note that the first person who welcomes Telemakhos back to Ithaca is Eumaios, another older loyal servant, a father figure for Telemakhos, the male counterpart of Eurykleia. See also below. For the "geometric" style of the composition in the Homeric epic see Whitman 1958.

Later on, in xix 4-13, Odysseus asks Telemakhos to put away the weapons. Telemakhos, in turn, calls Eurykleia and asks her to shut up the women in their rooms, while he lays away in the storeroom the weapons of his father to protect them from the smoke (xix 14-20). Although Odysseus' directions were to use the pretext of the smoke for the suitors, Telemakhos presents it to Eurykleia as well. Even on this occasion, when he is not telling the truth, he explains his acts to her, as he did before (ii 349-56). Note also that he calls her *maia* 'nurse' (xix 16). This address, in connection with the word *nêpios* 'infant', which Telemakhos uses in accepting his irresponsibility in the past (ἐγὼ δ' ἔτι νήπιος ἦα "but I was still a *nêpios*, an infant," xix 19), emphasizes the boy/nurse relationship that he is now relinquishing.[38] Eurykleia responds accordingly, calling him *teknon* 'child' (xix 22), but at the same time she is happy to see him taking care of the house and guarding his possessions (xix 22-23). She still worries who will light his way if the maids are not around (xix 24-25):

αἲ γὰρ δή ποτε, τέκνον, ἐπιφροσύνας ἀνέλοιο
οἴκου κήδεσθαι καὶ κτήματα πάντα φυλάσσειν.
ἀλλ' ἄγε, τίς τοι ἔπειτα μετοιχομένη φάος οἴσει;
δμῳὰς δ' οὐκ εἴας προβλωσκέμεν, αἵ κεν ἔφαινον.

Odyssey xix 22-25

How I wish, my child, that you would take charge one day
and take care of your house and guard all your possessions.
But come, who will go with you and hold the light?
You did not let the maids come out who would light your way.

Telemakhos, however, tells her not to worry, for the stranger (Odysseus) will help him (xix 26-28), an explanation that, inaccurate as it may seem, is actually a hint at the very truth.[39]

In this episode between Eurykleia and Telemakhos, after the return from this crucial trip, which is for him the passage from boyhood to adulthood, Eurykleia expresses her approval for what she thinks is Telemakhos' decision—to take care of his father's possessions. In fact, she had already anticipated and told Penelope that Telemakhos would soon assume such responsibilities (iv 756-770). After her small concern (who would light his way) is put at rest by his reasonable

---

[38] On the different uses and connotations of the word *nêpios*, see Edmonds 1976.

[39] Russo 1992.76 sees Telemakhos' reaction as one more example of his newly acquired independence and cool aloofness. Instead, I see here Telemakhos' caring effort to put at rest the concerns of the old Nurse with a little lie—still, a lie closest to the truth.

22 Chapter 1

answer, she follows his orders without any further objections, helping him again to grow up and act like the man of the house. Note also that Telemakhos makes a special effort to show immediate consideration for Eurykleia's concern, although a little later (xvi 147-151) his first reaction to Eumaios' concerns and suggestions is to ignore them, at least in the beginning.[40] This is all the more important, in light of the fact that Eumaios is a father-like figure to Telemakhos (Telemakhos even calls him *atta* 'daddy', 'father', xvi 31, 57, 130, and xvii 6, 599); moreover, their reunion after Telemakhos' return from his trip is compared to the reunion of a father with his long-lost son (xvi 11-35).

Telemakhos' consideration for the suggestions of Eurykleia indicates that he has more respect for her and her advice; it also suggests that before the present stage of his coming of age, she had more control and authority over him as his nurse and first Teacher, and her impact on him is still compelling.

3. The Recognition of the Old Master

3.1. *Eurykleia and the Stranger*

In xix 317-319 Penelope calls her maids to wash the stranger (Odysseus) and make him a bed, but he rejects her offer (xix 336-345). "Unless there is some devoted (*kedna iduia*) old woman" (εἰ μή τις γρηῦς ἔστι παλαιή, κεδνὰ ἰδυῖα, xix 346), he adds, who has suffered in her heart as many hardships as he has; he would not begrudge *her* to touch his feet (xix 346-348).[41] Penelope responds to Odysseus' request by suggesting for the task Eurykleia, a wise old woman who nursed her husband:

ἔστι δέ μοι γρηῦς πυκινὰ φρεσὶ μήδε' ἔχουσα.
ἣ κεῖνον δύστηνον ἐὺ τρέφεν ἠδ' ἀτίταλλε,

---

[40] Only later does he show consideration for Eumaios' suggestion (xvi 152-153).

[41] xix 346-8 were rejected first by the Alexandrian philologists Aristarchus, Aristophanes, and Zenodotus, and later by Wilamowitz. Büchner 1931.129-136 efficiently refuted the various objections. For a detailed summary of the main objections and their refutation, see Russo 1992.93-94. Stanford 1965 II.327-328, among others, accepts xix 346-348 as genuine and remarks that Odysseus was seeking a trustworthy accomplice among the women of the household. I also accept these lines—and further suggest that Odysseus meant Eurykleia in particular, but he did not expect her to recognize him.

δεξαμένη χείρεσσ', ὅτε μιν πρῶτον τέκε μήτηρ,
ἥ σε πόδας νίψει, ὀλιγηπελέουσά περ ἔμπης.

Odyssey xix 353-356

I have <u>an old woman with dense thoughts in her mind</u>
[*grêüs pukina phresi mêde' ekhousa*]
who <u>nursed [*trephen*]</u> and reared him, hapless one,
and took him to her arms when his mother bore him;
she will wash your feet, feeble though she is.

This passage identifies Eurykleia as the *trophos* (cf. *trephein*, 354), the 'nurse' of Odysseus as well. She is presented as a wise old woman. She is the wise Nurse of a wise master. The 'old woman with dense thoughts in her mind' (γρηῦς πυκινὰ φρεσὶ μήδε' ἔχουσα) is the Nurse to Odysseus 'of the dense thoughts' (πυκινὰ φρονέοντι) of ix 445.[42] The choice of this epithet for Eurykleia, similar to that of Odysseus, may be suggesting that Odysseus owes his wisdom and his shrewdness to his first Teacher, his Nurse.

Penelope encourages Eurykleia to wash the feet of the stranger, who is the same age as her master; Odysseus' hands and feet may be alike, grown old in misfortune, she remarks (xix 357-360).[43] She addresses her respectfully as *periphrôn* 'wise', 'prudent' (περίφρων, xix 357) —her own standing epithet.[44] She proudly introduces Eurykleia, honoring the guest by asking the wise old woman who nursed and raised her husband to wash his feet. Penelope's words also indicate that it is an equal honor for 'wise' Eurykleia to wash the stranger's feet, who is the same age as her master.

And indeed the old woman covers her face with her hands and, moved to tears (xix 361-362), addresses absent Odysseus in lamentation (xix 363-369).[45] Then, turning and addressing the

---

[42] Cf. also the similar epithet of Odysseus εἰδὼς...μήδεα πυκνά in the *Iliad* (III 202).

[43] We notice that Penelope recognizes the same age and the resemblances between the hands and feet of Odysseus and the stranger. As we will see further (xix 380-381), Eurykleia recognizes more resemblances. Stanford 1965 II.330 remarks how Homer portrays women as more perceptive than men, e.g., Helen recognizing Telemakhos in iv 149-150. We should notice that in both cases hands and feet are important recognition features (cf. also Aeschylus' *Libation-Bearers*). There are different theories on whether or to what extent Penelope recognizes Odysseus before he reveals himself. For a summary of the arguments see Murnaghan 1985.103-113. Murnaghan 1987.15ff. and 51ff. supports convincingly a partial and unconscious recognition.

[44] See e.g., i 329, iv 787, v 216; also used of queen Arete (xi 345); of Eurykleia see also xix 491 = xx 134, and xxi 381 (Eumaios addressing Eurykleia).

[45] Her address refers to the absent Odysseus. Still, as Stanford 1965 II.330 remarks,

24 Chapter 1

stranger (xix 370-374), she comments in open disapproval on the *kunes* (κύνες), the 'bitches', the maids who insulted the beggar, just as Odysseus may have been equally insulted by foreign women.[46] But she will wash his feet *ouk aekousa* 'not unwillingly' (οὐκ ἀέκουσαν, xix 374), not only for Penelope's sake, but also for his, for her heart within is stirred with sorrow (ἐπεί μοι ὀρώρεται ἔνδοθι θυμὸς / κήδεσιν, xix 377-378). She even bids the stranger to listen to her words, for many strangers have come to the palace, but none yet resembling, as he does, the form, the voice, and the feet of Odysseus (xix 378-381):

> ... ἀλλ' ἄγε νῦν <u>ξυνίει</u> ἔπος, ὅττι κεν εἴπω·
> πολλοὶ δὴ ξεῖνοι ταλαπείριοι ἐνθάδ' ἵκοντο,
> ἀλλ' οὔ πώ τινά φημι ἐοικότα ὧδε ἰδέσθαι
> ὡς σὺ <u>δέμας</u> <u>φωνήν</u> τε <u>πόδας</u> τ' Ὀδυσῆϊ ἔοικας.
>
> *Odyssey* xix 378-381

> But come now, <u>listen</u> to my words, whatever I tell you;
> indeed, many strangers have come here,
> but, I say, I have seen none yet resembling
> as you do, the <u>form</u>, the <u>voice</u>, and the <u>feet</u> of Odysseus

Eurykleia's long and authoritative speech in xix 363-381, her "speech-act" for the stranger, shows her importance in the poem. Other servants simply wash visitors silently, as we see in other similar instances (as in the case of Telemakhos in Sparta and Odysseus among the Phaeacians). She makes it clear that she will wash his feet not only because Penelope asked her, but also because she feels inclined to do it (see xix 377-378). And furthermore, using an imperative (378), she bids the stranger to *listen* to her words, as she tells him of his resemblances with her master. As a matter of fact, Eurykleia observes more resemblances than his own wife. She adds

---

her words would give the audience a shock: at first they would think that she is addressing the stranger and not her absent master. Russo 1992.94-95 notices that this is another example of dramatic effect, creating in the audience the illusion that Eurykleia recognized the beggar.

[46] This observation is very perceptive of Eurykleia, who has instinctively guessed her master's humiliation, only not in foreign lands but in his own palace. Notice here the language of blame: *kunes* 'bitches'. Eurykleia openly expresses her disapproval of the maids; later she volunteers to assist Odysseus in their punishment. On the language of blame see further Nagy 1979.226-227.

to the resemblance of the *podes* 'feet' the resemblance of the *demas* 'form' and the *phônê* 'voice' (xix 381).[47]

Odysseus praises her perceptiveness and agrees with her comments (xix 383-385): "Old woman, so say those who have seen us both with their eyes, that we look alike."[48] And he continues, recognizing the authoritative quality of her speech, "as you yourself in wisdom profess" (ὡς σύ περ αὐτὴ ἐπιφρονέουσ' ἀγορεύεις, xix 385).

Eurykleia's long and authoritative speech (xix 363-381) is indeed a virtual speech performance, what Martin calls a "speech-act," as Odysseus' comments of approval suggest, especially the use of the term *agoreuein*. The verb *agoreuein* (ἀγορεύειν) literally 'make a speech in the *agora* (the 'assembly'), speak in public', praises the rhetorical but also the authoritative quality of Eurykleia's speech.[49]

3.2. The Recognition

With his observation about the close resemblance, Odysseus is, in fact, trying to trick or mislead the clever old woman. But to no avail. As Eurykleia mixes cold and hot water, in order to wash Odysseus' feet, he sits close to the hearth but suddenly turns toward the darkness, lest she discover the scar and everything be exposed. She draws near and begins washing him, and at once she recognizes the scar:

ὣς ἄρ'ἔφη, γρηῢς δὲ λέβηθ' ἕλε παμφανόωντα
τοῦ πόδας ἐξαπένιζεν, ὕδωρ δ' ἐνεχεύατο πουλὺ
ψυχρόν, ἔπειτα δὲ θερμὸν ἐπήφυσεν. αὐτὰρ Ὀδυσσεὺς
ἷζεν ἐπ' ἐσχαρόφιν, ποτὶ δὲ σκότον ἐτράπετ' αἶψα·
αὐτίκα γὰρ κατὰ θυμὸν ὀΐσατο, μή ἑ λαβοῦσα
οὐλὴν ἀμφράσσαιτο καὶ ἀμφαδὰ ἔργα γένοιτο.
νίζε δ' ἄρ' ἆσσον ἰοῦσα ἄναχθ' ἑόν· αὐτίκα δ' ἔγνω
οὐλήν, τήν ποτέ μιν σῦς ἤλασε λευκῷ ὀδόντι

Odyssey xix 386-393

---

[47] Cf. xix 358-60.

[48] Odysseus' first address to Eurykleia, supposedly an old servant unknown to him, as 'old woman' (ὦ γρηῦ) should be taken as a formal and normal address to an old woman, and by no means derogatory. It is rather the equivalent to ὦ γύναι 'woman' (xix 107, 221), with which Odysseus regularly addresses Penelope under his false identity.

[49] Cf. xix 352, Penelope's praise of Odysseus' speech (ὡς σὺ μάλ' εὐφραδέως πεπνυμένα πάντ' ἀγορεύεις). On the special connotations of *agoreuein* cf. Martin 1989.37, who observes the association of this verb with the authoritative speech-act.

26 Chapter 1

So he spoke, and <u>the old woman</u> took the shining cauldron
she used for foot washing, and poured in plenty of cold water,
and then she added the hot. Now Odysseus
<u>was sitting</u> close to the fire, but <u>quickly</u> he <u>turned</u> to the dark,
for <u>immediately</u> he <u>deemed</u> in his heart lest, as she touched him,
she might feel the scar, and his schemes be revealed.[50] Coming
close, she <u>was washing</u> her lord; but <u>at once</u> she <u>recognized</u>
the scar which once the boar had dealt him with his white tusk.[51]

At this crucial point, the main narrative is interrupted by a long digression on how young Odysseus got this scar during a boar hunt (xix 393-466).[52] In the same lines (xix 399-409), we also learn how Odysseus got his name. In this event Eurykleia has an active participation. She presents the young boy to his grandfather, Autolykos, and even probably indirectly suggests a name for him:

Αὐτόλυκος δ' ἐλθὼν Ἰθάκης ἐς πίονα δῆμον
παῖδα νέον γεγαῶτα κιχήσατο θυγατέρος ἧς·
τόν ῥά οἱ Εὐρύκλεια φίλοις ἐπὶ γούνασι θῆκε
παυομένῳ δόρποιο, ἔπος τ' ἔφατ' ἔκ τ' ὀνόμαζεν·
"Αὐτόλυκ', αὐτὸς νῦν ὄνομ' εὕρεο ὅττι κε θῆαι
παιδὸς παιδὶ φίλῳ· <u>πολυάρητος</u> δέ τοί ἐστι."

Odyssey xix 399-404

Now Autolykos, coming once to the rich country of Ithaca,
had found that a child was newly born to his daughter;
and, as he finished his evening meal, Eurykleia laid him
upon his knees and spoke to him a word and said:
"Autolykos, find now yourself the name you will bestow on your
own child's dear child, for he is surely <u>much-prayed-for
[poluarêtos]</u>."

---

[50] I agree with Russo 1992.95 that the adverbs 'quickly' (αἶψα) and 'immediately' (αὐτίκα), as well as the use of the Aorist (Past) tense 'turned' (ἐτράπετο) and 'deemed' (ὀίσατο) after the Imperfect 'was sitting' (ἷζεν) prove that Odysseus did not want to be recognized.
[51] The contrast between Imperfect and Aorist in the verbs 'was washing... recognized' (νίζε...ἔγνω) is intensified by the adverb 'at once' (αὐτίκα), which stresses the surprise of Eurykleia's recognition. Notice also the parallel tense pattern at xix 389 'was sitting...turned' (ἷζεν...ἐτράπετο), and xix 392 'was washing...recognized' (νίζε...ἔγνω), which provides a dramatic contrast between his effort to hide and the sudden impact of her recognition.
[52] For an insightful comparative discussion of this famous digression see Auerbach 1953.3-23. For more recent discussions, see Pucci 1987.23-24, Dimock 1989.256-259, and Peradotto 1990.94, and 145ff. For a comprehensive analysis with further bibliography, see also Russo 1992.95-98.

Eurykleia, the Predecessor 27

As Murnaghan notes, the child of his daughter, whom Autolykos has come to see, is presented to him by Eurykleia, who poses a question the answer to which, however, is addressed to Odysseus' father and mother: therefore, there is confusion created around the identity of Eurykleia and Odysseus' real mother (see especially lines 400-401).[53] Eurykleia, as Murnaghan notes, probably even attempts to suggest a name for the boy: *Poluarêtos* (πολυάρητος) 'the much prayed for' (404), to which Autolykos suggests the name 'Odysseus' (405-409).[54]

It is important to note that Eurykleia is present at this crucial moment of Odysseus' life, his first experience of pain and, most important, his passage, through the boar-hunt experience, from boyhood to manhood. It is interesting that the old Nurse was also the main accomplice in Telemakhos' passage from boyhood to manhood through his trip in search for news of his father. In both cases, it is she, the Nurse, and not the mother, who plays this important role. For Eurykleia, then, the scar is not a superficial recognition token but a tie with Odysseus' first experience and destiny of pain, implied by his name 'Odysseus'—in the process of the choice of which she is also an important participant.[55]

It is also important to note here that, as Nagy has suggested, the recognition of the *sêma*—the scar in this case—requires an act of interpretation in which the *noos* is involved. Note the cognitive verb 'know', (ἔγνω and again γνῶ in xix 392, 468).[56] It is Eurykleia's mental abilities, the skills of 'the old woman with the dense thoughts' (γρηῢς πυκινὰ φρεσὶ μήδε' ἔχουσα), that defeated Odysseus' *mêtis*. Despite his cleverness, he had not anticipated that she could recognize him before he revealed himself at the moment of his own choice, in contrast to everybody else in Ithaca.[57]

---

[53] Murnaghan 1987.39-41 suggests that in this passage Eurykleia is virtually identified with Odysseus' mother and is presented, like Eumaios, more as a relative than as a servant.

[54] Murnaghan 1987.41. The rejection of her suggestion is not a surprise, especially regarding such an important issue; the real surprise is her suggestion itself, even so carefully presented.

[55] On the meaning of the name Odysseus, connected by the formulaic system with *odunê* (ὀδύνη) 'pain', see the discussion in Russo 1992.96-97.

[56] Nagy 1983. 36, 45-50. Cf. also the revised version in Nagy 1990b.202-222.

[57] On Odysseus' effort to prevent a premature, uncalculated recognition see xix 388-389. For a more detailed discussion see further my conclusion at the end of the chapter.

3.3 The Competition for Authority

Eurykleia, the main narrative continues, recognizes the scar. She lets the foot drop, and the bronze clatters and shakes.[58] Filled at the same time with joy and grief, in tears and with broken voice, she greets Odysseus:

> τὴν γρηῦς χείρεσσι καταπρηνέσσι λαβοῦσα
> γνῶ ῥ' ἐπιμασσαμένη, πόδα δὲ προέηκε φέρεσθαι·
> ἐν δὲ λέβητι πέσε κνήμη, κανάχησε δὲ χαλκός,[59]
> ἂψ δ' ἑτέρωσ' ἐκλίθη· τὸ δ' ἐπὶ χθονὸς ἐξέχυθ' ὕδωρ.
> τὴν δ' ἅμα χάρμα καὶ ἄλγος ἔλε φρένα, τὼ δέ οἱ ὄσσε
> δακρυόφι πλῆσθεν, θαλερὴ δέ οἱ ἔσχετο φωνή.
> ἁψαμένη δὲ γενείου Ὀδυσσῆα προσέειπεν·
> "ἦ μάλ' Ὀδυσσεύς ἐσσι, φίλον τέκος· οὐδέ σ' ἐγώ γε
> πρὶν ἔγνων, πρὶν πάντα ἄνακτ' ἐμὸν ἀμφαφάασθαι."
>
> *Odyssey* xix 467-475

This[60] the old woman touched with the palms of her hands,
and she recognized [*gnô*] as she handled it; she let the foot drop;
the leg fell into the basin, and the bronze clattered and shook,
and the water was spilt out on the ground.
At the same time joy and grief seized her heart.[61] Her eyes

---

[58] On the dangerous exposure of the bath ritual and its implications for Odysseus, see the stimulating discussion of Charles Segal 1967.331-342 (reprinted in Segal 1974.474-376). Segal observes that, like other transitional situations, the bath has an essential ambiguity; it is physically pleasant, yet it involves a potentially dangerous exposure. A bath, therefore, may also be partially accepted, as in the case of Odysseus' bathing by Eurykleia, as a ritual not fully or perfectly performed. This is why Odysseus does not allow himself to be washed by the younger servants, but only by an old servant "with whom he has the greatest bond of suffering." Segal also sees the bath as ritual entrance to another world and as a means of revealing identity. Eurykleia's recognition indicates the interruption of the proper ritual and underlines the danger of his re-entrance and, correspondingly, the revelation of his identity. It recalls a similar situation of danger, his bathing by Helen of Troy, in iv 252ff., when he entered the city in disguise. The similarity is "bitterly paradoxical" as he is now in Ithaca as much in the house of his enemies as he was in Troy. As Segal concludes, Odysseus' complete and final bath, in xxiii 152, seals the fulfillment of his return as it precedes the recognition by his wife. On this final bath and Eurykleia's suggestion see my comments below.

[59] The vivid details of this dramatic moment are intensified by the effect of assonance and alliteration of κ and χ in the narration of xix 469-470, especially in xix 469 (κανάχησε...χαλκός).

[60] The pronoun "this" (τήν), referring to the scar, signals the end of the digression and brings back the narrative to the recognition scene.

[61] The confusion of her feelings indicates her great emotion (cf. Stanford 1965 II.334). Furthermore, we should view her emotion as even more intensified by the memories of

were filled with tears and her rich voice was broken.
Touching Odysseus by his beard, she spoke to him: [62]
"Indeed, you are Odysseus, my dear son; and I did not
know [egnôn] you before, not until I touched my king all over."

She tries to find Penelope with her eyes and let her know that her husband is there, but Athena has turned Penelope's mind elsewhere (xix 476-479).

Odysseus' reaction is both violent and dramatic. He tries to secure Eurykleia's silence by all means. Feeling for her throat, he clasps it with his right hand, while, with the other, he pulls her closer and abruptly cuts her short (xix 479-481):

"μαῖα, τίη μ' ἐθέλεις ὀλέσαι; σὺ δέ μ' ἔτρεφες αὐτὴ
τῷ σῷ ἐπὶ μαζῷ· νῦν δ' ἄλγεα πολλὰ μογήσας
ἤλυθον εἰκοστῷ ἔτεϊ ἐς πατρίδα γαῖαν.
ἀλλ' ἐπεὶ ἐφράσθης καί τοι θεὸς ἔμβαλε θυμῷ,
σίγα, μή τίς τ' ἄλλος ἐνὶ μεγάροισι πύθηται.
ὧδε γὰρ ἐξερέω, καὶ μὴν τετελεσμένον ἔσται·
εἴ χ' ὑπ' ἐμοί γε θεὸς δαμάσῃ μνηστῆρας ἀγαυούς,
οὐδὲ τροφοῦ οὔσης σεῦ ἀφέξομαι, ὁππότ' ἂν ἄλλας
δμωὰς ἐν μεγάροισιν ἐμοῖς κτείνωμι γυναῖκας."

Odyssey xix 482-490

"Nurse [maia], do you want to destroy me? You nursed me
    [trephein] yourself
at your own breast; and now, having suffered many toils
after twenty years I finally came back to my homeland.
But since you found out and some god put it in your heart,
keep quiet [siga], so that nobody else in the house finds out.
For, I am telling you, and take my word for it,
if a god subdues for me the lordly suitors,
I will not spare even you, my own nurse [trophos], when I kill
the other servant women [dmôias] in my halls."[63]

---

the incident of the boar-hunt that the scar triggered, as they revived the nurse/boy ties.

[62] This is an element of a formal supplication (cf. *Iliad* I 501, VIII 371, X 454). On this occasion, I believe, it indicates Eurykleia's awe at the overwhelming emotion of the recognition of her master who is not only her 'dear son' (xix 474) but also her king (xix 475).

[63] This is one more indication that Eurykleia, though the Nurse of Odysseus (xix 354-355, 489), is still considered among the maids (xix 490). Cf. Eurykleia's introduction as a Nurse of Telemakhos, but also as one of the maids (i 434-435).

30   Chapter 1

Odysseus is so desperate that he tries every possible way. He first tries physically to keep Eurykleia silent, then he tries the power of speech.[64] By calling her *maia* 'nurse', he first appeals to her motherly affection and the physical bond between them since, as he stresses, she actually 'nursed' him with her own milk (xix 481-482). Then he appeals to her pity for his miseries, and reminding her that her discovery was through the help of some god, he appeals to her confidentiality. In case all these are not enough, he even threatens her with death, a threat that the pressure of his hand on her throat makes all the more believable, reminding her that although she is his nurse she is still a *dmôiê* 'servant'.[65]

There is a ring composition pattern, in Odysseus' reaction and plea for Eurykleia's silence in xix 79-90: it starts with a demonstration of violence (479-81), followed by an appeal to her as his Nurse (482-483), followed by a reference to divine intervention (485); then he pleads for her silence (486); then, again, he emphasizes divine help (488), her role as his Nurse (489), and finally his potential for violence (489-490). Thus, his appeal for silence is framed by references to divine means, to their nurse/child connection, and to his potential for violence. If Eurykleia is not scared by his clasp, if she is not moved by his appeal to their bond, if she is not convinced by his references to divine intervention, she should remember that he has unquestionable power and authority over her as her master.

Eurykleia, however, is not in the least intimidated. On the contrary, she faces Odysseus as an opponent in an agonistic speech which matches his at every point: she reacts with a rhetorical question matching that of Odysseus in xix 482, and right after that, like a Homeric hero about to enter battle, she confirms her *menos* 'strength' (and truly her reaction itself is clearly a proof of it).[66] In

---

[64] By contrast, the Nurse in *Hippolytus* (603-606) tries to achieve silence from Hippolytus by using first speech and then physical means of a very different kind—supplication. Speech, in any form, is women's most effective mode of influence.

[65] A servant has to obey his or her master to avoid punishment. Cf. Eurykleia's words to Penelope in iv 743-744. Cf. also the execution of the unfaithful maids and that of Melanthios (xxii 465-477).

[66] The word *menos* (μένος) indicates a driving force, strength, perseverance. It is still used in Modern Greek with a comparably strong meaning. Nagy 1974.266-268 compares the Greek *menos* 'power, faculty' with the Latin *mens* 'mind' and proposes that the noun *menos* is derived from the verbal root *men-*. In order to fight bravely, the Homeric hero has to be reminded of his *menos*, his power. Cf. the connections Nagy makes in the transformations of Athena as Mentes and Mentor as she is fusing *menos* into Telemakhos. See above (n28).

fact, she is declaring her *menos* to Odysseus before she enters this verbal fight or contest. Indeed, in answer to Odysseus' words in xix 487-490, she replies in xix 495-498 on equal terms, as one who is equally determined. And she finishes her speech by announcing what she will do for him:

> "τέκνον ἐμόν, ποῖόν σε ἔπος φύγεν ἕρκος ὀδόντων.
> οἶσθα μὲν οἷον ἐμὸν <u>μένος</u> ἔμπεδον οὐδ' ἐπιεικτόν,
> ἕξω δ' ὡς ὅτε τις στερεὴ λίθος ἠὲ σίδηρος.
> ἄλλο δέ τοι <u>ἐρέω</u>, σὺ δ' ἐνὶ φρεσὶ <u>βάλλεο</u> σῇσιν·
> εἴ χ' ὑπὸ σοί γε θεὸς δαμάσῃ μνηστῆρας ἀγαυούς,
> δὴ τότε τοι <u>καταλέξω</u> ἐνὶ μεγάροισι γυναῖκας,
> αἵ τέ σ' ἀτιμάζουσι καὶ αἳ νηλείτιδές εἰσι."
>
> *Odyssey* xix 492-498

> "my child, what a word escaped the barrier of your teeth?
> You know how my <u>strength [*menos*]</u> is solid and unyielding.
> I will be as firm as stone or iron.
> And <u>I will tell</u> you something else and <u>put</u> it in your mind;
> if through you a god subdues the illustrious suitors,
> then <u>I will name</u> to you the women in the halls,
> those who dishonor you and those who are guiltless."

Indeed, with this "speech-act," to use Martin's term, Eurykleia enters a verbal fight, or rather, a verbal contest, an agonistic speech performance, as she tries to answer all Odysseus' points. Her speech corresponds in every part with Odysseus' speech. Her rhetorical question in xix 492 is a response to Odysseus' rhetorical question in xix 482; xix 493-494, where she confirms her *menos*, is an answer to his request for silence in xix 482-486; xix 495 is her determined reaction to his announcement in xix 487; xix 496 is a repetition of xix 488; and xix 497-498 is her suggestion as an answer to his menace of xix 489-490.[67]

Eurykleia's agonistic speech and imperative tone (notice the future tense in ἐρέω, xix 495, καταλέξω, xix 497, and the imperative βάλλεο, xix 495) surprises and irritates Odysseus, as his reaction reveals. He retorts with one more rhetorical question and continues with assertion:

> "<u>μαῖα</u>, τίη δὲ σὺ τὰς μυθήσεαι; οὐδέ τί σε χρή.

---

[67] xix 495-498 correspond to xix 487-490, not only in length of message, but also in subject matter: "You will punish me with the other maids? I'll tell you what: <u>I will tell you</u> which maids you should punish."

εὖ νυ καὶ αὐτὸς ἐγὼ φράσομαι καὶ εἴσομ' ἑκάστην·
ἀλλ' ἔχε σιγῇ μῦθον, <u>ἐπίτρεψον δὲ θεοῖσιν</u>."

Odyssey xix 500-502

"<u>Nurse</u>, why will you name them? You do not need to.
I, myself, too, will mark them easily and know each one;[68]
but keep quiet and <u>leave it to the gods</u>."

Eurykleia makes no more attempts at a reply, and it seems that Odysseus has had the last word. In fact, his last word is to "leave it to the gods." The old woman complies with his request. She goes to bring more water, since she had spilt it all previously in her emotion at the recognition of Odysseus, and anoints him with oil (xix 503-505). She quietly becomes Odysseus' ally and accomplice, as she did with Telemakhos before.[69] After the threat of Odysseus (xix 489-490) she has no other safe choice); but she must also have been convinced by Odysseus' arguments. Especially faced with such a plea, in which Odysseus puts divine help before Eurykleia's merely human help (xix 502), she cannot but be persuaded.[70]

4. Eurykleia in Full Authority

4.1. *Eurykleia defends Penelope*

At the end of book xix, Penelope tells Odysseus that she is going upstairs to her room to sleep, and he can sleep in the hall, either making his bed on the floor or letting the maids set a bedstead for him (xix 588-599). Odysseus chooses to make his bedding in the forehall, where later Eurynome covers him with a cloak (xx 1-4). Soon after, Telemakhos asks Eurykleia if they honored the guest in the house with bed and food, because, he says, criticizing his mother, it is her way, "prudent though she is, strangely to honor one who is worse

---

[68] In fact, Odysseus has the chance to find them out soon (xx 6-8). Still, when the moment of the punishment comes, he actually asks Eurykleia to name the unfaithful maids for him (xxiii 417-418). On Odysseus' initial rejection of Eurykleia's suggestions see my discussion below.

[69] Cf. ii 349-380.

[70] Cf. the similar allusion to divine intervention that Telemakhos used to secure her help and cooperation in ii 372: "this is not without a god's will" (οὔ τοι ἄνευ θεοῦ ἥδε γε βουλή).

and send away a better man unhonored" (xx 129-133).[71] *Periphrôn* 'wise' Eurykleia reproaches him for blaming his mother (xx 134).[72] "You should not blame one who is not to blame" (οὐκ ἄν μιν νῦν, τέκνον, ἀναίτιον αἰτιόῳο, xx 135), she protests, and she continues explaining her version of what happened (xx 134-143).[73]

Eurykleia, here, not only reprimands Telemakhos, but also defends Penelope, changing the true account of events. From her speech, it seems that Penelope actually asked her maids to make a bed for Odysseus but he refused. The truth is, however, that she actually suggested, rather indifferently, that Odysseus could "make his own bedding or have the maids make it for him" (xix 598-599). It was more natural that Odysseus, a beggar, would take her first suggestion rather than pursue the second. Still, Eurykleia is telling the truth, since in xix 317-319 Penelope initially asked her maids to wash Odysseus and make a bed for him, both of which he refused at that time (xix 336-345). Eurykleia adds, "but we covered him with a cloak." 'We' (ἡμεῖς), refers to the servants, including herself. One would think then that Eurykleia, herself, was involved in this. Still, the narrator has told us already that it was Eurynome who covered him (xx 4). Not only the epithet *periphrôn* 'wise', but all the epithets that refer to Eurykleia's mental skills, are substantiated in this episode. She proves herself, although on a smaller scale, an expert in presenting lies in a truthful fashion, like her master, Odysseus, in xix 203, who "presented many lies resembling the truth" (ἴσκε ψεύδεα πολλὰ λέγων ἐτύμοισιν ὁμοῖα). One could suspect that probably he learned this skill of lying skillfully from his Nurse and first Teacher, Eurykleia.

Telemakhos' attempt to question his mother's hospitality is faced with Eurykleia's rebuttal in defense of her mistress. He has nothing to say in return. Defeated, he leaves without a word to attend to men's matters in the marketplace (xx 144-146), while Eurykleia attends to women's matters in the house: she now triumphantly displays her authority over the maids. At this point, quite purposefully, I believe,

---

[71] He addresses Eurykleia, as usual, as *maia* 'nurse', this time *maia philê* 'dear nurse'.

[72] This epithet, a standing epithet of Penelope, used also of queen Arete, is used here in a formula (xx 134= xix 491) as an intelligent choice to underscore her wisdom and intelligence, as her skillful speech suggests. As a form of address to Eurykleia, the epithet is first used by Penelope in xix 357 and then by Eumaios in xxi 381.

[73] The optative (αἰτιόῳο) makes her disapproval milder.

34 Chapter 1

Homeric poetry provides another instance, and another aspect, of Eurykleia's authority.

4.2. In Charge of the Maids

As soon as Telemakhos leaves, "*dia gunaikôn* 'noblest of women' Eurykleia, the daughter of Ops, son of Peisenor" (xx 147-148), calls the maids and orders them to clean and prepare the hall for the feast.[74]

This is in fact the third introduction of Eurykleia with father's and grandfather's names (see also i 428 and ii 347). I believe that this is not a coincidence, but a display of a poetic intention to emphasize her importance again now, and from now on, especially as Eurykleia is portrayed here in full authority in charge of the maids and their education. We should also notice that every time her father's and grandfather's names are mentioned, they follow a new attribute of Eurykleia's personality—a new epithet (κεδνά ἰδυῖα, i 428-429, γυνὴ ταμίη...νόου πολυϊδρείῃσιν, ii 345-347, δῖα γυναικῶν, xx 147-148)—as well as a new facet of her role—Telemakhos' nurse, the housekeeper, and now the person in charge of the maids and their *paideia*:

ἡ δ' αὖτε δμῳῇσιν ἐκέκλετο δῖα γυναικῶν,
Εὐρύκλει', Ὦπος θυγάτηρ Πεισηνορίδαο·
"ἀγρεῖθ', αἱ μὲν δῶμα κορήσατε ποιπνύσασαι,
ῥάσσατέ τ', ἔν τε θρόνοις εὐποιήτοισι τάπητας
βάλλετε πορφυρέους· αἱ δὲ σπόγγοισι τραπέζας
πάσας ἀμφιμάσασθε, καθήρατε δὲ κρητῆρας
καὶ δέπα ἀμφικύπελλα τετυγμένα· ταὶ δὲ μεθ' ὕδωρ
ἔρχεσθε κρήνηνδε, καὶ οἴσετε θᾶσσον ἰοῦσαι.
οὐ γὰρ δὴν μνηστῆρες ἀπέσσονται μεγάροιο,
ἀλλὰ μάλ' ἦρι νέονται, ἐπεὶ καὶ πᾶσιν ἑορτή."
Ὣς ἔφαθ', αἱ δ' ἄρα τῆς μάλα μὲν κλύον ἠδ' ἐπίθοντο.

Odyssey xx 147-156

But she called to the maidens, the noblest of women [*dia gunaikôn*] Eurykleia, the daughter of Ops, son of Peisenor. "Come, some of you busily sweep the hall, and sprinkle it with water, and put the purple coverlets over the well-wrought chairs. Some others, wipe thoroughly all the tables with sponges, and clean the mixing-bowls

---

[74] *Dia gunaikôn* (δῖα γυναικῶν, xx 147), like Penelope in i 332, xxi 42, 63, Helen iv 305, III 171, 228, 423, and Alcestis II 714. Eurykleia is the only servant in the *Odyssey* or the *Iliad* who shares this epithet with famous noble women.

and the wrought double cups; and others, <u>go</u>
to the spring for water and <u>fetch</u> it quickly back.
For the suitors will not long be absent from the palace,
but will arrive very early, since this is a feast-day for all."
So she spoke and they listened to her and obeyed.

Here we have the chance to observe Eurykleia as she exercises her traditional domestic and unquestionable authority over the maids, who are subordinate to her in hierarchy, as she instructs them with her orders. This is another facet of an older woman's tasks in a household, as described in the *Hymn to Demeter* 144 (see above). Notice here the series of imperatives (underlined in xx 149-154, above), revealing through her fussy and authoritative tone her authority over them.[75] As we are reminded of her father's and grandfather's names for the third time we may anticipate another important role for her in the story. It is conceivable that Eurykleia's function in the *Odyssey* is not merely to recognize Odysseus. This third introduction emphasizes another aspect of her power and authority—that over younger women of less experience, like the maids here, and even her own mistress, Penelope, as we will see later.

Her interaction with a group of younger women from a superior stance recalls indeed female choral performances in early lyric poetry like that of Alcman PMG 1. This interaction suggests a background of choral tradition, especially as those choral performances were part of a girl's *paideia*. The maids in this passage embody the members of the *khoros* aggregate, especially as Eurykleia, the older experienced female figure, instructs them in what to do.[76]

But even in the absence of younger women, we can still see her as the crystallization of a *khorêgos* figure who steps out of the *khoros* circle, maintaining, however, her basic characteristic of an authority derived from the hierarchical relationship with younger members as defined in the archaic Greek *khoros*. Her involvement in the *paideia* of her younger mistress or masters—even in the absence of the context of the archaic *khoros*—endows her with the same hierarchical authority as defined in the archaic Greek choral constructs.

---

[75] Stanford 1965 II. 348 notes that part of the excitement is due to her knowledge of Odysseus' presence now. I suggest that it is also in view of the punishment of a number of them through her cooperation with Odysseus.

[76] Cf. Eurykleia's words to Odysseus later (xxii 422-423), when she explains how she and Penelope taught the girls the household duties (see below).

36 Chapter 1

It is her role in the *paideia* of her masters that enhances her authority and influence over them. In the following lines we will trace such authority not only over the maids but also over Penelope, a younger female figure. Even more interesting, we will observe her effort to exercise her authority—acquired in the past and derived from her role as Nurse and Teacher—over a male figure of socially superior authority, her master, and king of Ithaca, Odysseus.

4.3. The 'Old Woman' as Odysseus' Accomplice

We will now have the chance to observe two similar characters, Eumaios and Eurykleia, interacting with each other for the first and only time. Eumaios is, like Eurykleia, an old faithful servant who in Odysseus' absence takes care of the estate, as Eurykleia takes care of his household. He is also a father figure for Telemakhos, whom he advises, protects and cares for, like Eurykleia.[77]

In xxi 378ff., in preparation for the archery contest, Eumaios, after bringing the bow to Odysseus, takes to Eurykleia the message that *Telemakhos* bids her to bar the doors of the hall, and, if the women within hear any din in the house, not to let them rush out, but to keep them there (xxi 381-385). In fact, it was *Odysseus* who had initially asked Eumaios to tell *the women* to close the doors and remain there (xxi 235-236). Eumaios, not knowing that Eurykleia already knows of Odysseus' presence, accommodates the message quite cleverly by changing the identity of the person who gave the orders; at the same time, he transfers the duty of carrying out the orders to Eurykleia, whom he respectfully addresses as *periphrôn* 'wise' (xxi 381).[78] Seeing how Eurykleia follows his directions without objection (xxi 386-387), we notice that he does not lack cleverness himself. Eumaios' clever address helps convince Eurykleia to follow Telemakhos' directions, which he conveys to her. In this sense, he is a real match for Eurykleia: he is her male counterpart.

A little later, in xxii 391-397, when the battle with the suitors is over, Odysseus asks Telemakhos to summon his Nurse. Telemakhos, indeed, summons Eurykleia, acknowledging his father's orders and, quite surprisingly, he addresses her in a new fashion:

---

[77] On the similarity of these two characters and their function in the *Odyssey*, see also Austin 1975.165ff. Cf. also my discussion above, and notes 14, 26, and 40.

[78] See also xix 357 and n44, and the summary of her epithets in Table II, at the end of the chapter.

"Δεῦρο δὴ ὄρσο, γρηῦ παλαιγενές, ἥ τε γυναικῶν
δμωάων σκοπός ἐσσι κατὰ μέγαρ' ἡμετεράων·
ἔρχεο· κικλήσκει σε πατὴρ ἐμός, ὄφρα τι εἴπῃ."

Odyssey xxii 395-397

"Get up, <u>old woman born of old</u>, you who are
the <u>guard of the servant women</u> in our house,
come, my father summons you to tell you something."

For the first and only time, Telemakhos calls Eurykleia 'old woman' (γρηῦ), intensified more with the epithet *palaigenês* 'born of old', instead of the usual 'nurse'.[79] Why does he not call her *maia* 'nurse', as usual, especially since his father told him to summon his 'nurse' (*trophos*, xxii 391)? Is this a novel (for Telemakhos) form of address, indicative of his excitement because of his father's presence, especially his achievement in killing the suitors? Is it a sign of his own proven manhood after his accomplishment and contribution, and therefore his new relation with his nurse? Or is it in anticipation of different tasks for her, especially considering her newly mentioned function as the 'guard of the maids' (xxii 396)? The explanation of such an address must be a combination of all these factors: (1) the excitement of the moment, (2) the new status of Telemakhos, and therefore this new relation to his old nurse (not boy/nurse anymore but grown up man/old woman), (3) in addition, a new kind of task for Eurykleia, in which the authority of her old age enhances and amplifies her hierarchical authority as the Nurse, as our further discussion will show.[80]

Without a word, Eurykleia follows Telemakhos into the hall, where she finds Odysseus blood-stained among the dead, like a lion feeding on his prey (xxii 398-406). When she sees the corpses and the blood, she is about to raise a yell of triumph at the sight of the great achievement (407-408). But Odysseus stays and checks her in her

---

[79] The disyllabic form γρηΰ instead of the monosyllabic diphthong γρηῦ (cf. xix 346, γρηῦς παλαιή), dictated by metrical restrictions, emphasizes more this new form of address by Telemakhos. For *palaigenês* (παλαιγενής) cf. *Iliad* XVII 561 (γεραιέ παλαιγενές), Menelaos' address of Phoenix; Phoenix is the equivalent male nurse/tutor figure to Achilles, who has special influence on him because of this bond, but also because of his old age. See also *Iliad* III 386, *Hymn to Hermes* 199, and especially *Hymn to Demeter* 101, 113, and the discussion above.

[80] See also the discussion on the term 'old woman' at the conclusion of the chapter. For a different interpretation see Russo 1992.288, who comments on "the humorous banter" of Telemakhos in elation at the triumph (the victory against the suitors).

38 Chapter 1

eagerness, calling her also 'old woman' (γρηῦ, 411):[81] "In your heart, rejoice, old woman; restrain yourself and don't yell in triumph; it is unholy to boast over slain men" (411-412). He further explains to her that they were destroyed through divine fate and through their reckless deeds (xxii 413-416).[82] And surprisingly, he now asks Eurykleia to do exactly what she had suggested previously (xix 496-498), and what Odysseus had initially rejected (xix 500-502), namely, to name for him the unfaithful maids:[83]

ἀλλ' ἄγε μοι σὺ γυναῖκας ἐνὶ μεγάροις κατάλεξον,
αἵ τε μ' ἀτιμάζουσι καὶ αἳ νηλείτιδές εἰσιν.

Odyssey xxii 417-418

but come, name for me the women in the house
both those who dishonor me and those who are guiltless.

And as Eurykleia sees that he has listened to her suggestion and that he needs her help, especially in a women's domain that belongs to her duties, she now answers him (xxii 420-429) by calling him again *teknon* 'child' (420), thus emphasizing her maternal authority over Odysseus both as his nurse and as an old woman. She promises to tell him the truth:[84] among the fifty servants whom they 'taught' (*didaskein*, 422), twelve have become shameless and respect neither her nor Penelope (420-425).[85] She finishes her report accounting for Telemakhos' inaction, thus expressing her own judgement, that it is time for him to take this responsibility (426-427):[86]

---

[81] Cf. xix 383 and xxii 481.

[82] For further references on the interpretation of Odysseus' reaction, see Stanford 1965 II.384.

[83] Note also that Telemakhos had advised Odysseus to identify the dishonest maids, xvi 316-317. Although Odysseus asks Telemakhos to give him the names of the suitors (xvi 235-236), he is rejecting Eurykleia's offer until now.

[84] This statement, emphasizing the truth of her words, strengthens my point that Eurykleia is capable of lies.

[85] Eurykleia's educational duties extended from the bringing up of Odysseus and Telemakhos to the teaching of the female servants. Among Eurykleia's tasks and responsibilities was the training of the maids. This was another task that an older woman performed in a household, as described in the *Hymn to Demeter* 144 (cf. the use of the same verb *didaskein* 'teach'). On the professional training of the servants, see Webster 1962a.459.

[86] xxii 425-429 have been condemned by Dünzer and van Herwerden; these lines are missing in a new papyrus published by Bartoletti in 1977, who also approves the omission. For more details see Fernández-Galiano 1992.294. Still, these verses are in full

Eurykleia, the Predecessor 39

τοιγὰρ ἐγώ τοι, <u>τέκνον</u>, ἀληθείην καταλέξω.
πεντήκοντά τοί εἰσιν ἐνὶ μεγάροισι γυναῖκες
δμωαί, τὰς μέν τ' ἔργα <u>διδάξαμεν</u> ἐργάζεσθαι,
εἴριά τε ξαίνειν καὶ δουλοσύνην ἀνέχεσθαι·
τάων δώδεκα πᾶσαι ἀναιδείης ἐπέβησαν,
οὔτ' ἐμὲ τίουσαι οὔτ' αὐτὴν Πηνελόπειαν.
Τηλέμαχος δὲ νέον μὲν ἀέξετο, οὐδέ ἑ μήτηρ
σημαίνειν εἴασκεν ἐπὶ δμῳῇσι γυναιξίν.

Odyssey xxii 420-427

Truly, I will tell you the truth, <u>my child</u>.
There are fifty servant women in the house,
whom <u>we taught [*didaxamen*]</u> their work,
how to card wool and endure slavery.
Twelve of them altogether set foot on shamelessness,
respecting neither me nor Penelope herself.
Telemakhos has only recently matured, and his mother
did not let him take command over the servants.

And then, unexpectedly, she offers a new suggestion—to tell Penelope of Odysseus' return (428-429):

ἀλλ' ἄγ' ἐγὼν ἀναβᾶσ' ὑπερώϊα σιγαλόεντα
εἴπω σῇ ἀλόχῳ, τῇ τις θεὸς ὕπνον ἐπῶρσε.

Odyssey xxii 428-429

But come, let me go to the bright upper chamber
and tell your wife in whom some god instilled sleep.

Odysseus this time objects mainly to the timing of her suggestion, and instead, he asks her to call the guilty women to his presence:[87]

Μή πω τήνδ' ἐπέγειρε· <u>σὺ</u> δ' ἐνθάδε εἰπὲ γυναιξὶν
ἐλθέμεν, αἵ περ πρόσθεν ἀεικέα μηχανόωντο.

Odyssey xxii 431-432

Don't wake her up yet; but <u>you [*su*]</u> tell the women to come here, those who have previously contrived shameful deeds.

I suggest that the emphatic use of 'you' *su* (σύ, 431) in the middle of his orders is intended to remind Eurykleia of *her* immediate task.[88]

---

agreement with Eurykleia's style and pattern of suggestions.

[87] Odysseus wants to spare Penelope from the gruesome spectacle that was to follow. See further Fenik 1974.239.

40 Chapter 1

The use of *su* reminds her of the completion of the task for which *she* had volunteered (cf. xix 496-498). Odysseus not only relies on her information regarding the unfaithful maids but also increases her authority over them by giving her the chance to more actively participate in their punishment. Indeed, Eurykleia has given him a sample of her tough and relentless *menos* 'strength' with her reaction at the sight of the punishment of the suitors (cf. xxii 407-408).

I see here a typical pattern of an initial rejection by Odysseus of Eurykleia's advice, which he follows later. Eurykleia, as her address *teknon* 'my son' (420) implies, has assumed her maternal influence and authority over Odysseus, and Odysseus initially reacts to it.[89] However, his resistance gradually diminishes, as he eventually follows her advice; compare his mild objection here, "don't wake her up yet" (xxii 431), with his clearly irritated and ironic previous objection (xix 500-501).

Indeed, the old woman, without further counter-suggestions, gladly follows Odysseus' order and goes to bring the women (xxii 433-434). Odysseus then asks Telemakhos and Eumaios to order the women to clean up the blood, then to take them out to the courtyard and kill them with their swords. Odysseus now allows Telemakhos to do what Penelope had not allowed him, namely, to deal with the maids, as Eurykleia very indirectly, carefully, and subtly hinted (see xxii 426-427).

Telemakhos, in turn, takes more liberty in suggesting that the 'clean' death by the sword be changed to death by hanging, as we see later (xxii 465ff.).[90] Telemakhos finally assumes the responsibility and the authority that his Nurse had expected of him (xxii 426-427).[91]

After the punishment of the maids (xxii 465-473) and that of Melanthios (xxii 474-479), Odysseus calls Eurykleia again and assigns

---

[88] This line (xxii 431) would flow unnoticed if the narrative had used instead simply the word ἀλλά 'but' (ἀλλ' ἐνθάδε εἰπὲ γυναιξίν).

[89] According to Olson 1992.226-227, rejection by the master of a servant's suggestion is typical in the *Odyssey*; servants may offer their advice, but they should expect no credit even if their suggestions are ultimately adopted. "Their task is to recognize the master's authority and thus to keep quiet and do what they are told." Eurykleia, however, as we see, does not follow this pattern.

[90] On the notion of an unclean death by hanging in contrast to a pure death by the sword see Loraux 1987.14-15.

[91] This would be the punishment for insulting himself and his mother and for sleeping with the suitors, as he started *agoreuein* 'announcing' (ἦρχ' ἀγορεύειν, xxii 461). The verb *agoreuein* (ἀγορεύειν) is indicative of Telemakhos' new authority. Cf. xix 385 and the following discussion.

Eurykleia, the Predecessor 41

to her a new errand—to cleanse the hall. And then, he asks her to do what she had suggested and he had postponed, namely, to call her mistress, and also all the maids in the house:

Οἶσε θέειον, <u>γρηΰ</u>, κακῶν ἄκος, οἶσε δέ μοι πῦρ,
ὄφρα θεειώσω μέγαρον· <u>σὺ</u> δὲ Πηνελόπειαν
ἐλθεῖν ἐνθάδ' ἄνωχθι σὺν ἀμφιπόλοισι γυναιξί·
πάσας δ' ὄτρυνον δμῳὰς κατὰ δῶμα νέεσθαι.

Odyssey xxii 481-484

Bring sulfur, <u>old woman</u>,[92] the cure of evils, and bring me fire
so I can purge the hall. And <u>you [su]</u>[93] tell Penelope
to come here with her attendant maids;
and urge all the women servants in the house to come.

Eurykleia, seeing that Odysseus is now following her advice to tell Penelope (see xxii 428-429), approves of Odysseus' words with maternal confidence (xxii 486).[94] Furthermore, as she regains her power of influencing and directing him, she has again something else to suggest, that he should change his clothes, while at the same time she expresses her disapproval of Odysseus' present looks (xxii 487-489). Note here her authoritative speech marked with the imperative "don't stand" (μηδ'... ἔσταθ', xxii 488-489). She continues her effort to direct Odysseus, while at the same time she freely expresses both her approval (xxii 486) and her disapproval (xxii 489):

"Ναὶ δὴ ταῦτα γε, <u>τέκνον ἐμόν</u>, κατὰ μοῖραν ἔειπες.
ἀλλ' ἄγε τοι χλαῖνάν τε χιτῶνά τε εἵματ' ἐνείκω,
μηδ' οὕτω ῥάκεσιν πεπυκασμένος εὐρέας ὤμους
ἔσταθ' ἐνὶ μεγάροισι· <u>νεμεσσητὸν</u> δέ κεν εἴη."

Odyssey xxii 486-489

"Indeed, you spoke these words <u>quite suitably, my child</u>.
But let me bring you a cloak and tunic,
and don't stand in the hall like this, your broad shoulders
covered with rags, for it would be <u>reproachable</u>."[95]

---

[92] Notice that he calls her γρηΰ 'old woman', and not just 'nurse', as he assigns to her a series of important tasks, especially to summon Penelope. Cf. xix 383 and xxii 411.

[93] Note again the emphatic 'you' (σύ) in the middle of his orders, which emphasizes that he now grants her the permission to do what *she* had suggested before.

[94] She addresses him 'my child' (τέκνον ἐμόν). Cf. xix 492 and xxii 420.

[95] On the importance of clothing for the recognition of Odysseus, see Block 1985.1-11. She discusses Odysseus' intentional revelations, that occur only by removing his rags. Block's careful discussion, however, does not account for Eurykleia's recognition of her

42 Chapter 1

Odysseus' resistance is now even more weak:

"πῦρ νῦν μοι πρώτιστον ἐνὶ μεγάροισι γενέσθω."

Odyssey xxii 491

"Now, first of all let me have a fire in my palace."

He answers briefly, neither opposing nor yet following Eurykleia's advice, only reminding her of his previous order of xxii 481.[96] And Eurykleia, as before, does not fail to do all that Odysseus asks. She brings fire and sulfur, and then she leaves the room to call all the maids, who welcome back Odysseus with great affection (xxii 492-496).

It is interesting to observe the emotional reunion scene between Odysseus and the other women servants (xxi 498-501), while Eurykleia and Odysseus never had an affectionate reunion. It is this lack of a natural outburst of affectionate emotion that makes the recognition scene between Odysseus and Eurykleia (xix 467ff.) even more powerful and dramatic. Eurykleia is, in fact, the only person who recognizes Odysseus unexpectedly and prematurely, despite his calculations. On all other occasions Odysseus chooses the moment and reveals himself to all the members of his household according to his plan: first to Telemakhos, then to Eumaios and Philoitios, and finally to Penelope and Laertes.

Odysseus' recognition by Eurykleia proves that she is the one person Odysseus does not manage to trick; on the contrary, she is the one who outwits him. Furthermore, from the moment she recognizes Odysseus, she uses what must have been her authority of the past and tries to direct him by suggesting what he should do. It is interesting to note that no other loyal servant (e.g., Eumaios or Philoitios) tries to direct or advise Odysseus.[97] We noticed how Odysseus confronts her in the beginning, ignoring her advice and her suggestions, but only temporarily. In the long run, he actually follows all her suggestions, only choosing his own timing. He always has a counter-suggestion or a different task for her. In xxii 491, as he is following the last of Eurykleia's suggestions, to have Penelope

---

master despite the beggar's clothes.

[96] He will see her point later, however, when he admits that his wife cannot recognize him because of his foul clothes (see xxiii 115-117 and the following discussion).

[97] For a complete list of servants' suggestions in the *Odyssey*, see Olson 1992.219-227.

Eurykleia, the Predecessor 43

awakened, he only briefly reminds her of one last necessary task, to purge the hall.

We should also note that when asked to perform, as an accomplice now, her more important tasks that require more authority and skill, Eurykleia is addressed as 'old woman', and not just 'nurse'. In fact, Odysseus calls Eurykleia 'old woman' more often than 'nurse'; he calls her *maia* 'nurse' only in the recognition scene when he appeals to her as his Nurse, and when he needs her protection as such through her silence. On all other occasions, he calls her 'old woman', and as such he asks for her active help in exercising her skills and her authority. By calling her 'old woman' he confirms her hierarchical authority.[98]

5. Eurykleia and the Reunion of the Couple

5.1. The Persuasion of Penelope

Book xxiii opens with Eurykleia's important errand to wake up Penelope and bring her the news. The old woman goes upstairs *kankhaloôsa* (καγχαλόωσα) 'laughing loud in exultation' to tell her mistress that her dear husband is at home.[99] Her knees are strengthened and her feet move quickly.[100] She stands above Penelope's head and speaks to her (xxiii 1-4).

The scene (xxiii 1-84) contains four exchanges of "speech-acts" between Eurykleia and Penelope (5-24, 25-38, 39-68, 69-84), which lead gradually to the recognition of Odysseus by Penelope. She affectionately addresses Penelope as 'dear child', and Penelope addresses Eurykleia as 'dear nurse'.[101] She brings forth the news of

---

[98] For a more systematic examination of the terms 'nurse' and 'old woman' (μαῖα, τροφός, γρηῦς), see Table III at the end of the chapter.

[99] Cf. *ololuzein* (ὀλολύζειν, xii 408, 411), another instance of Eurykleia's exultation at the feat of Odysseus.

[100] I prefer Aristarchus' reading, 'moved quickly' (ὑπερικταίνοντο) to Hesychius' reading 'were shaking' (ὑποακταίνοντο glossed as ἔτρεμον) especially in conjunction with 'laughing loud in exultation' (καγχαλόωσα). Eurykleia is rejuvenated with joy in anticipation of her masters' reunion.

[101] In response to Eurykleia's affectionate 'dear child' (φίλον τέκος, xxiii 5 and τέκνον φίλον, xxiii 26), and 'my child' (τέκνον ἐμόν, xxiii 70), Penelope addresses Eurykleia as 'dear nurse' (μαῖα φίλη, xxiii 35, 59, 81). Her relation with Penelope, in contrast to that with Telemakhos and Odysseus, does not go further than the old nurse/younger woman relationship. See also the forms of address in Table III at the end

44 Chapter 1

Odysseus' arrival, adding her own assessment of his late arrival and showing Penelope that she understands the difficulty of the situation (xxiii 5-8).[102] Then she accurately and efficiently summarizes the facts and adds another assessment of Odysseus' acts, approving the punishment of the suitors (xxiii 8-9):

> Ἔγρεο, Πηνελόπεια, <u>φίλον τέκος</u>, ὄφρα ἴδηαι
> ὀφθαλμοῖσι τεοῖσι τά τ' ἔλδεαι ἤματα πάντα.
> <u>ἦλθ'</u> Ὀδυσεὺς καὶ οἶκον <u>ἱκάνεται</u>, ὀψέ περ <u>ἐλθών</u>.
> μνηστῆρας δ' ἔκτεινεν ἀγήνορας, οἵ θ' ἑὸν οἶκον
> κήδεσκον καὶ κτήματ' ἔδον βιόωντό τε παῖδα.
>
> *Odyssey* xxiii 5-9

> Wake up, Penelope, <u>dear child</u>, to see with your own eyes
> what you have been longing for all your days.
> Odysseus <u>came</u>; he has <u>arrived</u> home, though indeed <u>coming</u> late.
> He has killed the haughty suitors who troubled
> his house, and consumed his property, and oppressed his son too.

Penelope finds this hard to believe and thinks that the gods took away Eurykleia's wits (xxiii 9-14):[103]

> <u>Μαῖα φίλη</u>, <u>μάργην</u> σε θεοὶ θέσαν, οἵ τε δύνανται
> <u>ἄφρονα</u> ποιῆσαι καὶ <u>ἐπίφρονά</u> περ μάλ' ἐόντα,
> καί τε <u>χαλιφρονέοντα</u> <u>σαοφροσύνης</u> ἐπέβησαν·
> οἵ σέ περ ἔβλαψαν· πρὶν δὲ <u>φρένας αἰσίμη</u> ἦσθα.
>
> *Odyssey* xxiii 9-14

> <u>Dear Nurse</u>, the gods have made you <u>crazy</u>; indeed, they can
> make <u>senseless</u> even one who is quite <u>sensible</u>,
> and to put the <u>simple-minded</u> on the way of <u>prudence</u>. They have
> driven you mad; though before now you were <u>sound in mind</u>.

Still she forgives her on account of her old age (σὲ δὲ τοῦτό γε γῆρας ὀνήσει, xxiii 24).[104]

---

of the chapter.
[102] Notice the triple repetition of the arrival verbs 'came', 'has arrived', 'coming' (ἦλθ'... ἱκάνεται ... ἐλθών, xxiii 7) that she uses to stress for Penelope the fact of Odysseus' arrival.
[103] Notice the terms 'crazy', 'senseless', sensible', 'simple-minded', 'prudence', 'sound in mind' (μάργην, ἄφρονα, ἐπίφρονα, χαλιφρονέοντα—a *hapax legomenon*—σαοφροσύνης, φρένας αἰσίμη), all pertaining to the qualities of her mind, her mental faculty; the wording implies that Eurykleia normally does possess such faculties.
[104] There is an irony here: Penelope thinks that Eurykleia's age reduced her mental abilities, although, in fact, her old age is an important factor that contributes to her

Eurykleia tells Penelope that she is not teasing her, she is telling her 'the truth' (*etumon*, xxiii 26):[105] the stranger is really Odysseus, as she is 'declaring in her speech' (*hôs agoreuô*, xxiii 27).[106] Telemakhos knew a long time ago, but 'prudently' (*saophrosunêisi*, xxiii 30), she continues adding her comment of approval again, he kept his father's plans secret until he punished the violent suitors (xxiii 26-31).[107]

Eurykleia's speech turns Penelope's incredulity to joy, but she still cannot believe how he, alone, overcame all the suitors. She embraces the old woman in tears (xxiii 32-34) and wants to know if she is "really telling *nêmertes* 'the truth'" (Εἰ δ' ἄγε δή μοι, μαῖα φίλη, νημερτὲς ἐνίσπες, xxiii 35); and, if he is really home, as she is 'declaring in her speech' (*hôs agoreueis*, xxiii 36), how he alone confronted the arrogant suitors (xxiii 35-38).[108]

Eurykleia honestly replies that she did not hear and she did not ask; she only heard the groaning of the slain. She continues with an account of the main events following the killing of the suitors. She gives Penelope a long report of what she saw when Telemakhos, following his father's order, called her to the hall, and of the purification, and of how Odysseus asked her to summon her mistress (xxiii 39-51). She concludes her speech urging Penelope to come with her and to rejoice also (xxiii 52-57):[109]

ἀλλ' ἕπευ, ὄφρα σφῶϊν ἐϋφροσύνης ἐπιβῆτον
ἀμφοτέρω φίλον ἦτορ, ἐπεὶ κακὰ πολλὰ πέποσθε.
νῦν δ' ἤδη τόδε μακρὸν ἐέλδωρ ἐκτετέλεσται·
ἦλθε μὲν αὐτὸς ζωὸς ἐφέστιος, εὗρε δὲ καὶ σὲ
καὶ παῖδ' ἐν μεγάροισι· κακῶς δ' οἵ πέρ μιν ἔρεζον

---

cleverness and shrewdness.

[105] Cf. also xxii 420. Eurykleia is also capable of lies (see xx 134-143).

[106] Cf. further xxiii 36. Cf. also xix 352 (on Odysseus), xix 383 (on Eurykleia), xxii 461 (on Telemakhos), and notes 49 and 91.

[107] This is a deliberate response to Penelope's comment on Eurykleia's *saophrosunê* (σαοφροσύνη) at xxiii 13.

[108] Cf. the use of the word for 'truth' also in Eurykleia's speech in xxiii 26: *etumon* (ἔτυμον). Note also the use of the verb *agoreuein* (ἀγορεύειν) by Penelope as a response to Eurykleia's words at xxiii 27. Also cf. Odysseus' praise of Eurykleia's correct speech at xix 385. Odysseus is a better judge of Eurykleia's speech capacities, being himself best at *agoreuein*. By contrast, Penelope, inferior in this capacity, as I will demonstrate further, misjudges Eurykleia's correct speech and is not fully capable of seeing the truth of it.

[109] The authenticity of Eurykleia's account at xxiii 40-57 has been questioned. I agree with Heubeck that the similarities in language and in the content of these lines and the narrative of the events in books xxi-xxii argue that this passage is genuine. See further references in Heubeck 1992.317.

46 *Chapter 1*

μνηστῆρες, τοὺς πάντας ἐτίσατο ᾧ ἐνὶ οἴκῳ.

Odyssey xxiii 52-57

> Come with me, then, so that you both can turn your dear hearts
> in the way of happiness, since you have both suffered much.
> But now, at last, this long desire has been fulfilled.
> He has come back alive at his hearth, and found you
> and his son in the palace; and the suitors who did evils
> to him, he punished them all in his house.

Eurykleia's words do not succeed in overcoming Penelope's incredulity. She advises Eurykleia not to exult yet (μαῖα φίλη, μή πω μέγ' ἐπεύχεο καγχαλόωσα, xxiii 59).[110] She does not believe her: "but your story is not true as you proclaim" (ἀλλ' οὐκ ἔσθ' ὅδε μῦθος ἐτήτυμος, ὡς ἀγορεύεις, xxiii 62).[111] She thinks that one of the immortal gods punished the suitors, and that Odysseus lost his chance of returning and is lost himself (xxiii 58-68).[112]

Now Eurykleia reacts as dramatically as she had reacted to Odysseus' threats when she recognized him from his scar (xxiii 70).[113] She reproaches Penelope for saying that her husband, who is present in his house at his own hearth, never returned home (xxiii 70-72). Seeing that she failed to convince Penelope with the facts, she now brings forth the 'very manifest sign' (*sêma ariphrades*, xxxiii 73)— the scar.[114] But 'with his much-knowing mind' (*poluidreiêisi nooio*, xxiii 77), she continues, he did not let her speak.[115] She ends her

---

[110] Cf. Odysseus' advice in xxii 411. Also cf. xxiii 1.

[111] On the truth of Eurykleia's account cf. xx 134-143, xxii 420, and xxiii 26. On the use of the verb *agoreuein* see xxiii 36 and note 108; cf. also xxiii 27 and note 106.

[112] Penelope's suspicion that it was a god, and not Odysseus, is partly correct in view of Athena's help in xxii 205-240, 272-273, 297-298.

[113] Eurykleia's reaction in xxiii 70 and in xix 492 is expressed, in fact, with the same formula: "my child, what a word escaped the barrier of your teeth" (τέκνον ἐμὸν ποῖον σε ἔπος φύγεν ἕρκος ὀδόντων).

[114] Although xxiii 73-77 have been considered interpolations by a number of scholars (Payne, Knight, Wilamowitz, von der Mühll), still, the correspondence with passages in book xix (e.g. xxiii 74 = xix 393) and the references to events in xix (e.g. xxiii 75 to xix 392 and xix 476-477; xxiii 76-77 to xix 488-490) confirm their authenticity; see further Heubeck 1992.319-320.

[115] Although a firm decision between the readings *poluidreiêisi* 'much-knowing' (πολυιδρείῃσι) and *polukerdeiêisi* 'much-devising' (πολυκερδείῃσι) is impossible (see Heubeck 1992.320), I am in favor of the first reading (πολυιδρείῃσι), especially in anticipation of Penelope's comment in xxiii 82 (μάλα περ πολύϊδριν ἐοῦσαν) referring to Eurykleia as being 'much-knowing'. Odysseus and Eurykleia share the same qualities of mind. Eurykleia calls upon her master's 'much-knowing mind' (πολυϊδρείῃσι νόοιο).

speech urging Penelope to come along. She confirms the truth of her words by saying: "if I am lying, I will surrender myself to you to kill with the most pitiful death" (xxiii 78-79):[116]

> Τέκνον ἐμόν, ποῖόν σε ἔπος φύγεν ἕρκος ὀδόντων,
> ἣ πόσιν ἔνδον ἐόντα παρ' ἐσχάρῃ οὔ ποτ'ἔφησθα
> οἴκαδ' ἐλεύσεσθαι· θυμὸς δέ τοι αἰὲν ἄπιστος.
> ἀλλ' ἄγε τοι καὶ σῆμα ἀριφραδὲς ἄλλο τι εἴπω,
> οὐλήν, τήν ποτέ μιν σῦς ἤλασε λευκῷ ὀδόντι.
> τὴν ἀπονίζουσα φρασάμην, ἔθελον δὲ σοὶ αὐτῇ
> εἰπέμεν· ἀλλά με κεῖνος ἑλὼν ἐπὶ μάστακα χερσὶν
> οὐκ ἔα εἰπέμεναι πολυϊδρείῃσι νόοιο.
> ἀλλ' ἕπευ· αὐτὰρ ἐγὼν ἐμέθεν περιδώσομαι αὐτῆς,
> αἴ κέν σ' ἐξαπάφω, κτεῖναί μ' οἰκτίστῳ ὀλέθρῳ.
>
> *Odyssey* xxiii 70-79

My child, what a word escaped the barrier of your teeth?
You said that your husband, who is here, beside the hearth,
would never come home; your heart is always mistrustful.
But come, and I will tell you another manifest sign,
the scar, that once the boar inflicted on him with his white tusk.
I recognized it while I was washing him, and I wanted
to tell you; but he seized my mouth with his hands
and would not let me tell you in the wisdom of his much-
knowing mind [*poluidreiêisi nooio*].
But follow me; and I will surrender myself here,
if I am deceiving you, to kill me with the most pitiful death.

Penelope, addressing Eurykleia again as *maia philê* 'dear nurse' (xxiii 81), still believes that Eurykleia, "no matter how wise she is" (μάλα περ πολύϊδριν ἐοῦσαν, xxiii 82), cannot understand the counsels of the gods (xxiii 81-82).[117] She is convinced, however, to go

---

Penelope, in turn, calls upon Eurykleia's similar skills (μάλα περ πολύϊδριν ἐοῦσαν). Cf. also ii 346, where Eurykleia is first introduced as a woman 'of the many skills of the mind/with the much-knowing mind' (νόου πολυϊδρείῃσιν). This word-play implies that Eurykleia is wise like her master.

[116] Cf. Odysseus/beggar trying to convince Eumaios of his master's return in xix 391-400. Cf. also Eurykleia's words in iv 743-744, indicating her courage in telling Penelope the truth regarding her knowledge of Telemakhos' secret trip.

[117] I do not believe that the choice of the term *poluidris* (πολύϊδρις, xxiii 82) is a coincidence after Eurykleia's characterization of Odysseus as *poluidreiêisi nooio* (πολυϊδρείῃσι νόοιο, xxiii 77), but rather a witty response by Penelope. Cf. also n115.

with Eurykleia and see the dead suitors and "whoever it was who killed them" (xxiii 83-84).[118]

The dialogue between Eurykleia and Penelope has a performative agonistic character. Their "speech-acts" resemble a four-round rhetorical contest, an *agôn*, in which Eurykleia tries to convince Penelope that Odysseus is present, and Penelope tries to convince Eurykleia that she is wrong, that she lost her brains, that the gods took her wits in her old age, and that she does not understand the counsels of the gods.[119] And although Penelope appears to have the last word, her actions—the fact that she goes to the hall to see for herself, as we will see—make Eurykleia the actual winner of this contest. She has accomplished her errand and her goal, to bring Penelope to the hall.

This agonistic performance in turn suggests a "background" of choral tradition where the two leading personalities, Penelope and Eurykleia, like Agido and Hagesikhora in Alcman PMG 1, have stepped out of the *khoros* circle and perform for a broader audience. Eurykleia's power of persuading Penelope reveals a hierarchical authority. This authority stems from her advisory role in the *paideia* of Penelope, a younger and less experienced female personality. The persuasion of Penelope suggests ties between epic and lyric choral compositions with performative agonistic or instructive character.

5.2. Tricking Odysseus

Indeed, Penelope comes down from her chamber and ponders whether she should stand afar and question her husband, or whether she should go up to him and take and kiss his head and hands (xxiii 85-87). As she crosses the threshold, however, she chooses to sit at a distance, especially as Odysseus was sitting by a pillar looking down, waiting to see what she would say when she saw him (xxiii 88-92). Moreover, she has difficulty recognizing him in his beggar's clothes:

---

[118] The fact that Penelope does not respond to Eurykleia's testimony of the scar does not mean that xxiii 73-77 are not genuine. On the contrary, the testimony of the scar provokes Penelope's comment at xxiii 81-82. For a detailed discussion, see Heubeck 1992.319-320. See also n115.

[119] This contest of words, although without an audience of judges, partially resembles the contest of words between Phaedra and her Nurse in *Hippolytus* 373-524, where the Nurse also tries to persuade her unwilling mistress. It also shares agonistic elements with the argument between Achilles and Agamemnon in *Iliad* I (although here, too, there is the presence of an audience of the Greek army). On the agonistic character of the "speech-acts" in the *Iliad*, see Martin 1989.

"and now she would examine him carefully in the face, and now, again, she would not recognize him in his foul clothing" (xxiii 94-95).

Eurykleia proves right in her advice once more. Her last suggestion, before she left Odysseus in order to summon Penelope, was that he should change cloak and tunic (ἀλλ' ἄγε τοι χλαῖνάν τε χιτῶνά τε εἵματ' ἐνείκω, xxii 487), but Odysseus disregarded her. Now Penelope would not recognize her husband as a consequence of his foul clothing, as Odysseus will soon admit himself (see xxiii 115-116). He will finally have to follow her advice.

Indeed, when Telemakhos rebukes his mother for being cruel by keeping such distance from his father (xxiii 103), Odysseus admits that Penelope cannot recognize him because of his foul clothes:[120]

νῦν δ' ὅττι ῥυπόω, κακὰ δὲ χροΐ εἵματα εἷμαι,
τοὔνεκ' ἀτιμάζει με καὶ οὔ πω φησὶ τὸν εἶναι.

Odyssey xxiii 115-116

Now, because I am dirty and have foul clothes on my body,
this is why she dishonors me and does not yet say I am he
[her husband].

He finally follows Eurykleia's advice, although he does not admit it, and does not give her credit. Eurykleia's wise advice triumphs in the end, although Odysseus never admits, especially in public, that it was her idea and that she was right.[121] Indeed, Eurynome washes Odysseus and anoints him with oil, putting about him a fair cloak and tunic (xxiii 154-155); even Athena adds her magic touch (xxiii 156-163).

Still, Odysseus, exasperated that his wife still keeps her distance from her husband, asks Eurykleia to make a bed for him, for Penelope's heart is made of iron (xxiii 171-172).[122] Penelope seizes this opportunity to test him with the secret of the bed that only the two of them share. She confirms Odysseus' order to Eurykleia, repeating the order and complementing it in such a way that it will

---

[120] Cf. above xxiii 94-95 but also Eurykleia's suggestion at xxii 487-489. Compare also Telemakhos' comment at xxiii 103 with Eurykleia's comment about Penelope's stubbornness in her incredulity at xxiii 72.

[121] It is not surprising that Eurykleia gets no credit for her wise advice. As a rule, servants get no credit from their masters even if their suggestions are sound (cf. Olson 1992.227).

[122] Cf. xxiii 172, Eurykleia's comment on her incredulity, and xxiii 103, Telemakhos' comment on his mother's cruelty.

50   Chapter 1

give her the chance for her own *peira* 'test' (πεῖρα, cf. also xxiii 114, 181), and her own more private *sêma* (σῆμα), that of their bed (xxiii 171, 177). She asks Eurykleia to move Odysseus' bed out of their chamber, intending to provoke his reaction that will prove to her his identity (xxiii 177-180).[123] Indeed, Odysseus takes this opportunity to prove his identity (xxiii 181-204).

With her silent cooperation, Eurykleia helps Penelope in tricking and testing Odysseus.[124] With her understanding silence, she now helps Penelope, as she first helped Telemakhos by not revealing his departure to his mother, and then Odysseus by not revealing his identity to his wife.

5.3. Eurykleia and the Reunion of the Couple

Eurykleia has one more chance to play a role in the happy reunion of Odysseus and Penelope, for which she has tried so hard already. Now Eurykleia (referred to as τροφός in xxiii 289 and γρηῦς in xxiii 292) and Eurynome—the two old nurse figures—together prepare a soft bed for Odysseus and Penelope "under the light of shining torches" (δαΐδων ὕπο λαμπομενάων, xxiii 290).[125] The presence of Eurykleia and Eurynome for the first and last time together is, I believe, symbolic of the couple's reunion, as Eurykleia is Odysseus' old nurse and Eurynome acts as Penelope's nurse (see xvii 495-499 and xviii 164-186, and below).

As Eurykleia's role has now been accomplished, she exits the scene, retiring to her own chamber (xxiii 292), as quietly as she first made her entrance preparing Telemakhos' bed (i 428 ff.), while Odysseus and Penelope, guided to their chamber by the torch of the chambermaid, Eurynome, spend the night together (xxiii 291-296):[126]

τόφρα δ' ἄρ Εὐρυνόμη τε ἰδὲ τροφὸς ἔντυον εὐνὴν
ἐσθῆτος μαλακῆς, δαΐδων ὕπο λαμπομενάων.
αὐτὰρ ἐπεὶ στόρεσαν πυκινὸν λέχος ἐγκονέουσαι,

---

[123] For a summary and further references on the textual and semantic difficulties on the removal of the bed, see Heubeck 1992.332.

[124] On Penelope's trick and her testing of Odysseus, by which she outwits him, see Murnaghan 1985.105.

[125] Compare Eurykleia's first appearance in the *Odyssey* holding the 'blazing torches' (αἰθομένας δαΐδας, i 428). Making the bed of her masters was one of the main tasks of an older woman in the household, as described in the *Hymn to Demeter* 143 (see above, section 2.1).

[126] This is in essence a preparation of a bridal chamber for the reunited couple led by the light of torches just as in a nuptial ceremony. See Segal 1994.75 and 193.

γρηῢς μὲν κείουσα πάλιν οἰκόνδε βεβήκει,
τοῖσιν δ' Εὐρυνόμη θαλαμηπόλος ἡγεμόνευεν
ἐρχομένοισι λέχοσδε, δάος μετὰ χερσὶν ἔχουσα·
ἐς θάλαμον δ' ἀγαγοῦσα πάλιν κίεν. οἱ μὲν ἔπειτα
ἀσπάσιοι λέκτροιο παλαιοῦ θεσμὸν ἵκοντο·

Odyssey xxiii 289-296

> Meanwhile, Eurynome and the nurse [*trophos*] were making
> the bed with soft coverings, under the light of shining torches.
> Then, when they had made a firm bed with their work,
> the old woman [*grêüs*] went away back to her own place
> while Eurynome, the chambermaid, guided them
> on their way to their bed, holding the torch in her hands;
> and when she had led them to their chamber, she came back.
> Then they gladly went to the place of their old bed.

In the ring composition pattern, Eurykleia, who was introduced as the 'old woman' who under the light of the torches prepared the bed for Telemakhos (i 428), after playing her role both as the 'nurse' and as the 'old woman', now exits the scene, after preparing the bed for Odysseus and Penelope under the light of the torches again.[127] This ring composition pattern, bringing together Eurykleia with Telemakhos first and then with Odysseus and Penelope, forms the frame within which Eurykleia's interaction with these characters, through her help and with her advice, helps develop the plot. She is present and active in the process of Telemakhos' growth; she is present and active in the success of the returning hero; she is present and active again in the reunion of the hero with his wife.

Now that Eurykleia's important role has been accomplished, Eurynome, the chambermaid, another nurse figure in the household of Odysseus, carries the torch and guides the couple to their bed (xxiii 293-294). This detail may suggest that Eurykleia does not simply retire to her room; she may also be retiring from action, partially at least, especially in consideration of the restoration of order in the house.

5.4. Eurynome, Another Nurse

Eurynome is a character similar to Eurykleia, but of considerably lesser importance. She is another *tamiê* 'steward' (ταμίη, xvii 497, xviii 169), as well as a *thalamêpolos* 'chambermaid' (θαλαμηπόλος,

---

[127] These two characteristics are brought together at xxiii 289 (*trophos*) and 292 (*grêüs*).

xxiii 293), attached to and caring for Penelope. She is first mentioned in xvii 495ff., when she joins in Penelope's prayer that Antinoos should be punished for striking the beggar Odysseus (xvii 496-497). In fact, Eurynome wishes that none of the suitors should "reach the dawn" ('Ηῷ ἵκοιτο, xvii 497).[128] Penelope responds to this daring comment by calling her *maia* 'nurse', and she agrees that they—the suitors—are all enemies, for they devise evils (xvii 499).[129]

A little later Penelope confesses to Eurynome her desire to show herself to the suitors and have a word with her son (xviii 164-168). Eurynome approves her plans and further advises her to wash and anoint her cheeks (xviii 170-176). She even calls her affectionately *tekos* 'child' (xviii 170). Penelope, however, does not listen to her advice; instead she asks her to call her two maids of honor to escort her to the hall (xviii 177-184). The old woman, without further comment, leaves the room in order to fulfill her orders (xviii 185-186).[130] Even so, Athena takes care of Penelope's good looks: a little refreshing nap makes up for the make-up that Eurynome had wisely advised.

Although Eurynome is not mentioned as Penelope's Nurse, from the words the two women use in addressing each other—*tekos/maia* 'child/nurse'—as well as from the tone of approval, concern, and advice that Eurynome shows for Penelope (although Penelope does not necessarily follow it), we may assume that this older servant is so attached to Penelope that she actually serves as another Nurse figure for her. Note that there is the same exchange of affectionate address between Penelope and Eurykleia (cf. xxiii 5, 11, 26, 35, 59, 81, 171). However, Penelope, as we have seen, is more eagerly convinced and influenced by Eurykleia, the Nurse of both her husband and her son, who, as the narrative shows, has more power than Eurynome.[131]

We may assume that Eurykleia's involvement in the *paideia* of both her male masters also included the *paideia* of Penelope, who once entered the household of Odysseus as a young bride (cf. her first address to Penelope as *numpha philê* 'dear bride' (νύμφα φίλη, iv 743).

---

[128] It is interesting that there is a similar folk curse expression in Modern Greek, used more commonly by elder women: *pou na mê xêmerôthei* "(I wish) that he/she may not see the daybreak" (πού νά μή ξημερωθεῖ).

[129] By calling Eurynome 'nurse', Penelope shows her affection and respect to this elder housekeeper, as she does later with Eurykleia.

[130] Cf. the similar formula for Eurykleia at xxii 495-496.

[131] See iv 750-766 and xxiii 1-84, especially 83-84.

This role gives Eurykleia the special authority and power over Penelope that Eurynome lacks.

6. Conclusions

Eurykleia, as the old Nurse in the household of Odysseus, has the authority to advise, praise, and blame Penelope, and, as we have seen, Penelope accepts her advice, praise, and blame (iv 758-766 and xxiii 83-84). Moreover, she has the power to convince and influence Penelope, the other woman who outwits Odysseus. We saw this more clearly in her successful effort to persuade Penelope to go and meet her husband. As I suggested, the long speeches between the two women resemble a rhetorical contest, an *agôn*, in which Eurykleia is the actual winner, as Penelope is in the end persuaded to go and meet Odysseus. These agonistic speech performances, these "speech-acts," in turn suggest a "background" of choral tradition where two leading personalities, Penelope and Eurykleia, similar to Agido and Hagesikhora in Alcman PMG 1, have stepped out of the chorus circle and perform for a broader audience.

Eurykleia is also in charge of the maids and their instruction, their *paideia*, and has the authority of a senior servant to give them orders, which they follow obediently. Here is another instance that suggests even more clearly the choral background of epic tradition: the maids in this passage embody the members of the *khoros* aggregate, as Eurykleia, the older experienced female figure, in charge of their *paideia*, instructs them what to do.

In the case of her two masters, at first sight, it seems that Eurykleia has more authority and success in advising Telemakhos, her younger master; she seems to have less authority and success in advising Odysseus, who, as the king of Ithaca, is a figure of much higher authority. A more careful examination, however, of all the instances of Eurykleia's interaction with each of these two male personalities reveals a different picture.

Telemakhos, despite his politeness and consideration for his old nurse's advice, in the end, does not follow it. There is, however, a pattern of respect and reassurance: (a) Telemakhos kindly makes a request providing good reasons; (b) Eurykleia expresses her concern; (c) Telemakhos eases her fears and reassures her; (d) Eurykleia, reassured, silently grants his request. Telemakhos, in the end, always has his way—an essential element in the process of his coming of age.

Does Eurykleia then have no power to direct Telemakhos? The first time Telemakhos does not listen to Eurykleia concerns his trip, which Athena herself advised. After his reassurance that such a trip is not without a god's will, she becomes his accomplice and helps him undertake it. Later Eurykleia praises Telemakhos' decision to put away the weapons but, at the same time, she has a concern, which Telemakhos alleviates with his reassurance. On both occasions she is proud of him and approves his growth and independence (see iv 754-770 and xix 22-23). Also, we should not forget that, when she scolds him for blaming his mother for her lack of hospitality to the stranger (xx 135), he does not present any objection but silently accepts her blame and disapproval. Eurykleia exercises her authority over Telemakhos in the form of advice, praise, and blame. Telemakhos accepts her praise and her blame, but not her advice when it contradicts his coming of age; instead, on these occasions, Eurykleia, by following his orders, becomes his accomplice and helps him grow. Indeed, she always expresses her praise and approval of the signs of his growth and independence.

Odysseus, on the other hand, despite his harshness and seemingly unchallenged authority, in the end, follows Eurykleia's suggestions. We have witnessed how Eurykleia finally has the last word in naming for him the unfaithful maids, a suggestion that Odysseus dismisses at first (cf. xix 497ff. and xxii 417ff.). Furthermore, it is Eurykleia who suggests to Odysseus, after the destruction of the suitors, that it is time to tell Penelope (xxii 328-329). And, although Odysseus thinks it is not the right time (xxii 431-432), still, when he gives her the word later (xxiii 1-84), she is the one who not only summons Penelope, but psychologically prepares her for her husband's presence and convinces her to come and see for herself. But even then, instead of obeying without objection, she suggests that Odysseus should first change into clean clothes and remove his rags (xxii 486-489). Odysseus again disregards her advice with a counter-suggestion (xxii 491), only to find himself later suggesting exactly the same thing (xxiii 130-132) when Penelope stays at a distance instead of falling into his arms—as her son thinks she should (xxiii 97-103).

Indeed, in all the scenes between Odysseus and Eurykleia, I see a contest for authority. Each wants to have the last word. Eurykleia is not scared by Odysseus' harsh language, not even when he threatens to strangle her if she speaks (xix 479-490). She reacts with a counter-suggestion—to name for him the unfaithful maids. She always reacts with a counter-suggestion. Odysseus, on the other hand, although he always seems to have the last word, in the end, follows the advice of Eurykleia, who, in the long run, has her quiet victory.

Eurykleia's recognition of Odysseus constitutes her first victory. As Murnaghan remarks, the recognition scenes between Odysseus and Telemakhos and Odysseus and Laertes, the only persons to whom he is related by blood, are the only direct recognitions. They frame the recognitions between people to whom he is not related by blood, Eurykleia, Eumaios, Philoitios, and Penelope: "these are more difficult relationships and their continuity over time is subject to question. Therefore, they take place, especially in the case of Eumaios and Penelope, after a long period of testing and renegotiation.... The tense moment of real danger to Odysseus' whole program created by Eurykleia's recognition dramatizes how much he needs to rely on her."[132] Following this line of thought, I concur that Odysseus invited the close encounter with Eurykleia in order to test her loyalty. His agony as he tries to hide in the dark reveals his fear before the impending danger of a premature recognition.

Odysseus, always in control, chooses when to reveal himself. The only exception is with Eurykleia; this is why he is so upset. He meant *her* to wash his feet but miscalculated *her* mental abilities. As Nagy has shown, the recognition of the *sêma* requires the act of interpretation in which the *noos* is involved.[133] It is Eurykleia's mental abilities, her *noos*, that defeated Odysseus' *mêtis*, his intelligence, and recognized the *sêma*, the scar. This feat encourages her to reestablish her status of power and control, especially as in her first encounter with Odysseus she outwits him. Steadily, to the very end, she keeps trying to direct him with suggestions, always one at a time, always in the right order. She skillfully and methodically prevents him from exercising his most important skill, his *mêtis*, on a number of important issues with which he has to deal, issues regarding his course of action with the women in the household, from the unfaithful maids to his own wife, Penelope. Odysseus always presents resistance in the beginning but nevertheless follows the Nurse's advice on one issue after the other, until the very last one. This, of course, does not mean that these decisions are merely based

---

[132] Murnaghan 1987.38-39.
[133] Nagy 1983.36 and 45-50. See also my previous discussion of the recognition scene.

on her suggestions. They would eventually be made at his own timing; still, Eurykleia's advice deprives him of the initiation and the originality of these decisions.

Let us also not forget that it is Eurykleia who suggests that Telemakhos has grown up and should be in charge of the punishment of the maids; Odysseus heeds this suggestion by assigning their punishment to him. Note finally that Eurykleia is also involved in Penelope's trick of the bed, another instance in which Odysseus is outwitted by a woman, this time his wife.[134]

Table I, with a summary of Eurykleia's interaction with the main characters in the *Odyssey* (see end of chapter) shows that she has the authority to give (a) *orders* to the maids, who are subordinate to her; (b) *suggestions* and (c) *advice* to all the other characters: Penelope, who always follows them, Odysseus, who rejects them in the beginning and follows them in the end, and Telemakhos, who, in view of his coming of age, does not follow them but always offers a good reason or excuse; Eurykleia expresses her (d) *judgement*, (e) *blame*, and/or (f) *praise* with all the characters: Penelope, Odysseus both as a beggar and as her master, and Telemakhos; even when she (g) *follows directions* (from Odysseus, Telemakhos, or Penelope), she is first convinced or feels inclined to follow them, as in the case of washing Odysseus' feet.

I suggest that Eurykleia, as Odysseus' first Teacher, played an important role in young Odysseus' ethical formation.[135] I also suggest that she may have inspired him and taught him the skill of telling convincing lies.[136] We know that Odysseus possessed this skill: "he spoke feigningly, telling many lies resembling the truth" (ἴσκε ψεύδεα πολλὰ λέγων ἐτύμοισιν ὁμοῖα, xix 203). It is possible that he may have learned this from his nurse and Teacher, Eurykleia who certainly possessed this skill herself, as her little lie to Telemakhos at xx 135-143 reveals, as Penelope at xxiii 62 suggests, and as her epithets confirm.

---

[134] For a summary of Eurykleia's interaction with the main characters in the *Odyssey* see Table I at the end of this chapter.

[135] Cf. Plato's observations in *Protagoras*, 325cd where he describes the first period of education at home, where *trophos*, and *paidagogos* , along with the parents, play a role in a child's early ethical formation.

[136] Cf. the Olympian Muses who inspired Hesiod in the skill of lying: "We know how to say many lies like to truth, and we know, whenever we wish, how to utter true things" (ἴδμεν ψεύδεα πολλὰ λέγειν ἐτύμοισιν ὁμοῖα, / ἴδμεν δ', εὖτ' ἐθέλωμεν, ἀληθέα γυρήσασθαι, *Theogony* 27-28). On lies and truth in female speech cf. Bergren 1985.69-96.

Eurykleia, the Predecessor 57

An overview of the epithets used of Eurykleia support these observations: *kedna iduia* (κεδνὰ ἰδυῖα) 'knowing caring feelings', 'with affectionate feelings', 'devoted'; *pukimêdês* (πυκιμηδής) 'with dense thoughts', 'shrewd in counsel'; *pukina phresi mêde' ekhousa* (πυκινὰ φρεσὶ μήδε' ἔχουσα) 'having dense thoughts in her mind', 'having shrewd devices in her mind'; *noou poluidreiêisin* (νόου πολυϊδρείῃσιν) 'of a mind knowing many things', 'of many skills of the mind'; *poluidris* (πολύϊδρις) 'of many skills', 'knowing much'; *periphrôn* (περίφρων) 'wise'; *dia gunaikôn* (δῖα γυναικῶν) 'noblest of women'. For a complete summary of the epithets of Eurykleia see Table II at the end of the chapter.

As Table II shows, there are two categories of epithets used of Eurykleia: (a) those referring to her gentle, wise, or noble character: *kedna iduia, periphrôn, dia gunaikôn* (κεδνὰ ἰδυῖα, περίφρων, δῖα γυναικῶν), which she shares only with women of noble birth: Penelope, Arete, Helen, Alcestis; and (b) those referring to her mental qualities, her cleverness and shrewdness: *pukimêdês, pukina phresi mêde' ekhousa, noou poluidreiêisin, poluidris* (πυκιμηδής, πυκινὰ φρεσὶ μήδε' ἔχουσα, νόου πολυϊδρείῃσιν, πολύϊδρις), which she shares with her master Odysseus and other tricky men (Triptolemos, Prometheus, and the Phoenician pirate who stole Eumaios). These epithets suggest that Eurykleia enjoys honor comparable to some extent to that of Penelope and other women of noble birth; as to her mental abilities, they are comparable to those of her master Odysseus. It is also interesting to observe that the number and the variety of her epithets exceed those used of Penelope.[137] This is another indication of her multifaceted personality and her impact and importance in the story.

A careful examination of her epithets in combination with the terms 'nurse' and 'old woman' shows that, by choice and beyond metrical constraints, if they pertain to her intelligence or her wisdom, they are combined with a reference to her old age beyond her role as a nurse. For a summary of the terms *trophos, maia* 'nurse', and *grêus* 'old woman', see Table III at the end of the chapter.[138]

---

[137] I am adding two more epithets (κεδνὰ ἰδυῖα, δῖα γυναικῶν) to the three epithets used of Penelope (περίφρων, ἐχέφρων, αἰδοίη) that Austin 1975.53-54 records.

[138] A careful observation of this table shows that in the narrative Eurykleia is more often referred to as *trophos* (τροφός) 'nurse': (sixteen times), most times in identical formulas, with a total of eleven variations: five times without an epithet and six times with the epithet *philê* (φίλη) 'dear'. The term *grêus* (γρηῦς) 'old woman' appears in the narrative thirteen times. Of those, the term is used ten times without an epithet and three times with three different epithets, one pertaining to her noble character or gentle

This evidence confirms my observation based on the close examination of the text, that the terms 'nurse' and 'old woman', mainly as forms of address, and less so in the narrative, reflect the differentiation of Eurykleia's skills, according to the role she is asked to perform. When it comes to skills of the role of a nurse, she is referred to as nurse; when it comes to skills that require more judgement, intelligence, and wisdom, she is referred to as 'old woman'. To Penelope she is always the *philê maia* 'dear nurse'. A *philos* in Homer is someone 'near' and 'dear', and Eurykleia, as a woman, is certainly closer to Penelope, another woman. For Odysseus and Telemakhos, she turns from 'nurse' to 'old woman', when it comes to more harsh and responsible tasks that require not only the affectionate care, confidence, and advice of a nurse, but the maturity and the wisdom of an older, experienced, tough, and clever old woman.

Either as 'nurse' or as 'old woman', Eurykleia is presented as a character of intelligence, wisdom, and nobility, who has the authority to advise, praise, or blame, and the power to influence all three of her masters in the house of Odysseus.

Her authority and power of persuasion stem from her important role in the *paideia* of her two masters and her advisory role in the *paideia* of Penelope, a less-experienced younger woman. Specifically, her power of persuasion over Penelope reveals a hierarchical authority that suggests the lyric background of the *Odyssey*, more clearly manifest in her directions to the maids. The agonistic character of her encounter with Odysseus, the persuasion of Penelope, and the instruction of the maids are manifestations of the ties with lyric choral traditions of agonistic or instructive character.

---

thoughts and the other two to the cleverness and wisdom of her mind. As a form of address, *maia* (μαῖα) 'nurse' is used by all three: Odysseus, Telemakhos, and Penelope, seven times without an epithet, and five with the epithet *philê* (φίλη) 'dear'. Among those, four belong to Penelope and one to Telemakhos. Penelope always addresses Eurykleia as 'dear nurse', Telemakhos addresses her once as 'nurse' and once as 'dear nurse', and Odysseus always addresses her as 'nurse'. 'Old woman', as a form of address, on the other hand, is never used by Penelope; it is used only once by Telemakhos, and three times by Odysseus. Among these, an epithet is used only once by Telemakhos ('born of old'). In particular, Eurykleia is addressed as 'old woman' on the following occasions: when Odysseus as beggar praises her perceptiveness (xix 383), when Telemakhos gives her the message that his father wants to speak to her (xxii 395), when Odysseus advises her to restrict her joy over the dead suitors (xxii 411), and when Odysseus assigns to her, among other tasks, the task of bringing Penelope (xix 481).

Table I: Eurykleia's Interaction with the Other Characters

1. Telemakhos

i	428-42:	She *helps* Telemakhos go to bed (lights his way, takes his clothes, shuts the door).
ii	361-70:	*Advises* Telemakhos not to take trip to Pylos and Sparta.
	377:	*Becomes* his *accomplice* with her *silence*.
	378-80:	Actively *helps* him prepare supplies for his trip.
xix	22-3:	*Praises* him for taking care of his property.
xx	134-5:	*Blames* Telemakhos for wrongly blaming his mother.
	136-43:	*Manipulates* the *truth* about Penelope's hospitality.
xxi	386-7:	*Follows* Telemakhos' *directions* conveyed by Eumaios.

2a. Odysseus/Beggar

xix	363-74:	*Expresses* her *disapproval* of his treatment by the maids.
	374-8:	*Agrees* to wash his feet because she also wants to do so.
	378-81:	*Bids* him to listen to her comments.

2b. Odysseus/Master

xix	467-75:	*Recognizes* Odysseus.
	492-4:	*Blames* Odysseus for his reaction.
	495-8:	*Suggests* naming the unfaithful maids.
	502-3:	*Becomes* his *accomplice* with her *silence*.
xxii	407-8:	*Praises* slaughter of the suitors.
	420-5:	*Reveals* to Odysseus the names of the unfaithful maids.
	426-7:	Indirectly *suggests* Telemakhos' taking charge of the unfaithful maids.
	428-9:	*Suggests* waking up Penelope.
	433-4:	*Summons* the unfaithful maids.
	486:	*Approves* Odysseus' directions to summon Penelope.
	487-9:	*Suggests* that Odysseus should change his clothes.
xxii	492-6:	*Brings* the faithful maids and fire.
xxiii	1-84:	*Brings* Penelope to Odysseus.

3. Penelope

iv	743-9	*Brings* her the *news* of Telemakhos' trip.
	750-3	*Advises* her to wash and pray to Athena for his safety.
	754	*Blames* her for suggesting to upset Laertes.
	754-7	*Expresses* her *judgement* on Telemakhos' growth.
xxiii	5-9	*Brings* Penelope the *news* of Odysseus' presence.
	25-31	Tries to *convince* Penelope of Odysseus' presence.
	39-57	Tries to *convince* Penelope of Odysseus' presence.
	70-2	*Blames* Penelope for her incredulity.
	73-84	*Convinces* Penelope of Odysseus' presence.
	177-80	*Becomes* her *accomplice* in testing Odysseus with her silence.
	289-91	*Prepares bed* for Odysseus and Penelope.
	292	*Retires* from action.

4. The Maids

xx	147-56	*Gives orders* to the maids.

Table II: Summary of the Epithets of Eurykleia

κεδνὰ ἰδυῖα (*kedna iduia*): 'knowing caring feelings', 'with affectionate feelings', 'devoted' (from κεδνός, a derivative of κήδομαι and εἴδω, οἶδα, i 428, xix 346, xx 57, xxiii 182, 232). Introductory characterization of Eurykleia that, along with her name, her father's name, and her grandfather's name, emphasizes her noble birth and the nobility of her character, especially since her name itself (Εὐρύκλεια) means 'one with broad fame'. This epithet appears five times, only in the *Odyssey*, twice of Eurykleia (i 428 and xix 346) and three times of Penelope (xx 57, xxiii 182, 232).

Eurykleia, the Predecessor 61

πυκιμηδής (*pukimêdês*): 'with dense thoughts', 'shrewd in counsel' (from πυκά and μήδεα, i 438). Along with her old age (γρηῦς *grêüs* 'old woman') comes an epithet characteristic of her cleverness and shrewdness. Note that this epithet is not used elsewhere in the *Odyssey* or in the *Iliad*. The only other use in the Homeric tradition is found at *Hymn to Demeter* 153 (of Triptolemos).

πυκινὰ φρεσὶ μήδε' ἔχουσα (*pukina phresi mêde' ekhousa*): 'having dense thoughts in her mind', 'having shrewd devices in her mind' (xix 353), used of Eurykleia only, again in conjunction with her old age (γρηῦς *grêüs* 'old woman'), similar to the previous epithet. Another similar epithet is used in the *Odyssey* (πυκινὰ φρονέων, ix 445) and another in the *Iliad* (εἰδὼς...μήδεα πυκνά, III 202), both referring to Odysseus.

νόου πολυϊδρείῃσιν (*noou poluïdreiêisin*): 'of the mind that knows many things', 'of many skills of the mind', in reference to Eurykleia's skills as the ταμίη *tamiê* 'housekeeper'. This epithet is used twice in the *Odyssey* only: at ii 346 of Eurykleia and at xxiii 77 of Odysseus by Eurykleia.

πολύϊδρις (*poluïdris*): 'of many skills', 'knowing much'. This epithet, similar to the one above and referring again to Eurykleia's mental skills, is used at xix 82 by Penelope of Eurykleia. It is used only once more in the *Odyssey* at xv 459 (referring to the Phoenician who helped steal little Eumaios from his nurse). Cf. also *Theogony* 616, used of Prometheus.

περίφρων (*periphrôn*): 'wise'. Introduced by Penelope as she urges Eurykleia to wash Odysseus' feet (xix 357). It is used of Eurykleia again at xix 491 = xx 134, and also at xxi 381 (Eumaios' address of Eurykleia). It is important to note that this is a standing epithet of Penelope (i 329, iv 787, v 216, xiv 373, etc.), also used once of queen Arete (xi 345).

δῖα γυναικῶν (*dia gunaikôn*): 'noblest of women'. An epithet used only once of Eurykleia in xx 147, when she calls the maids and assigns them their duties. This epithet is used elsewhere only of Penelope (i 332, xxi 42, 63) and Helen (iv 305) in the *Odyssey*, and of Helen (III 171, 228, 423) and Alcestis (II 714) in the *Iliad*.

Table III: Summary of the Terms 'Nurse' and 'Old Woman'

I. OLD WOMAN (ΓΡΗΥΣ)

1. In the narrative (thirteen times, three with an epithet, ten without):

i 438	καὶ τὸν μὲν <u>γραίης</u> <u>πυκιμηδέος</u> ἔμβαλε χερσίν
xix 346	εἰ μή τις <u>γρηῦς</u> ἔστι <u>παλαιή</u>, <u>κεδνὰ ἰδυῖα</u>
xix 353	ἔστι δέ μοι <u>γρηῦς</u> <u>πυκινὰ φρεσὶ μήδε' ἔχουσα</u>
ii 377	ὣς ἄρ' ἔφη, <u>γρηῦς</u> δὲ θεῶν μέγαν ὅρκον ἀπώμνυ
xix 361	ὣς ἄρ' ἔφη, <u>γρηῦς</u> δὲ κατέσχετο χερσὶ πρόσωπα
xix 386	ὣς ἄρ' ἔφη, <u>γρηῦς</u> δὲ λέβηθ' ἕλε παμφανόωντα
xix 503	ὣς ἄρ' ἔφη, <u>γρηῦς</u> δὲ διὲκ μεγάροιο βεβήκει
xxii 433	ὣς ἄρ' ἔφη, <u>γρηῦς</u> δὲ διὲκ μεγάροιο βεβήκει
xix 467	τὴν <u>γρηῦς</u> χείρεσσι καταπρηνέσσι λαβοῦσα
xxii 495	<u>γρηῦς</u> δ' αὖτ' ἀπέβη διὰ δώματα κάλ' Ὀδυσῆος
xxiii 1	<u>γρηῦς</u> δ' εἰς ὑπερῷ' ἀνεβήσετο καγχαλόωσα
xxiii 292	<u>γρηῦς</u> μὲν κείουσα πάλιν οἰκόνδε βεβήκει
xxiii 33	<u>γρηΐ</u> περιπλέχθη, βλεφάρων δ' ἀπὸ δάκρυον ἧκεν

2a. As a form of address by Odysseus (three times):

xix 383	ὦ <u>γρηῦ</u> οὕτω φασὶν ὅσοι ἴδον ὀφθαλμοῖσιν
xxii 411	ἐν θυμῷ, <u>γρηῦ</u>, χαῖρε, καὶ ἴσχεο μήδ' ὀλόλυζε
xxii 481	οἶσε θέειον, <u>γρηῦ</u>, κακῶν ἄκος, οἶσε δέ μοι πῦρ

2b. As a form of address by Telemakhos (only once):

xxii 395	δεῦρο δὴ ὄρσο, <u>γρηῦ</u> <u>παλαιγενές</u>, ἥ τε γυναικῶν δμῳάων σκοπός ἐσσι κατὰ μέγαρ' ἡμετεράων

II. NURSE (ΤΡΟΦΟΣ)

1. In the narrative (sixteen times, ten with an epithet, six without):

xxii 480	αὐτὰρ ὅ γε προσέειπε <u>φίλην τροφὸν</u> Εὐρύκλειαν
iv 742	τὴν δ' αὖτε προσέειπε <u>φίλη τροφός</u> Εὐρύκλεια
xxiii 25	τὴν δ' αὖτε προσέειπε <u>φίλη τροφός</u> Εὐρύκλεια

Eurykleia, the Predecessor 63

xxiii 39	τὴν δ' αὖτε προσέειπε <u>φίλη τροφὸς</u> Εὐρύκλεια
xix 21	τὸν δ' αὖτε προσέειπε <u>φίλη τροφὸς</u> Εὐρύκλεια
xxii 419	τὸν δ' αὖτε προσέειπε <u>φίλη τροφὸς</u> Εὐρύκλεια
xxii 485	τὸν δ' αὖτε προσέειπε <u>φίλη τροφὸς</u> Εὐρύκλεια
xxiii 69	τὴν δ' ἠμείβετ' ἔπειτα <u>φίλη τροφὸς</u> Εὐρύκλεια
ii 361	ὣς φάτο, κώκυσεν δὲ <u>φίλη τροφὸς</u> Εὐρύκλεια
xxii 492	ὣς ἔφατ', οὐδ' ἀπίθησε <u>φίλη τροφὸς</u> Εὐρύκλεια
xix 15	ἐκ δὲ καλεσσάμενος προσέφη <u>τροφὸν</u> Εὐρύκλειαν
xxi 380	ἐκ δὲ καλεσσάμενος προσέφη <u>τροφὸν</u> Εὐρύκλειαν
xxii 394	κινήσας δὲ θύρην προσέφη <u>τροφὸν</u> Εὐρύκλειαν
xxii 301	Τηλέμαχ', εἰ δ' ἄγε μοι κάλεσον <u>τροφὸν</u> Εὐρύκλειαν
xvii 31	τὸν δὲ πολὺ πρώτη εἶδε <u>τροφὸς</u> Εὐρύκλεια
xxiii 289	τόφρα δ' ἄρ' Εὐρυνόμη τε ἰδὲ <u>τροφὸς</u> ἔντυον εὐνὴν

III. NURSE (MAIA)

1a. As a form of address by Odysseus (three times, without an epithet):

xix 482	<u>μαῖα</u>, τί ἦ μ' ἐθέλεις ὀλέσαι; σὺ δέ μ' ἔτρεφες αὐτὴ
xix 500	<u>μαῖα</u>, τί ἦ δὲ σὺ τὰς μυθύσεαι; οὐδέ τι σε χρή
xxiii 171	ἀλλ' ἄγε μοι <u>μαῖα</u>, στόρεσον λέχος ὄφρα καὶ αὐτὸς

1b. As a form of address by Telemakhos (four times, one time with an epithet, three times without):

ii 349	<u>μαῖ'</u>, ἄγε δή μοι οἶνον ἐν ἀμφιφορεῦσιν ἄφυσσον
xix 16	<u>μαῖ'</u>, ἄγε δή μοι ἔρυξον ἐνὶ μεγάροισι γυναῖκας
ii 372	θάρσει, <u>μαῖ'</u>, ἐπεὶ οὔ τοι ἄνευ θεοῦ ἥδε γε βουλή
xx 129	<u>μαῖα φίλη</u>, τὸν ξεῖνον ἐτιμήσασθ' ἐνὶ οἴκῳ

1c. As a form of address by Penelope (four times, with an epithet):

xxiii 11	<u>μαῖα φίλη</u>, μάργην σε θεοὶ θέσαν, οἵ τε δύνανται
xxiii 59	<u>μαῖα φίλη</u>, μή πω μέγ' ἐπεύχεο καγχαλόωσα
xxiii 81	<u>μαῖα φίλη</u>, χαλεπόν σε θεῶν αἰειγενετάων
xxiii 35	εἰ δ' ἄγε δή μοι, <u>μαῖα φίλη</u>, νημερτὲς ἐνίσπες

2

Nurse Characters in Aeschylus, Sophocles, and Euripides

1. Introduction

This chapter discusses the nurse characters in Aeschylus' *Libation-Bearers (Choephoroi)*, Sophocles' *Women of Trachis (Trachiniai)*, and Euripides' *Andromache* and *Medea*. The first part considers the role of the Nurse in Aeschylus' *Libation-Bearers*, who has an important part and a multiple function. The second part considers the Nurse of Deianeira in Sophocles' *Women of Trachis*, who, despite her short part in the beginning, triggers the action in the play. The third part considers both the Nurse of Hermione and the Handmaid of Andromache in Euripides' *Andromache*. A careful comparative examination of these two similar characters is important as it highlights the differences between them. Finally, the fourth part discusses the Nurse of Medea in *Medea*, the precursor of the Nurse in *Hippolytus*.

2. Kilissa and the Change of Klytaimnestra's Orders in Aeschylus' *Libation-Bearers*

Among the surviving tragedies of Aeschylus, the only one containing a nurse character is the *Libation-Bearers*.[1] The Nurse in the *Libation-Bearers* has a small but important part. She even has a name, Kilissa—a unique case in Greek tragedy, where all the other Nurses

---

[1] In the *Suppliant Maidens* there is a chorus of attendants with a similar advisory role.

Nurse Characters in Aeschylus, Sophocles, and Euripides 65

are referred to by the anonymous and generic term *trophos* 'Nurse'.[2] By following the directions of the chorus and agreeing to change Klytaimnestra's orders she triggers the reversal, the *peripeteia*.

As I will demonstrate, by bidding Aigisthos to come alone, without his bodyguard, she *deliberately* participates in a conspiracy against her masters, which results in their destruction. Moreover, her participation in their destruction is even more substantial. I suggest that with her remarks and her criticism and disapproval of Klytaimnestra and Aigisthos, especially with the expression of her hatred for Aigisthos, she actually *invites* the intervention of the chorus on behalf of Orestes. Her hatred, originating from her love for Orestes, drives her to conspire with the chorus. She will take this high risk of disobeying her mistress and changing her orders in order to harm Orestes' enemies, who are also her enemies.

In the *Libation-Bearers*, Orestes' nurse, Kilissa, is introduced after Orestes, disguised as a traveler from Daulis, brings to Klytaimnestra the fake news of her son's death (674-690). After Klytaimnestra's mixed reaction to the news (691-699), she leaves the stage announcing that she will impart the news to the master of the house, Aigisthos, since she has no lack of *philoi* 'friends' (κοὐ σπανίζοντες φίλων, 717), to take counsel with him concerning this present misfortune (βουλευσόμεσθα τῆσδε συμφορᾶς πέρι, 718).[3]

The chorus of slave-women, who have already shown their loyalty to Electra and Orestes from the beginning of the play, express their impatience as to when they will show the power of their speech, literally their mouths (στομάτων ἰσχύν), for Orestes' good:[4]

---

[2] Presumably a toponymic; she or her family come from Cilicia (Kilikia). Pindar, in *Pythian* ii.15ff., also mentions the nurse of Orestes, but calls her Arsinoe; she is Laodamia in Pherecydes (*FGrH* 3 F 134) as also in Stesichorus (*PMG* 218) according to Σ *Cho.* 133. Pindar's Arsinoe rescues Orestes at his father's murder, and Pherecydes' Laodamia also saves Orestes but loses her own son. An archaic relief from Melos of the 470s or 460s (Paris, Louvre MNB 906), which portrays the recognition of Electra and Orestes, has Electra accompanied by her nurse and Orestes by two men, one of them presumably Talthybios. For further details, see Garvie 1986.xxi-xxiv and 244.

[3] This passage (716-718) prepares us for the mission of the Nurse to summon Aigisthos, Klytaimnestra's only 'friend' (not only 'near and dear' but also loyal). With Kilissa's intervention, however, Klytaimnestra's message will ironically turn against herself.

[4] The speaker of these lines (719-721) is more probably the chorus-leader, who, in this play, not only leads the other members of the chorus, but also directs first Electra, then Orestes, and finally the Nurse. Orestes has asked the chorus either to keep silent or to speak *ta kairia* 'the suitable words, what the occasion requires' (581-582). Therefore the

66 Chapter 2

> εἰέν, φίλιαι δμωίδες οἴκων,
> πότε δὴ <u>στομάτων</u>
> δείξομεν <u>ἰσχὺν</u> ἐπ' Ὀρέστῃ;
>
> Libation-Bearers 719-721
>
> come, dear handmaids of this house,
> when shall we show our <u>mouths'</u>
> <u>power</u> [*stomatôn iskhun*] for Orestes?

As if in answer to their prayers to *Peithô dolia* 'deceiving Persuasion' (Πειθὼ δολία) and Hermes (722-728), they see Kilissa, the Nurse of Orestes, coming in tears.[5] They want to find out the reason for her *amisthos* 'sincere' grief (733):[6]

> τροφὸν δ' Ὀρέστου τήνδ' ὁρῶ κεκλαυμένην·
> ποῖ δὴ πατεῖς, Κίλισσα, δωμάτων πύλας;
> λύπη δ' ἄμισθός ἐστί σοι ξυνέμπορος.
>
> Libation-Bearers 731-733
>
> But here I see the Nurse of Orestes in tears;
> Where are you going, Kilissa, at the palace gates,
> with unhired grief for your partner?

In answer to the chorus' question, Kilissa explains the purpose of her presence at the gates: her mistress bade her to summon Aigisthos so that he may hear the news (734-737). She continues commenting on Klytaimnestra's pretense of sorrow before the servants at the bad news, while underneath she laughs, as things have turned out well for her (737-741).[7] Now she (Kilissa) is bringing the news to

---

'power of their mouths' can refer to any verbal power they possess—prayer or song—but also the power of persuasion, which they have successfully exercised so far with both Electra and Orestes, and which they will exercise soon with the Nurse; these lines foreshadow the change of Klytaimnestra's message. For more details on the role of the chorus-leader in this play see my conclusion at the end of this section. On the "force of language" see also Goldhill 1984.169.

[5] Deceitful Persuasion here refers both to Orestes' deceit and to their own power of persuasion through the power of their speech (στομάτων... ἰσχύν); see also n4. For references on the importance of persuasion in the whole trilogy see Garvie 1986.241-242.

[6] *amisthos* (ἄμισθος) 'unhired, unbidden, spontaneous'; see Thomson 1966b II.166. The spontaneous grief of the Nurse is in contrast to Klytaimnestra's feigned grief, at least as Kilissa reports further (737-741).

[7] If Klytaimnestra is sad before the servants, Kilissa is only guessing her joy. However, we should trust her interpretation, for she knows why Klytaimnestra gave Orestes away; his death should bring her relief rather than grief.

Aigisthos, who will certainly rejoice, she concludes (742-743), as she shares her feelings with the chorus:

> Αἴγισθον ἡ κρατοῦσα τοῖς ξένοις καλεῖν
> ὅπως τάχιστ' ἄνωγεν, ὡς σαφέστερον
> ἀνὴρ ἀπ' ἀνδρὸς τὴν νεάγγελτον φάτιν
> ἐλθὼν πύθηται τήνδε. <u>πρὸς μὲν οἰκέτας</u>
> <u>θέτο σκυθρωπῶν πένθος ὀμμάτων, γέλων</u>
> <u>κεύθουσ' ἐπ' ἔργοις διαπεπραγμένοις καλῶς</u>
> <u>κείνη</u>, δόμοις δὲ τοῖσδε παγκάκως ἔχειν,
> φήμης ὕφ', ἧς ἤγγειλαν οἱ ξένοι τορῶς.
> <u>ἦ δὴ κλύων κεῖνος εὐφρανεῖ νόον,</u>
> <u>εὖτ' ἂν πύθηται μῦθον.</u>
>
> Libation-Bearers 734-743

The mistress bade me to summon Aigisthos for the strangers
with all speed, so that more clearly,
man from man, the tidings that have just arrived
he may learn by coming by. <u>Before the servants
she has put on a sad face hiding a smile in her eyes
over deeds that have worked well
for her</u>; though, for this house, things are terrible,
after the rumor that the strangers announced clearly.
<u>He [Aigisthos] will certainly rejoice listening,
when he hears the news/story [*muthos*]</u>.[8]

Then, changing tone, she laments for Orestes, recalling all the intimate details of her affection, her care, and her labors as his nurse (743-763). And as she concludes her memories of Orestes when he was a baby, she remembers her task (764-765):[9]

> ...ὦ τάλαιν' ἐγώ,
> ὥς μοι τὰ μὲν παλαιὰ συγκεκραμένα
> ἄλγη δύσοιστα τοῖσδ' ἐν Ἀτρέως δόμοις
> τυχόντ' ἐμὴν ἤλγυνεν ἐν στέρνοις φρένα.
> ἀλλ' οὔτι πω τοιόνδε πῆμ' ἀνεσχόμην·
> τὰ μὲν γὰρ ἄλλα τλημόνως ἤντλουν κακά·

---

[8] The irony here is that her *muthos*—Kilissa's story, instead of Klytaimnestra's original orders—will bring just the opposite result. Also notice here the redundancy "listening, when he finds out" (κλύων... εὖτ' ἂν πύθηται). Redundancy of speech, common in tragedy, is characteristic of common people, but it also suggests emotional agitation (cf. Garvie 1986.247). Furthermore, I believe, the repetition here is intentional: Kilissa wants to emphasize Aigisthos' joy at the sound of the news, in contrast to her own grief, and so, indirectly, to express her disapproval.

[9] Cf. 734-737.

φίλον δ' Ὀρέστην, τῆς ἐμῆς ψυχῆς τριβήν,
ὃν <u>ἐξέθρεψα μητρόθεν δεδεγμένη</u>,
καὶ νυκτιπλάγκτων ὀρθίων κελευμάτων
καὶ πολλὰ καὶ μοχθήρ' ἀνωφέλητ' ἐμοὶ
τλάσῃ· <u>τὸ μὴ φρονοῦν</u> γὰρ ὡσπερεὶ βοτὸν
<u>τρέφειν</u> ἀνάγκη, πῶς γὰρ οὔ; <u>τροφοῦ φρενί</u>·
οὐ γάρ τι φωνεῖ παῖς ἔτ' ὢν ἐν σπαργάνοις,
εἰ λιμός, ἢ δίψη τις, ἢ λιψουρία
ἔχει· νέα δὲ νηδὺς αὐτάρκης τέκνων.
τούτων πρόμαντις οὖσα, πολλὰ δ', οἴομαι,
ψευσθεῖσα παιδὸς σπαργάνων φαιδρύντρια,
γναφεὺς τροφεύς τε ταὐτὸν εἰχέτην τέλος.
ἐγὼ διπλᾶς δὲ τάσδε χειρωναξίας
ἔχουσ' Ὀρέστην <u>ἐξεδεξάμην πατρί</u>·
τεθνηκότος δὲ νῦν τάλαινα πεύθομαι.
στείχω δ' ἐπ' ἄνδρα τῶνδε <u>λυμαντήριον</u>
οἴκων, <u>θέλων</u> δὲ τόνδε <u>πεύσεται λόγον</u>.

Libation-Bearers 743-765

...Poor me!
How the old sorrows of all sorts
so hard to bear, that befell this house of Atreus,
have caused pain in my heart within my chest!
But never before have I endured a blow like this.
For all the other troubles I bore patiently;
but my dear Orestes, how he wore away my soul,
whom <u>I nursed after I took him from his mother</u>
  [*exethrepsa mêtrothen dedegmenê*].[10]
And his night cries that kept me awake[11]
—many and bothersome I endured fruitlessly![12]
For one must <u>nurse the senseless thing [*to mê phronoun...trephein*]</u>
like a dumb animal, how else—by following the <u>nurse's sense</u>
  [*trophou phreni*];[13] for a baby still in swaddling clothes

---

[10] Kilissa was not his only wet-nurse, as Klytaimnestra's words at her murder scene (896-898) reveal.

[11] An echo of 524, Klytaimnestra's terror at the snake dream. Orestes makes both women wake up for him, but for different reasons: his nurse on account of sincere care, his mother on account of guilty fear. On Klytaimnestra's dream cf. Spatz 1982.119 and Devereux 1976.321-340. Devereux suggests that the dream reveals that Klytaimnestra is a bad mother.

[12] Fruitlessly for her, but also for Orestes, whom she believes dead.

[13] For the ms. reading *tropôi phrenos* (τρόπῳ φρενός) "by way of reasoning," I prefer Thomson's reading: *trophou phreni* (τροφοῦ φρενί) forming a chiastic construction: *to mê phronoun... trephein...trophou phreni* (τὸ μὴ φρονοῦν...τρέφειν ...τροφοῦ φρενί) "that which

Nurse Characters in Aeschylus, Sophocles, and Euripides 69

cannot say whether it is hunger, thirst, or wetting,
for a baby's inside acts instinctively.
Making a guess on these, quite often, I think,
I was mistaken; washer of the child's linen
—laundress and nurse had the same duty.
With these two handicrafts, I received
Orestes [to raise him] for his father [*exedexamên patri*].[14]
Poor me, now I find out he is dead! But now I am on my way
to fetch the man, the destroyer [*lumantêrion*] of this house,[15]
and willingly he will hear the word [*thelôn peusetai logon*].[16]

The speech of the Nurse, like the speech of the Herald in *Agamemnon*, is, as Garvie comments, "a mixture of elevated poetic language (749ff., 756) and almost incoherent anacolutha, which characterize the speech of ordinary characters under emotional strain."[17] Particularly disturbed are lines 749-762, starting with her memories of nursing Orestes, constituting an unusually long sentence (its verb found only in 762 after a repetition of its object 'Orestes'). This sentence is "interrupted by a series of rambling parentheses and explanatory clauses as new ideas come into Kilissa's head," as Conacher also notes.[18] Especially since the subject matter of her speech is about ordinary things that are found nowhere else in extant Greek tragedy, it is difficult to tell how far the incoherences are the result of textual corruption, and how far they are to be attributed to Aeschylus' deliberate intention to characterize the Nurse as an ordinary person in a state of agitation and excitement, Conacher

---

has no reason should be nurtured by its nurse's reason." Even with the reading *tropôi phrenos*, I suggest that the reference applies to the nurse's reasoning and not to the baby's.

[14] Here, again, I prefer the reading *patri* (πατρί) 'for his father', stressing Kilissa's loyalty to Agamemnon, to the reading *patros* (πατρός) 'from his father', especially in view of 750: *exethrepsa mêtrothen dedegmenê* (ἐξέθρεψα μητρόθεν δεδεγμένη) "after I took him from his mother."

[15] Cf. Klytaimnestra's use of the same adjective of Agamemnon (*Agamemnon* 1438): One who causes destruction has to be destroyed. Cf. the chorus' advice to Electra: τὸν ἐχθρὸν ἀνταμείβεσθαι κακοῖς (123), according to the general Greek ethical belief "help your friends and harm your enemies." On this idea see Blundell 1989.26-59.

[16] Kilissa repeats her guess that Aigisthos will be pleased at the news, which she expressed already at the beginning of her speech (742), thus indirectly emphasizing her discontent. Note that now, referring to the news of Orestes' death, she uses *logos* 'word' instead of *muthos* 'story' (743). Cf. also n8.

[17] Garvie 1986.243. I find 760 (γναφεὺς τροφεύς τε ταὐτὸν εἰχέτην τέλος), underscored by the use of the dual, a most archaic and elevated line.

[18] Conacher 1987.7.

70 Chapter 2

further notes.[19] A comparison, however, with the Herald's speech in the *Libation-Bearers* (551ff. and 636ff.) and the Watchman's speech in *Agamemnon* (12ff.) makes the latter possibility more likely.[20]

Despite the textual incoherences, which govern the emotional memories of nursing Orestes, there is, however, a carefully wrought geometric pattern of a ring composition in Kilissa's speech (734-765):

A	734-43	Αἴγισθον ... μῦθον	She explains her errand to summon Aigisthos (to hear news pleasing to him).
B	743-48	ὢ τάλαιν' ἐγώ ... κακά	She expresses her pain at Orestes' death.
C	749-62	φίλον δ' Ὀρέστην... ὃν ἐξέθρεψα μητρόθεν δεδεγμένη... Ὀρέστην ἐξεδεξάμην πατρί	She describes her pains in nursing Orestes, whom she received from his mother to raise for his father.
B	763	τεθνηκότος δὲ νῦν τάλαινα πεύθομαι	She expresses again her pain at Orestes' death.
A	764-65	στείχω δ' ἐπ' ἄνδρα... λόγον	She repeats her errand to summon Aigisthos (to hear news pleasing to him).

It is important that, in her conclusion, Kilissa not only repeats her errand to fetch Aigisthos, but also that he will be pleased at the news of Orestes' death; and even more important, she expresses her hatred and contempt for him, "the man who wrecked the house" (ἄνδρα... λυμαντήριον οἴκων, 764). This wording is an invitation for the chorus to seize the opportunity and help Orestes, and so prove the power of their speech, a wish they expressed before ("when shall we show Orestes the power of our mouths?" 720-721).

---

[19] Conacher 1987.7 notices how the Nurse is "unobtrusively naturalistic" as she describes the baby's needs.

[20] For a comparison with the Watchman's speech, see Rosenmeyer 1982.217-218. Cf. also the Guard's speech in Sophocles' *Antigone* (223-277).

Nurse Characters in Aeschylus, Sophocles, and Euripides 71

Indeed, the chorus-leader tells Kilissa to change Klytaimnestra's message and to ask Aigisthos to come alone, without his bodyguard (766-773).[21] The chorus-leader speaks in riddles that Kilissa does not seem to understand. She asks in disbelief if the chorus women are really glad at the news. She cannot understand how things can change for the better if Orestes, *elpis domôn* 'the hope of the house', is gone (774-776).[22] The chorus-leader responds with one more riddle (777). Kilissa starts suspecting that the chorus knows more (778), but the chorus-leader, instead of giving her more hints, urges her to go on with her errand and leave the rest to the gods (779-780). Kilissa, without objection, heeds the chorus' words, putting her trust in the gods (781-782), and leaves the stage:

ΧΟΡΟΣ   πῶς οὖν κελεύει νιν μολεῖν ἐσταλμένον;
ΤΡΟΦΟΣ τί πῶς; λέγ' αὖθις, ὡς μάθω σαφέστερον.
ΧΟΡΟΣ   εἰ ξὺν λοχίταις εἴτε καὶ μονοστιβῆ.
ΤΡΟΦΟΣ ἄγειν κελεύει δορυφόρους ὀπάονας.
ΧΟΡΟΣ   μή νυν σὺ ταῦτ' ἄγγελλε δεσπότου στύγει·
        ἀλλ' αὐτὸν ἐλθεῖν, ὡς ἀδειμάντως κλύῃ,
        ἄνωχθ' ὅσον τάχιστα γαθούσῃ φρενί.
        ἐν ἀγγέλῳ γὰρ κυπτὸς ὀρθοῦται λόγος.
ΤΡΟΦΟΣ ἀλλ' ἦ φρονεῖς εὖ τοῖσι νῦν ἠγγελμένοις;
ΧΟΡΟΣ   ἀλλ' εἰ τροπαίαν Ζεὺς κακῶν θήσει ποτέ.
ΤΡΟΦΟΣ καὶ πῶς; Ὀρέστης ἐλπὶς οἴχεται δόμων.
ΧΟΡΟΣ   οὔπω· κακός γε μάντις ἂν γνοίη τάδε.
ΤΡΟΦΟΣ τί φής; ἔχεις τι τῶν λελεγμένων δίχα;
ΧΟΡΟΣ   ἄγγελλ' ἰοῦσα, πρᾶσσε τἀπεσταλμένα.
        μέλει θεοῖσιν ὧνπερ ἂν μέλῃ πέρι.
ΤΡΟΦΟΣ ἀλλ' εἶμι καὶ σοῖς ταῦτα πείσομαι λόγοις.
        γένοιτο δ' ὡς ἄριστα σὺν θεῶν δόσει.

Libation-Bearers 766-782

CHORUS How then dispatched does she bid him come?
NURSE   What how? (What do you mean by how?)[23] Say that again, so I can understand it better.

---

[21] Such intervention of the chorus that affects the outcome of the plot is very rare in Greek tragedy (only here and in Euripides' *Ion*); cf. Vellacott 1984.113, Garvie 1986.243, Conacher 1987.20.

[22] Ironically, Orestes is also called *elpis* 'hope' by Klytaimnestra in the preceding scene (698-689). As Kilissa now uses the same word in sincerity, Klytaimnestra's pretense is emphasized even more. See also Conacher 1987.120-121.

[23] I prefer the reading 'what how' (τί πῶς) to 'or how' (ἦ πῶς). It is a colloquial expression, more common in comedy and still used in Modern Greek.

CHORUS With his bodyguard, or perhaps unattended?
NURSE   She bids him bring his escort of spearmen
CHORUS Now, do not give this message to our <u>hated master
        [despotou stugei]</u>; but with all speed and <u>with a
        cheerful heart [gathousêi phreni]</u> bid him come alone
        so that he may hear the news without alarm.[24] <u>In a
        messenger's mouth a crooked message turns straight.</u>[25]
NURSE   Are you really glad at the news?
CHORUS <u>If Zeus will ever make the ill wind change.</u>
NURSE   And how? Orestes, <u>the hope of the house is gone.</u>
CHORUS Not yet;<u> he were an ill seer that would interpret so.</u>[26]
NURSE   What are you saying? Do you know something separate
        from what has been said?
CHORUS Go give your message; do what you've been told.
        <u>The gods are taking care of what should be taken care of.</u>
NURSE   Well, I am going, and I will listen to your bidding.
        <u>May all turn out for the best with the gods' blessings.</u>

The Nurse in the *Libation-Bearers*, at first sight, basically only follows orders—first Klytaimnestra's orders to summon Aigisthos, then the chorus' orders to bid him come without his bodyguards. Still, in trusting the chorus and agreeing to change Klytaimnestra's orders, she shows disrespect and disobedience to Klytaimnestra; in agreeing to accept a change of orders, she takes on a big responsibility and a high risk. Moreover, with her disapproval of Klytaimnestra and Aigisthos, she invites the chorus' intervention.

Indeed, Kilissa, upon her appearance on stage, immediately expresses her criticism of Klytaimnestra, and so, indirectly, she displays her disapproval and her negative feelings for her (737-741). She also openly manifests her disapproval, contempt, and hatred for

---

[24] *gathousêi phreni* 'with a cheerful heart' may refer to either Kilissa or Aigisthos. For the arguments for both interpretations see Garvie 1986.252-253. I see in this phrase an echo of Kilissa's comment on Aigisthos' joy in 712. Still, I believe it refers to the Nurse: she should look but also be cheerful in anticipation of the outcome of her mission. Kilissa's response in 774 "are you really glad at the news?" (ἀλλ' ἦ φρονεῖς εὖ τοῖσι νῦν ἠγγελμένοις) supports this view.

[25] This proverbial line, attributed elsewhere to Euripides, was rejected by Verrall as a gloss; for references, see Thomson 1966b II.167. For a detailed discussion of the textual problems see Garvie 1986.253.

[26] This is an answer to Kilissa's remark that she is not a very good *mantis*, as she already conceded at 758-759. For similar passages, see Thomson 1966b II.167. For the enigmatic character of the chorus' speech in 766-782 see Goldhill 1984.171.

Aigisthos at the end of her speech to the chorus (764). At the same time she demonstrates her ability to read the laughter Klytaimnestra hides under her feigned sad eyes before the servants (737-740), and from Klytaimnestra's own words about her relief at the news of Orestes' death (696-699) we know that Kilissa's guess is right. Her guess in anticipating Aigisthos' joy at the news of Orestes' death (742-743, 765) is also very accurate. With the repetition of Aigisthos' anticipated joy at the beginning and the end of her speech, she emphasizes her criticism of Aigisthos. The expression of her hatred and contempt for Aigisthos at the end of her speech to the chorus is particularly important. Her comments invite and induce the chorus to take this opportunity and use "the power of their mouths" (720-721), the power of speech and persuasion, and change Klytaimnestra's orders in favor of Orestes' case.

It is true that Kilissa does not appear to understand the questions of the chorus in 766, or to observe their meaningful proverb of 773. Instead, she is surprised that the chorus are glad at the news. Still, after the chorus' enigmatic remarks of 775 and 777, she begins to suspect that they know something about Orestes beyond her knowledge. She pursues this suspicion with further questions until the chorus bid her to change the message and leave the rest to the gods (781). Only then does she hasten to deliver her message to Aigisthos, following the chorus' advice and trusting the rest to the gods (782). Divine assistance is very important for Kilissa: at the sound of the gods' name, she stops asking further questions; she trusts the gods and, as the chorus suggests, she will leave the rest to them.[27] Furthermore, she trusts the chorus and their hidden knowledge. She also knows that they share her feelings of hatred toward Aigisthos, as they openly called him "hated master" in 770. Consequently, she gladly agrees to change the message of Klytaimnestra for Aigisthos, knowing—or at least suspecting—that, by doing so, she will bring harm to him.

Therefore, I suggest, by disobeying her mistress and changing her orders, she consciously and deliberately participates in a conspiracy against Aigisthos and Klytaimnestra. Her hatred for them, originating from her love for Orestes, drives her to take the high risk of

---

[27] Cf. Eurykleia's compliance with Telemakhos' wish and with Odysseus' orders, when they both invoke the help of the gods (*Odyssey* ii 372, xix 502).

disobedience and to use the power of her changed message to harm them.[28]

In addition, by exhibiting her care and sincere love for Orestes, she provides a vivid contrast to Klytaimnestra's cold indifference.[29] At the news of Orestes' death, she reacts with sincere tears, in contrast to Klytaimnestra's faked sorrow. Her true love and sincere sorrow for Orestes' death originated from her care for him as a baby, which she explains to the chorus in detail (749-762). This speech is essential for the interpretation of Apollo's provocative statement during the trial of Orestes in the last play of the Oresteian trilogy, *Eumenides* 658-659, that "the mother is not the so-called parent of the child, but merely the nurse, the *trophos* of the newly planted embryos (οὐκ ἔστι μήτηρ ἡ κεκλημένη τέκνου / τοκεύς, τροφὸς δὲ κύματος νεοσπόρου). In the case of Klytaimnestra—Apollo failed to observe—she was not even the nurse. If she had cared for Orestes as a mother or even as a nurse, like Kilissa, the audience and half of the members of the jury—those who voted for Orestes' acquittal—would probably have been less favorable to Orestes.

Beyond her role as a messenger, the Nurse in the *Libation-Bearers* performs three more important functions: 1) she triggers the outcome of the plot; 2) she provides a contrast to Klytaimnestra and alienates us from her; 3) she presents the human, innocent side of Orestes, a contrast to the cold, scheming avenger of the previous and following scenes.[30]

Although in the *Libation-Bearers* Orestes' Nurse does not advise or help Orestes directly in avenging his father's death, indirectly, she helps him decisively, by willingly changing Klytaimnestra's message at the bidding of a wiser advisor, the chorus, and in particular the chorus-leader.

Indeed, the chorus-leader in the *Libation-Bearers* does not direct only Kilissa. She directs Electra, who seeks the chorus' advice at the

---

[28] A servant's infidelity is severely punished. Cf. the punishment of the unfaithful maids in the *Odyssey* (xxii 465-473).

[29] Cf. Rosenmeyer 1982.218, Garvie 1986.243-244, and Conacher 1987.120-121. As Conacher observes, Kilissa's speech provides an unconscious commentary on the preceding scene of Klytaimnestra's grief, and it "prepares us for the minimizing of the maternal relationship."

[30] For the multiplicity of the functions of the Nurse cf. Rosenmeyer 1982.218, Garvie 1986.243-244, and Conacher 1987.20-21.

Nurse Characters in Aeschylus, Sophocles, and Euripides 75

beginning of the play.[31] She advises and directs Electra until Orestes takes charge.[32] Clearly, the chorus-leader directs Electra and Kilissa—both female characters—but even partially Orestes in 264-268, when she advises both Orestes and Electra to be quiet and cautious.[33] Moreover, she even directs Orestes on how to give them directions, and so she directs the action: "Let it be so. But as to the rest, explain to your friends, telling them what some should do and what others should not do" (γένοιτο δ' οὕτως. τἄλλα δ' ἐξηγοῦ φίλοις / τοὺς μέν τι ποιεῖν, τοὺς δὲ μή τι δρᾶν λέγων, 552-553).

As I have stated in the Introduction, one of my goals is to trace the development of the lyric *khorêgos* of early choral compositions. Elaborating on Nagy and Calame's notions on the development of the lyric *khorêgos* in Athenian drama, I suggest that this play offers itself as a case in point for the evolution of the lyric *khorêgos* into the dramatic chorus-leader.[34] In an attempt to trace the persona of the lyric *khorêgos* in the *Libation-Bearers*, I suggest that it is crystallized in the personality of the chorus-leader who, as I noted above, displays manifestations of her leading role in directing not only Electra or Kilissa, both female characters, but also Orestes, a younger male character.[35]

In light of the above observations, it is better understood why the Nurse so easily obeys the orders and accepts the higher authority of the chorus, specifically the chorus-leader. This higher authority is not

---

[31] See 84ff., and especially 118 "what shall I say? Instruct me and explain to me for I am ignorant" (τί φῶ; δίδασκ' ἄπειρον ἐξηγουμένη).

[32] He suggests that Electra should go inside and the chorus keep his plans secret (τήνδε μὲν στείχειν ἔσω· / αἰνῶ δὲ κρύπτειν τάσδε συνθήκας ἐμάς, 554-555). After exposing his plans he suggests again that they should "keep a discrete tongue, be silent where necessary, and speak what the occasion bids" (ὑμῖν δ' ἐπαινῶ γλῶσσαν εὔφημον φέρειν,/ σιγᾶν θ' ὅπου δεῖ καὶ λέγειν τὰ καίρια, 581-582).

[33] The chorus as a whole encourages Orestes and Electra in the great kommos (306-478).

[34] Calame 1977.437-439 [=Calame 1997.255-258] has suggested that the *khoros* is a microcosm of social hierarchy, within which a majority of younger members act out a pattern of subordination to a minority of older leaders, in most instances embodied in the central persona of the *khorêgos* 'the leader of the *khoros*', as in the Spartan songs that are sung and danced by the *khoros* of Spartan girls. Such a song is dramatized in Alcman PMG 1. Furthermore, Nagy 1990a.377-379 has suggested that the early lyric *khorêgos* has survived in the Athenian drama in both an undifferentiated form as the chorus-leader, and in a differentiated form as one of the actors. See also Introduction.

[35] This challenging issue, however, is beyond the scope and the limitations of this book.

76 Chapter 2

due to a higher social position, since they are all servants, but rather to the chorus' knowledge in contrast to her ignorance.

Still, the responsibility for changing her mistress' orders is beyond the traditional authority of her role as the Nurse. Besides, with her criticism of Klytaimnestra and Aigisthos, she invites the intervention of the chorus, and by conspiring with them against her masters she brings about the *peripeteia* resulting in the destruction of Orestes' and her enemies. Her influence in the outcome of the play is such that we should not be surprised that Aeschylus even gave her a name.

3. The Nurse Triggers the Action in Sophocles' *Women of Trachis*

Among the surviving tragedies of Sophocles the only one containing a Nurse character is the *Women of Trachis*.[36] The first part of the *Women of Trachis* contains Deianeira's monologue, her dialogue with the Nurse, and the dialogue between Deianeira and Hyllos, her son. Deianeira comes on stage, followed by the Nurse.[37] Deianeira does not address her but, in a monologue, complains about her past and present miseries, and the long absences of Herakles, especially the present one; he has been away for fifteen months without any news, and she fears for him (1-48).

This introductory *rhesis*, of a kind common in Euripides, is without parallel in Sophocles' work.[38] Deianeira's monologue, however, is closely attached to the Nurse's interaction, while Euripides characteristically sets his prologue speech apart.[39] The closest parallel *rhesis* is Andromache's speech in Euripides' *Andromache*.[40] Still, Andromache's Handmaid is only bringing to her evil news as a

---

[36] Sophocles is in favor of a sister character as a foil to his heroines; see Ismene in *Antigone* and Chrysothemis in *Electra*. Both sisters represent the conservative voice of common sense, which is usually what the traditional voice of the Nurse represents (see for example Hermione's Nurse in *Andromache* and Medea's Nurse in *Medea*).

[37] Although there is confusion in the manuscripts between *trophos* 'Nurse' and *therapaina* 'Handmaid', the advice and the authority that the character displays support that she is a *trophos*.

[38] See Kamerbeek 1970.10.

[39] See Scodel 1984.32.

[40] The many similarities with Euripides' plays (*Andromache, Medea, Alcestis*) testify to the close interaction between Sophocles and Euripides; the influence, however, is likely to have been mutual, and no evidence has been found that clarifies the chronology. See Easterling 1982.22.

Nurse Characters in Aeschylus, Sophocles, and Euripides 77

messenger, while here the Nurse advises Deianeira to send her oldest son, Hyllos, in search of news about his father, and so initiates the action of the play.

After Deianeira's *rhesis*, the Nurse addresses her troubled mistress and indirectly criticizes her passivity, while at the same time she advises action.[41] Instead of complaining, she should send her son, Hyllos, to find out about his father. In indirect criticism she comments on Deianeira's complaining, and tactfully she offers her advice, a servant's advice, as she says: Deianeira should send one of her children in quest of her husband.[42] And narrowing down her advice, she suggests Hyllos in particular. At that moment she sees Hyllos approaching opportunely.[43] Then, repeating the notion of the validity of her advice which she expressed in the beginning of her speech, she concludes that Deianeira can use it now:[44]

δέσποινα Δηάνειρα, πολλὰ μέν σ' ἐγὼ
κατεῖδον ἤδη πανδάκρυτ' ὀδύρματα
τὴν Ἡράκλειον ἔξοδον γοωμένην·
νῦν δ', εἰ δίκαιον τοὺς ἐλευθέρους φρενοῦν
γνώμαισι δούλαις, κἀμὲ χρὴ φράσαι τὸ σόν·
πῶς παισὶ μὲν τοσοῖσδε πληθύεις, ἀτὰρ
ἀνδρὸς κατὰ ζήτησιν οὐ πέμπεις τινά,
μάλιστα δ' ὅνπερ εἰκὸς Ὕλλον, εἰ πατρὸς
νέμοι τιν' ὥραν τοῦ καλῶς πράσσειν δοκεῖν;
ἐγγὺς δ' ὅδ' αὐτὸς ἀρτίπους θρώσκει δόμους,
ὥστ' εἴ τί σοι πρὸς καιρὸν ἐννέπειν δοκῶ,
πάρεστι χρῆσθαι <u>τἀνδρὶ</u> τοῖς τ' ἐμοῖς λόγοις.

Women of Trachis 49-60

Deianeira, my mistress, many times have I
marked your tearful lamentations,
moaning at the departure of Herakles.
But now, if it is proper for the free-born to get advice
from slaves, then I should speak for your good.
How come and though you have so many children, still

---

[41] As Seale 1982.184 remarks, the lack of movement in Deianeira's monologue is made dramatically significant by the role of the Nurse; the Nurse's embarrassment in advising Deianeira stresses the queen's passivity. On the passivity and inaction of Deianeira see also Bowra 1944.120.

[42] Cf. the old servant's tactful advice in *Hippolytus* 88-89.

[43] The opportune arrival of Hyllos precipitates the setting in motion of the action. This is what Halleran 1985.43 calls a "talk of the devil" entrance of a new character.

[44] 59-60 correspond to 52-53 and frame her advice.

78 Chapter 2

> you do not send one of them in quest of your husband,
> especially the one it is natural to send, Hyllos,
> if he cares for news for his father's well being.
> But here he comes hurrying towards the house with timely step.
> So if you think I speak in season,
> you can use the man [t'andri] and my advice.[45]

Deianeira approves the Nurse's speech and comments on her wisdom: original (authoritative) words (*muthoi*), she says, may come from humble people; the Nurse, although a slave, has spoken a free word (*logos*):[46]

> ὦ τέκνον, ὦ παῖ, κἀξ ἀγεννήτων ἄρα
> μῦθοι καλῶς πίπτουσιν· ἥδε γὰρ γυνὴ
> δούλη μέν, εἴρηκεν δ' ἐλεύθερον λόγον.
>
> *Women of Trachis* 61-66

> My child, my boy, even from humble people
> original words [*muthoi*] may come wise; this woman is a
> slave, but she has spoken a free word [*logos*].

Deianeira uses both the words *muthos* (μῦθος) and *logos* (λόγος) to refer to the Nurse's advice, while the Nurse herself uses *logos* (60). In epic language, which Sophocles favors, *muthos* has a more important connotation than *logos*: *muthos* stands for "marked speech," original, authoritative speech, while *logos*, stands for "unmarked speech," everyday speech.[47] The use of the word *muthos* by Deianeira is a commentary on the Nurse's original speech.

Hyllos asks readily for instructions, thus accepting the wisdom and the authority of the Nurse, although indirectly—through the judgement of his mother. Deianeira transfers the Nurse's advice to her son: it brings *aiskhunê* 'shame', she says, that when his father has been away so long, he has not tried to learn where he is (65-66). By using the word *aiskhunê* (αἰσχύνη) 'shame', Deianeira verbalizes the Nurse's criticism of Hyllos' lack of action, rephrasing and interpreting it at the same time.[48]

---

[45] With the use of the word 'man', she indicates that she sees him as a grown man already, mature and ready for responsibility.

[46] Cf. the comments of Orestes in Euripides' *Electra* (367-372) on Electra's husband, whose words, despite his low birth, reveal a noble character.

[47] See Martin 1989.1-26 and Nagy 1990a.31ff.

[48] On the Nurse's criticism of Hyllos' lack of action, see also Davies 1991.71. On the dramatically significant rephrasing of the Nurse's words at 56-57 in order to create a

Although the Nurse's part is not long, it is powerful and instrumental. Her idea to send Hyllos to get word of his father sets the tragedy in action. She has no difficulty convincing Deianeira, who follows her advice literally without a word. Her short but crucial speech is compelling in its rhetorical organization and power of persuasion. It starts with a *captatio benevolentiae*: in an effort to dispose her mistress favorably toward her forthcoming advice she expresses her understanding of Deianeira's woes (49-51). This *captatio benevolentiae*, however, is at the same time, very cleverly, her indirect but effective criticism and disapproval of Deianeira's inaction. Then, with rhetorical skill, she tells her that, even though a slave, she has the thoughts of a free-born, and she tactfully suggests that it would be profitable for Deianeira to listen to her (52-53). Then she proceeds to her suggestion in the form of a rhetorical question (54-57). In this question, in only four lines, she is making a number of points: why don't you get information about your husband; you have many children who can do this for you; you have a son who is, in particular, the right person to do this; he should care to find out where his father is.[49] This last point expresses her criticism of Hyllos' inaction—in addition to his mother's—a point that, as she sees Hyllos, she reinforces by calling him a 'man', implying that he is old enough. The timely arrival of Hyllos marks her peroration (59-60), in which she also skillfully repeats the importance of her advice.

The opening scene of the *Women of Trachis* recalls the *Odyssey*.[50] Deianeira shares the fear and passivity of Penelope; however, at the Nurse's suggestion, she does send Hyllos to seek word of his father, while Telemakhos goes in search for word of his father secretly, without telling his mother.[51] I suggest that the Nurse here, in advising that Hyllos travel in quest of news of his father, can be paralleled to Athena, who, in the form of an old friend, advises Telemakhos to undertake a similar trip in quest for news of his father.[52]

---

sense of urgency and in order to avoid the impression that Deianeira weakly repeats the Nurse's advice, see Easterling 1977.122-123.

[49] Her advice is stated in general terms at the beginning (54-55), and then narrowed down (56-57).

[50] On the parallels with the *Odyssey* cf. Segal 1977.125.

[51] See Scodel 1984.31.

[52] Athena appears to Telemakhos first as Mentes and then as Mentor, a figure with 'mental' skills, a Tutor (note also the meaning of the word 'mentor' today). Advice for action in both cases comes from an older figure with advisory role, a Tutor or a Nurse.

80 Chapter 2

We see the Nurse again in the fourth episode (871-996), this time as a messenger with the news of Deianeira's suicide. The episode consists of one scene that starts with a *kommos* between the Nurse and the chorus and continues with a long *rhesis* of the Nurse, which serves as a messenger's speech.[53] The chorus hears lamentations from within the house and announces the entrance of the old woman coming outside, distressed with the bad news she is 'about to reveal' (*sêmanousa*, 870).[54]

The Nurse addresses the chorus as *paides* 'children' (871), talking to them with maternal authority, while the chorus addresses her as *geraia* 'old woman' (873).[55] The Nurse establishes over them the authority that her old age and her knowledge give her. (Note the chorus' use of the verb *sêmainein* 'to reveal', 870.)[56] In possession of the knowledge of Deianeira's death, she imparts it in dark riddles, obscure to the ignorant chorus. The chorus women do not understand her unclear words (871-872) and ask her to explain (873). In an ambiguous statement the Nurse indicates to them that Deianeira is dead: "Deianeira has walked the last of all roads with a motionless foot" (βέβηκε Δηάνειρα τὴν πανυστάτην / ὁδῶν ἁπασῶν ἐξ ἀκινήτου ποδός, 874-875).[57] And when the chorus women need more clarifications she gets impatient and her answers become laconic.[58] Throughout the dialogue she seems impatient and authoritative in her speech to the chorus. She possesses the knowledge and she is in charge of speech, like Phaedra's Nurse in her interaction with the chorus.[59]

The Nurse describes Deianeira's suicide in a long dramatic narrative (899-946). As an eye-witness, she gives a poignant picture of the suicide. The speech of the Nurse stresses Deianeira's devotion to her house and her marriage, and so the story is more effective, coming from the woman who has been closer to Deianeira than

---

For more details on the names Mentes and Mentor, see Appendix A in Nagy 1974.266-268. See also my discussion in chapter 1, p.16 n28.

[53] Cf. *Oedipus Tyrannus* 1237-1285.

[54] See below.

[55] Cf. the address 'old woman' of Eurykleia in the *Odyssey*.

[56] *sêmainein* 'to reveal' from *sêma*; cf. the discussion on *sêma* in the *Odyssey* in chapter 1, pp.27, 46, 55.

[57] On Deianeira's death see Loraux 1987.13-17.

[58] Cf. 876 "you heard it all," 877 "you hear it for the second time," and 892 "I speak clearly."

[59] Cf. *Hippolytus* 267-270 (see chapter 3).

anybody else.[60] As Kamerbeek remarks, this is an occasion to admire Sophocles' economy. The Nurse was present before Hyllos entered this scene, and now, in a symmetrical pattern, she appears after him. Hyllos' departure was her advice. Deianeira's suicide has resulted from Hyllos' curse and the news that he brought. The Nurse warns Hyllos and is witness to his repentance when he hears of Deianeira's innocence (932 ff.). The use of the Nurse as the messenger of Deianeira's suicide thus enhances the unity of the play.[61] Furthermore, "there seems to be a deliberate design in having the Nurse, who opened the play with Deianeira, present the final chapter of her mistress' life. Apart from the external aspect of balance, Sophocles re-creates the domesticity of the opening scene and so frames Deianeira's stage existence in a special way."[62]

There is one more reason why the Nurse should announce Deianeira's death. The whole drama is precipitated by her advice and her directions. With Hyllos' mission for news of his father, Deianeira finds out about Herakles' infidelity, and, with her love charm, unwillingly poisons him and then kills herself in despair. If Hyllos had not been sent for news of his father, Herakles would not have been poisoned, and Deianeira would not have died. The Nurse offered a plan as a solution to Deianeira's lamentations; but since this plan proved destructive, it is highly dramatic if she, who initiated it, brings the news of the destruction to the audience. It is not a coincidence that the last words of the speech of the Nurse (943-946) echo Deianeira's opening lines:[63]

Λόγος μὲν ἔστ' ἀρχαῖος ἀνθρώπων φανεὶς
ὡς οὐκ ἂν αἰῶν' ἐκμάθοις βροτῶν, πρὶν ἂν
θάνῃ τις, οὔτ' εἰ χρηστὸς οὔτ' εἴ τῳ κακός

Women of Trachis 1-3

There is an old saying in existence among men
that you may not completely learn a mortal's life until
one dies, whether it is noble or base.

---

[60] Cf. Seale 1982.203.
[61] Kamerbeek 1970.20.
[62] Seale 1982.203.
[63] Cf. the same maxim of conventional wisdom at the end of *Oedipus Tyrannus*. On the importance of this maxim at the beginning of the play see Easterling 1982.58-59. For further references on the same *topos* in Greek tragedy see Davies 1991.220.

The Nurse's last words recall the reflection of her mistress, which is now ironically substantiated:

τοιαῦτα τἀνθάδ' ἐστίν· ὥστ' εἴ τις δύο
ἢ καί τι πλείους ἡμέρας λογίζεται,
μάταιός ἐστιν· οὐ γὰρ ἔσθ' ἥ γ' αὔριον,
πρὶν εὖ πάθῃ τις τὴν παροῦσαν ἡμέραν.

Women of Trachis 943-946

Such are things here. So if one counts
on two or more days, he is foolish,
for there is no tomorrow, till
the present day is safely past.

Thus, the Nurse in the *Women of Trachis* has a double role: in the beginning she advises Deianeira and, as Deianeira follows her advice without hesitation, she sets the action in motion. Through her second function, that of a messenger, she provides a commentary of the tragedy that she herself, although unwillingly, triggered with her advice.

The Nurse's advice to her mistress stems from interest for her well-being; it is meant to offer a solution to her problem and cure her worries. In the long run, however, with Deianeira's gift, the Nurse's benevolent advice produces a destructive outcome.[64] In this, Deianeira's Nurse resembles Phaedra's Nurse in *Hippolytus*, although the degree of involvement is very different. Despite their good intentions, instead of offering a cure, both Nurses bring about or precipitate the destruction of their mistresses.

Although her role as an advisor to her mistress is short and she has no further involvement in the plot—except reporting her mistress' suicide—Deianeira's Nurse is almost as effective as Phaedra's Nurse. She has authority to advise and criticize Deianeira.[65] More important, with her cleverness and her skill to impose her ideas with rhetorical persuasion, she has the power to convince her. Indirectly, she also advises and criticizes Hyllos. She addresses the younger women of the chorus with the authority and superiority that her old age, her knowledge, and also her function in the house as Deianeira's Nurse involved in her *paideia*, confers on her.

---

[64] This explains why she shows no awareness of her responsibility, but blames Deianeira's gift as a cause of all the evils (cf. 871-872). The Nurse triggers the *peripeteia*, but not Deianeira's decision to send the fatal gift.

[65] In contrast to Phaedra's Nurse, she does this with tact and subtlety.

The Nurse's interaction with the younger Deianeira, and especially with the younger members of the chorus, suggests here, too, a "background" of choral tradition. The Nurse, like Hagesikhora in Alcman PMG 1, a more experienced member of the choral aggregate, has a leading role over the younger and less experienced members, while the leader of the chorus, like Agido, is a second leading personality.

4. Nurse and Handmaid in Euripides' *Andromache*

In Euripides' *Andromache*, two secondary female characters complement the two heroines, Andromache and Hermione; Andromache is complemented by her *therapaina*, her Handmaid, while Hermione is complemented by her *trophos*, her Nurse. A discussion of the role of both these secondary female characters will reveal the element of authority, present in a Nurse, but absent from a Handmaid, even one old and loyal to her mistress.

The prologue in *Andromache* contains Andromache's *rhesis* and her dialogue with her Handmaid.[66] *Andromache* starts, like the *Women of Trachis*, with a monologue of Andromache, exposing her lamentable situation (1-55). A Handmaid enters the stage unannounced and engages in a dialogue with Andromache.[67] She addresses Andromache as *despoina* 'mistress' and confirms how *eunous* 'loyal' she has been to her and to her husband (Hector), when he was alive in Troy (εὔνους δὲ καὶ σοὶ ζῶντί τ' ἦ τῷ σῷ πόσει, 59).[68] She then brings forth *neous logous* 'the news' (60).[69] Menelaos and his daughter are plotting against Andromache (56-63).

---

[66] The format of the prologue, consisting of a *rhesis* followed by a dialogue, resembles the format of the prologue in the *Women of Trachis*, and it is common in Euripides; cf. *Trojan Women, Medea, Hippolytus, Alcestis*. On the Euripidean prologue, in general, see Erbse 1984.1-20; on *Andromache*, in particular, 130-143.

[67] Stevens 1971.100 remarks that the entrance of slaves, as a rule, is not announced in Euripides; they indicate their status by addressing their masters as *despoina* or *anax* (e. g., in *Hippolytus* 88). Moreover, Andromache is alone on stage, and, as Halleran 1985.6 notes, announcements rarely occur with only one person on stage.

[68] Slaves in Greek tragedy are loyal "almost by definition" (Stevens 1971.100). Cf. also the use of the same adjective *eunous* 'loyal' by the Nurse in *Hippolytus* 698 (ἔθρεψά σ' τ' εὔνους τ' εἰμί).

[69] This is used euphemistically with a sinister connotation; cf. *Medea* 37. The sinister connotation of any news, in general, is manifested in the English common expression "no news is good news."

84 Chapter 2

Andromache, now in the same condition as her former slave, calls her 'dearest fellow slave' (*philtatê sundoulê*) and asks further questions (64-67). She wishes to know what *mêkhanai* 'devices' they (Hermione and her father) 'plot/knit' (*plekousin*) against her again (ποίας μηχανὰς πλέκουσιν αὖ).[70]

A more animated dialogue between Andromache and her Handmaid follows (68-95) in which the rest of the essentials of the plot are revealed. The Handmaid tells her that they are planning to kill her child, and Andromache laments her desperate situation, especially now that the boy's father (Neoptolemos) is at Delphi (68-76). The Handmaid agrees that it would be better if he were present, but now, she observes, Andromache is without *philoi* 'friends' (νῦν δ' ἔρημος εἶ φίλων, 77-78).[71] Andromache thinks of another friend who could help; she asks if there is any news from Peleus. The Handmaid remarks that he is too old to be of any use (80). Andromache does not take her remark into consideration, and, instead, she asks her to go and find him for her (81-83).[72] The old Handmaid is hesitant because she does not know what excuse to use if she is seen out of the house (84). Andromache assures her that, being a woman, she can find many excuses, literally *mêkhanai* 'devices', (πολλὰς ἂν εὕροις μηχανάς· γυνὴ γὰρ εἶ, 85).[73] The Handmaid is still hesitant because

---

[70] Burnett 1971.132-133 remarks that the splitting of the villain in two redoubles the effect of the portrayal of the cruelty against Andromache. *Mêkhanai* (μηχαναί) are here women's 'devices', as the notion of a woman's *plekein* 'plotting/knitting' (πλέκειν lit. 'knit') suggests; Andromache verifies this idea with her words to her maid in 85. Hermione's Nurse also uses a similar verb *raptein* 'sew' (ῥάπτειν), referring to Hermione's deadly contrivances against Andromache (φόνον ῥάψασα, 836). For the connotations of *mêkhanê* (μηχανή) and *plokos* (πλόκος) see also *Medea* 408-409, and *Hippolytus* 481 and 514.

[71] Her *philos* 'friend' is Neoptolemos, whom Andromache mentioned in 75-76.

[72] As the continuation of the plot shows, Andromache was right in her judgement to rely on Peleus and her Handmaid was not. Peleus' arrival saves Andromache and her son from the plots of Hermione and Menelaos. The Handmaid's remark was based on the common belief that the aged are weak. Peleus' heroic stature is a surprise. Burnett 1971.130-156 views *Andromache* as a play of surprise and "mixed reversal."

[73] Cf. the same idea expressed by Phaedra's Nurse: "being women we will find devices" (...γυναῖκες μηχανὰς ἐξευρήσομεν, *Hippolytus* 481). Cf. also *Andromache* 66 above, where Andromache is referring to the devices of another woman, Hermione; and *Medea* 408-409 "and besides, we are born women, for good things *amêkhanôtatai* 'most uninventive' but most clever inventors of all evils" (πρὸς δὲ καὶ πεφύκαμεν / γυναῖκες, ἐς μὲν ἐσθλ' ἀμηχανώταται, / κακῶν δὲ πάντων τέκτονες σοφώταται).

she finds it risky knowing that Hermione is a careful guard (86).[74] In order to convince her, Andromache has to rely on the fidelity of her servant. She complains that her Handmaid is denouncing her *philoi* 'friends' in their misfortune, implying herself (ὁρᾷς; ἀπαυδᾷς ἐν κακοῖς φίλοισι σοῖς, 87).[75] The Handmaid reacts strongly; she will not accept this blame from her mistress: "not so; you will not *oneidisêis* 'blame' me for this" (οὐ δῆτα·μηδὲν τοῦτ' ὀνειδίσῃς ἐμοί, 88).[76] She decides to go, commenting with sad realism that her life as a slave-woman is not so important, after all (89-90). The prologue ends with Andromache's reflections on the nature of women, who are prompt to express their woes through tears and endless lamentations (91-95).

The Handmaid serves as a messenger who warns her mistress of impending evil.[77] She expresses her compassion and her loyalty and she offers her comments (78, 80), which, however, have no effect.[78] Despite her reservations and her hesitation before the risk of being blamed as disloyal by her mistress, she obeys and undertakes the dangerous errand. By contrast, Hermione's Nurse, who advises her mistress and disapproves of her exaggerations, has more authority over her than Andromache's Handmaid, as our discussion will show.

The Nurse's entrance marks the second part of the play.[79] The manuscripts assign this character as *trophos* 'Nurse', or *therapaina*

---

[74] The Handmaid's caution and hesitation are sensible since Hermione is also a woman and therefore dangerous; she also knows women's devices.

[75] The Handmaid's *philos* 'friend' is Andromache. Andromache appeals to her Handmaid as a 'friend', not as a slave.

[76] On denouncing a master cf. also above, n68. Note also here the language of blame: Andromache blames her Handmaid; by contrast, it is the Nurse who regularly blames her mistress or expresses her disapproval, as we have seen with the Nurse characters already, and we will see in this play with Hermione's Nurse as well.

[77] Cf. Klytaimnestra's old servant in *Iphighenia at Aulis* 855-895, who warns his mistress of Agamemnon's plots; see also the tutor in *Medea* 61-73, who warns the Nurse of the impending danger for Medea.

[78] Especially her disapproval of Andromache's idea to summon Peleus is totally disregarded and ignored by Andromache, just as the old servant's advice is ignored by Hippolytus in *Hippolytus* 113. A servant may advise but is generally ignored; the Nurse, however, has a different effect.

[79] The bipartite action in the drama raises problems of unity. On the blending of the two actions see Friedrich 1953.47ff. For a summary of the attempts to solve the problem of unity in this play see Erbse 1966.276-297. On the structure of the play and its problems see also Kovacs 1980.45-49. As Halleran remarks, the unprepared entrance of the Nurse is not surprising: if Andromache has a slave, we should not be surprised if Hermione has her Nurse along with her; the Nurse's news however is more surprising, as in the second

'Handmaid', but it is generally accepted as *trophos*. Her address to Hermione as *teknon/pai* 'child' as well as her tone of advice, approval and disapproval, and, more important, Hermione's compliance, support this choice. She comes as a messenger to announce to the chorus what is happening inside the house in describing Hermione's plight. Her speech to the chorus before the entrance of Hermione functions as the prologue to the second part of the play. It partially resembles in function and content the Nurse's prologue in *Medea* 1-48.

As Hermione's Nurse comes on stage, she addresses the women of the chorus as *philtatai gunaikes* 'dearest women' (802), and she tells them of Hermione's troubles. Now that her father has abandoned her, Hermione regrets plotting the death of Andromache and her son, and she wants to kill herself for fear of her husband.[80] She is afraid that he will punish her "for seeking to kill those that she had no right to" (802-810).[81] The servants can hardly keep her from hanging herself and take the sword from her hand (811-813).[82] This is how 'she regrets' (*metalgei*, 814).[83] The Nurse now addresses the chorus women

---

part of the play Hermione, who was Andromache's persecutor, now turns into the victim (Halleran 1985.39).

[80] Kovacs 1980.71 remarks: "The scene marks a departure in the action and involves a slight irrationality. Menelaos had promised in unmistakable terms that he would return to discuss matters with Neoptolemos." Still, Hermione's fears may be exaggerated, but they are not irrational. In Menelaos' absence anything could happen, and, besides, Menelaos is not to be trusted. As Burnett 1971.139 remarks, "Hermione is both pathetic and dangerous because she is genuinely self-deceived, but her father and her erstwhile suitor...intentionally deceive others." Burnett 1971.144 further comments that the second drama has been compressed into a single episode, but although the heroine's danger and helplessness are described first by the Nurse and then by Hermione, still the violence that threatens the heroine is not satisfactorily defined. However, as Lesky 1983.252 pointedly remarks, "the transition from self-confidence, as long as Menelaos stood behind her, to unbridled despair is harsh and abrupt but thoroughly plausible, given the woman's character as the poet reveals it."

[81] Line 810, where the Nurse expresses her criticism and disapproval of Hermione's treatment of Andromache and her son, is bracketed by Diggle, suspected as spurious. But cf. Kilissa expressing her disapproval of Klytaimnestra and Aigisthos to the chorus in *Libation-Bearers* 737-743 and 765.

[82] The Nurse's words are verified later by Hermione (841-844), although in reverse order. Hanging and death by the sword are the traditional ways of committing suicide. Still, as Loraux 1987.13-17 has demonstrated, hanging is the traditional way of "killing a woman," in contrast to the sword, which is the traditional men's method of suicide. Hermione and Deianeira are the only exceptions in Greek tragedy (while Dido in Vergil's *Aeneid* is the most famous example in Latin literature).

[83] Cf. *sunnoia* (805) 'remorse'; Andromache does not feel remorse out of moral considerations but out of regret at the realization that what she has done would look bad

as *philai* 'friends', emphasizing their bond of friendship as women (cf. 802 'dearest women'), and she asks for their help, complaining that she cannot restrain her mistress from killing herself.[84] She finishes her speech with a *sententia* which implies that Hermione, unstable as she is, may be more willing to listen to new friends than to old ones (818-819):

ὦ φίλταται γυναῖκες, ὡς κακὸν κακῶν
διάδοχον ἐν τῇδ' ἡμέρᾳ πορσύνεται.
δέσποινα γὰρ κατ' οἶκον, Ἑρμιόνην λέγω,
πατρός τ' ἐρημωθεῖσα συννοίᾳ θ' ἅμα
οἷον δέδρακεν ἔργον Ἀνδρομάχην κτανεῖν
καὶ παῖδα βουλεύσασα, κατθανεῖν θέλει,
πόσιν τρέμουσα, μὴ ἀντὶ τῶν δεδραμένων
ἐκ τῶνδ' ἀτίμως δωμάτων ἀποσταλῇ,
[ἢ κατθάνῃ κτείνουσα τοὺς οὐ χρὴ κτανεῖν].
μόλις δέ νιν θέλουσαν ἀρτῆσαι δέρην
εἴργουσι φύλακες δμῶες ἔκ τε δεξιᾶς
ξίφη καθαρπάζουσιν ἐξαιρούμενοι.
οὕτω μεταλγεῖ καὶ τὰ πρὶν δεδραμένα
ἔγνωκε πράξασ' οὐ καλῶς. ἐγὼ μὲν οὖν
δέσποιναν εἴργουσ' ἀγχόνης κάμνω, φίλαι·
ὑμεῖς δὲ βᾶσαι τῶνδε δωμάτων ἔσω
θανάτου νιν ἐκλύσασθε· τῶν γὰρ ἠθάδων
φίλων νέοι μολόντες εὐπιθέστεροι.

Andromache 802-819

O dearest women [*philtatai gunaikes*], how on this day
evil falls upon evil.
For my mistress in the house, Hermione I say,
abandoned by her father and also in remorse [*sunnoia*]
for what a terrible thing she did planning to murder
Andromache and her son, wants to die,
fearing her husband, lest, for what she did,
she'll be thrown out of the house in dishonor
[or killed for trying to kill those that she should not].
Now the guards in the house can barely restrain her,
as she is trying to knot a rope on her neck,

---

to others, especially her husband, whose punishment she fears. See Stevens 1971.192 and Kovacs 1980.71-72 and 102-104.

[84] The Nurse addresses the women of the chorus in equal terms, unlike the Nurse in *Women of Trachis* 71, who addresses the chorus from a superior stance as 'children'. The complaining Nurse is a familiar theme expressing a common trend among nurses. Cf. Kilissa in *Libation-Bearers* 743-762 and Phaedra's Nurse in *Hippolytus* 250-266.

88   *Chapter 2*

> and snatch the sword from her right hand.
> This is how she <u>regrets [*metalgei*]</u>, and she realizes that
> what she did before was not right. And I am quite exhausted
> trying to keep my mistress from the halter, my friends.
> Now you, going into the palace,
> plead with her not to destroy herself; <u>for new friends
> have more persuasion than accustomed ones.</u>

At this point, the chorus can hear the cries of the servants as Hermione is rushing onto the stage; this saves the chorus from heeding the Nurse's urging and leaving the orchestra. This would be highly unusual, although not impossible, for the conventions of Greek tragedy. Indeed, Hermione enters the stage in a frantic condition. She wants to tear her hair and lacerate her cheeks (825-827). The Nurse tries to avert her: "child (*pai*), what are you about? Will you disfigure yourself?" (828).[85] Hermione wants to remove her veil (829-831), but the Nurse advises her to cover herself: "my child (*teknon*), cover your bosom, fasten your dress" (832). Hermione, however, does not see the reason why she should cover herself, if all her schemes are *dêla* 'clear', *amphiphanê* 'revealed', and *akrupta* 'unconcealed' (833-835).[86] The Nurse reconfirms Hermione's guilt (836): "do you regret plotting murder for the other wife?" Hermione curses herself for her destructive daring, but the Nurse tells her that her husband will forgive her misconduct, her error (840).[87]

Hermione now appeals to her Nurse as a *philê* 'friend'. The bond between the Nurse and Hermione is a bond of friendship between women like the bond of friendship between the Nurse and the women of the chorus. (Compare also Penelope's address to Eurykleia as *maia philê* 'dear Nurse' in *Odyssey* xxiii 11, 35, 59, and 81). She asks the Nurse to give her back the sword and not to prevent her from

---

[85] Note that in maternal tone she calls her 'child'; cf. also 832, 866, and 880. This is a typical address of a Nurse to her mistress: cf. Phaedra's Nurse in *Hippolytus*. Eurykleia in the *Odyssey* also uses the same maternal address with Telemakhos, Odysseus, and Penelope.

[86] Cf. *Hippolytus* 201-202, where Phaedra also wants her maids to loosen her hair. Cf. also *Hippolytus* 243-245, where, however, Phaedra wants her Nurse to cover her; she does not want to reveal her secrets. Hermione, on the contrary, does not mind being uncovered because her secrets are out already. Note how the three synonymous adjectives in 834—'clear' (δῆλα), 'revealed', literally 'visible all around' (ἀμφιφανῆ), and 'unconcealed' (ἄκρυπτα)—emphasize the notion of the revelation of what should remain concealed. On the literal and metaphorical meaning of concealment and revelation see my discussion in chapter 3.

[87] Cf. *Hippolytus* 462-467, where the Nurse also tells Phaedra of forgiving husbands.

Nurse Characters in Aeschylus, Sophocles, and Euripides 89

hanging herself (841-844), verifying the Nurse's description to the chorus at 811-816. The Nurse will not let her die, for she is not in her right mind (845).[88] Hermione thinks of more spectacular and unconventional methods of dying. She considers first fire and then hurling herself from a rock into the sea or "to the woods of the mountains" (846-850).[89] The Nurse advises her to calm down, and concludes with a *sententia*: "why do you suffer? Misfortunes are god-sent to human beings at one time or another" (τί ταῦτα μοχθεῖς; συμφοραὶ θεήλατοι/ πᾶσιν βροτοῖσιν ἢ τότ' ἦλθον ἢ τότε, 851-852).[90] Hermione in a more peaceful tone now abandons the idea of killing herself and, calling upon her father who deserted her, laments her miserable fate (854-865).

In this dialogue the Nurse responds to Hermione's emotional lyric cries with sensible spoken iambics. In a motherly protective tone, she calmly tries to reason with her and avert her from killing or hurting herself. She also tries to keep her from exposing herself to the public eye.[91] She tries to inspire in her caution, moderation, and good sense. Indeed, Hermione stops her thoughts of killing or hurting herself and calmly mourns her sad fate (854-865).

At this point, the Nurse, seeing that Hermione is now calm enough to be able to listen, addresses her mistress in a longer speech in which she uses all her rhetorical skill at persuasion. She starts calling Hermione 'child' (*pai*) again, and, without hesitation, she directly expresses her disapproval, both for her excessive behavior with Andromache before, and for her excessive fear now (866-868).[92] Then

---

[88] Cf. *Hippolytus* 324, where Phaedra's Nurse expresses the same concern for Phaedra's sanity. In the eyes of a reasonable Nurse, suicide is insane by definition.

[89] The fantasies of Hermione's suicide resemble the fantasies of Phaedra's delirium; cf. the images of the woods and especially the wording in 849 "...to the woods of the mountains" (...καθ' ὕλαν ὀρέων), similar to that of *Hippolytus* 215 "send me to the mountain; I am going to the woods" (πέμπετέ μ' εἰς ὄρος· εἶμι πρὸς ὕλαν). Both women fantasize escape, although of a different kind. For different interpretations of Hermione's other choices of suicide see Stevens 1971.193; for an insightful discussion see Loraux 1987.19.

[90] Cf. the philosophizing Nurse at *Hippolytus* 437-439 and especially at 203-207.

[91] Phaedra's Nurse shows the same concern for Phaedra, although in a different context (*Hippolytus* 212-214). She worries because of Phaedra's inappropriate words in public during her delirium, while Hermione's Nurse worries about the physical exposure of her mistress.

[92] The use of the verbs *epainein/ainein* (ἐπαινεῖν/αἰνεῖν) 'praise', 'approve' —here used in the negative form (οὔτ'...ἐπῄνεσα, 266)—is central in praise/blame poetry. Cf. Nagy 1989.10-11.

90 Chapter 2

she presents her argumentation, which is characterized by down-to-earth common sense: first, her husband will not listen to the barbarian slave he brought from Troy instead of the noble wife who came with a big dowry from a fortunate city (869-873), and, second, her father will not abandon her (874-875).[93] She finishes her speech with a peroration, advising her to go inside the house and not to cause a scandal by being seen outside (876-878):[94]

> ὦ παῖ, τὸ λίαν οὔτ' ἐκεῖν' ἐπῄνεσα,
> ὅτ' εἰς γυναῖκα Τρῳάδ' ἐξημάρτανες,
> οὔτ' αὖ τὸ νῦν σου δεῖμ' ὃ δειμαίνεις ἄγαν.
> οὐχ ὧδε κῆδος σὸν διώσεται πόσις
> φαύλοις γυναικὸς βαρβάρου πεισθεὶς λόγοις.
> οὐ γάρ τί σ' αἰχμάλωτον ἐκ Τροίας ἔχει,
> ἀλλ' ἀνδρὸς ἐσθλοῦ παῖδα σὺν πολλοῖς λαβὼν
> ἕδνοισι, πόλεώς τ' οὐ μέσως εὐδαίμονος.
> πατὴρ δέ σ' οὐχ ὧδ' ὡς σὺ δειμαίνεις, τέκνον,
> προδοὺς ἐάσει δωμάτων τῶνδ' ἐκπεσεῖν.
> ἀλλ' εἴσιθ' εἴσω μηδὲ φαντάζου δόμων
> πάροιθε τῶνδε, μή τιν' αἰσχύνην λάβῃς
> [πρόσθεν μελάθρων τῶνδ' ὁρωμένη, τέκνον].

Andromache 866-880

O child [*pai*], I did not approve [[*out'...epêinesa*] of your excesses
then, when you wronged the Trojan woman,
nor do I now (approve of) your excessive fear.
Your husband will not repudiate your marriage like this
persuaded in the wicked words of a barbarian woman.
For he did not get you prisoner from Troy,
but he got the daughter of a noble man with much
dowry, from a city not moderately fortunate.
And your father, having not forsaken you like this, as you fear,
my child [*teknon*], will not let you be thrown out of this house.
But get inside and do not make a scene in front of the house
lest you cause shame for yourself
[if you are seen here in front of the palace, my child {*teknon*}].[95]

---

[93] On the different barbarian characters in Greek tragedy and the attitude of the Greeks toward them see Hall 1989; specifically on Andromache, see 132-214. On Hermione's reasons for believing that her father has abandoned her, see Kovacs 1980.71.

[94] A woman's place is in the house; her presence outside the house signals disorder and is a cause for scandal.

[95] The repetition in the beginning, the middle, and the end of her speech of the address 'child' (*pai/teknon*) strengthens its power of persuasion. This line was deleted by Nauck and is bracketed by Diggle. However, although it may seem superfluous, it is

Nurse Characters in Aeschylus, Sophocles, and Euripides 91

The Nurse's final speech, although short, is well organized and rhetorically convincing. It provides logical argumentation for the Nurse's point: Hermione's fears are unsubstantiated and therefore she should not consider suicide but calm down and go inside. Unlike Deianeira's Nurse in the *Women of Trachis,* instead of employing a *captatio benevolentiae,* Hermione's Nurse starts with a remark of open disapproval and scolding.[96] Then she presents her arguments against Hermione's unreasonable fears. Her first argument is strongly supported with realism, which can even be seen as cynicism: Neoptolemos will not listen to a barbarian woman instead of a wife from a noble family and especially with a big dowry.[97] Her second argument, however, that her father will not abandon her, lacks any support. This can be explained in two ways: either the argument speaks for itself (a father will not betray and abandon his daughter) or, most probably, the Nurse knows Menelaos too well. This second interpretation is preferable, as it agrees with the Euripidean realism manifested in all servants. In any case, her speech, as a whole, is solid enough to convince Hermione to go inside.

Obeying the Nurse, Hermione starts going inside, but, caught by the entrance of the stranger, she withdraws behind the chorus members, and, only when she hears that the newcomer is Orestes (889) does she come forward and speak to him; or, she is almost off stage with the Nurse and returns at 889.[98] The unexpected arrival of Orestes (881ff.) represents the *peripeteia* of the second part of the play and provides the solution to both the personal and dynastic problems

---

needed, especially as it frames the Nurse's speech and, with its redundancy, it adds special emphasis to the Nurse's rebuke. Cf. also Stevens 1971.199.

[96] It is typical for a Nurse to express her disapproval (see also above, n76). Moreover, Hermione is younger, and her frantic condition allows for such treatment.

[97] This is not a new idea for Hermione. As Vellacott 1975.117-118 remarks, "Hermione accepts the economic aspect of marriage without question," as her opening lines reveal when she boasts of the rich dowry Menelaos gave her; the Nurse, in comforting Hermione (871-873), reminds her of her big dowry. Stevens 1971.198-199 characterizes the Nurse's comments as cynical, while Kovacs 1980.72 sees them as spoken in "worldly wisdom."

[98] According to Lesky 1983. 252-253, "Hermione has entered the house or she is just about to. Since a restless coming and going hardly suited the poet's purpose, we must best imagine that she remained standing at the door, overheard the conversation with Orestes, and now falls at his feet hoping for deliverance." On this scene see also Stevens 1971.199.

of Hermione; instead of committing suicide she will follow Orestes for an immediate escape. [99]

In contrast to Andromache's Handmaid, Hermione's Nurse has authority over her mistress. She has more influence on Hermione than the Handmaid has on Andromache. She advises her mistress and openly expresses her disapproval of her excessive behavior. She is not carried away emotionally by Hermione's frenzy, but, calmly, reasonably, and even almost cynically (like Phaedra's Nurse), she manages to calm down Hermione and to reason with her; so when the Nurse advises her to go inside, Hermione listens to her and obeys. The Nurse in *Andromache* has the same degree of authority that the Nurse in the *Women of Trachis* has in reproving and advising her mistress and in being respected and obeyed by her; and, although less subtle and tactful, she is equally efficient and effective.

Regarding her interaction with the women of the chorus, the Nurse treats them on equal terms as 'friends' and asks their help in preventing Hermione from killing herself. It is important to observe here that there is a bond of friendship, not only between the Nurse and Hermione (note how Hermione calls the Nurse her 'friend'), but also between her and the women of the chorus, as well as between them and Hermione. As the Nurse says, these friends are newer to Hermione and, therefore, she will be more easily convinced by them (cf. 818-819). The Nurse counts on this bond in asking the chorus to influence Hermione and stop her from killing herself. This bond of friendship among the women is also the link among the members of the female aggregate which we find in archaic choral compositions like Alcman PMG 1, and it stresses once more the lyric 'background' of women's poetics in tragedy. The setting is also similar. Two leading female personalities, Hermione and her Nurse, like Agido and Hagesikhora in Alcman PMG 1, are performing in the presence of a female aggregate.

---

[99] Orestes' role corresponds to Peleus' role in the first part (see Lesky 1983. 252). On Orestes' unexpected appearance see Mastronarde 1979.26 and Halleran 1985.39. On the personal and the dynastic levels of this play, see Conacher 1967.166. As Burnett 1971.144 observes, "Hermione... at once sees in him the opportunity of immediate flight. Death is no longer an interesting alternative, since Orestes can remove her from her husband's roof and put her out of his reach."

5. The Nurse in Euripides' *Medea*: The Nurse who Foreshadows her Mistress

Following the pattern of the Euripidean prologues, *Medea* starts with a long *rhesis*, a long speech, containing basic information about the play, the setting, and the background, delivered by the Nurse. This *rhesis* contains foreshadowing comparable to the foreshadowing in the *rhesis* of Aphrodite in *Hippolytus*, and the foreshadowing in other plays with divine, or non-divine, prologues.[100] The *rhesis* of the prologue is followed by a dialogue between Medea's Nurse and the Tutor of Medea's children, the closest parallel to which is found in *Andromache*, where Andromache's *rhesis* is followed by a dialogue with her Handmaid.

The Nurse's speech can be divided into three parts, each of them starting with a general statement that summarizes her main point and ending with a conclusion that she expresses in the form of a reflection or a *sententia*. The first part starts with an account of what happened from the moment that Medea fell in love with Jason until now (1-15). The second part describes at length Medea's devastation at Jason's betrayal (16-35). In the third part the Nurse expresses her fears for Medea's children, and about her revenge in general; this part ends with the arrival of the children accompanied by their Tutor, the *Paidagogos* (36-48).

The Nurse's speech starts with a long contrary-to-fact wish (1-15): she wishes that Medea should never have met Jason, loved him, and followed him to Corinth; then her mistress, Medea, would not have sailed to Iolkos, "her heart pierced through with love for Jason."[101] The Nurse does not omit that, before Medea came to Corinth, she had

---

[100] Cf. Apollo's *rhesis* in the prologue to *Alcestis*, Hermes' in *Ion*, Dionysus' in *Bacchae*, and Poseidon's in *Trojan Women*; also Iphighenia's (in her dream) in *Iphighenia in Tauris*, Helen's (in Hermes' prophesy) in *Helen*, and the ghost of Polydoros in *Hecuba*. Hamilton 1978. 277-302 does not include *Medea* in his list of Euripides' plays containing a prediction in the prologue (277), as *Medea* does not fit his two categories of prologue either by a god or a spirit. Indeed, the prediction in *Medea* by the Nurse is quite exceptional, especially if the problematic lines 38-43 are not omitted. On the Euripidean prologue, in general, see Erbse 1984.1-20, and on the prologue to *Medea*, 103-118.

[101] *Medea* is the only drama that starts with a regret which introduces an 'unreal desire'. The formal frame of her recollection makes the past events appear as negative and regretful. See Pucci 1980.33. The length of the Nurse's first sentence containing her multiple wish reveals her emotional condition; at the same time it reveals Medea's past in a very lively way.

94 Chapter 2

persuaded the daughters of Pelias to kill their father, a remark that warns of Medea's dangerous nature from the very beginning of the play. She continues her speech with a remark on how, at first, when she came to Corinth with her husband and children, Medea found favor with the Corinthians, "complying with Jason in all things." She concludes her long wish with a *sententia*: the best security for a woman is not to be in conflict with her husband (14-15):[102]

> Εἴθ' ὤφελ' Ἀργοῦς μὴ διαπτάσθαι σκάφος
> Κόλχων ἐς αἶαν κυανέας Συμπληγάδας,
> μηδ' ἐν νάπαισι Πηλίου πεσεῖν ποτε
> τμηθεῖσα πεύκη, μηδ' ἐρετμῶσαι χέρας
> ἀνδρῶν ἀριστέων οἳ τὸ πάγχρυσον δέρας
> Πελίᾳ μετῆλθον. οὐ γὰρ ἂν δέσποιν' ἐμὴ
> Μήδεια πύργους γῆς ἔπλευσ' Ἰωλκίας
> ἔρωτι θυμὸν ἐκπλαγεῖσ' Ἰάσονος,
> οὐδ' ἂν κτανεῖν πείσασα Πελιάδας κόρας
> πατέρα κατῴκει τήνδε γῆν Κορινθίαν
> ξὺν ἀνδρὶ καὶ τέκνοισιν, ἁνδάνουσα μὲν
> φυγῇ πολιτῶν ὧν ἀφίκετο χθόνα,
> αὐτή τε πάντα ξυμφέρουσ' Ἰάσονι·
> <u>ἥπερ μεγίστη γίγνεται σωτηρία,</u>
> <u>ὅταν γυνὴ πρὸς ἄνδρα μὴ διχοστατῇ·</u>

Medea 1-15

How I wish that the Argo had never reached the land
of Colchis, through the blue Symplegades,
nor that the smitten fir tree had ever fallen in the glades
of Pelion, nor that it had furnished the oars for the hands
of heroes who came for the golden fleece
in Pelias' name. Then my mistress,
Medea, would not have sailed to the towers of Iolkos,

---

[102] Although a barbarian, like Medea, the Nurse shares contemporary Athenian values; this does not suggest Euripides' inconsistency; it is rather a proof of the universality of attitudes on a woman's role in ancient times. On the different treatment of barbarians and Greeks see Hall 1989. Hall (203) sees Medea as the "paradigmatic 'transgressive' woman" whose "overbearing nature cannot fully be understood without reference to her barbarian provenance." Shaw 1975.255-266 also argues that one of the most important themes of the play is Medea's cultural isolation, and that her subordination of her female instinct as a mother to her 'masculine' desire to dominate is what makes her fully 'barbarian'. On the other hand, Knox 1979.306-311 questions Medea's portrayal as an oriental witch. In the same trend, March 1990.63 sees Medea treated with compassion rather than condemnation.

her heart pierced through with love for Jason,
nor would she have persuaded the daughters of Pelias to kill
their father, and now be living here in Corinth
with her husband and children, pleasing the people
whose land she reached in exile,
while complying with Jason in all things;
<u>and this becomes the best security,</u>
<u>when a woman is not in conflict with her husband.</u>

Then the Nurse gives an account of Medea's present situation: Jason has betrayed her for the daughter of Kreon, and Medea, dishonored, invokes their oaths and their pledges. She describes at length Medea's misery: she lies unfed, melting in tears, neither raising her eye nor lifting her face from the earth; she does not listen to friends who try to reason with her, but in lamentation she calls to herself, her father, her country, and her home, which she betrayed for a husband who has now dishonored her. She concludes her account of Medea's misfortunes with a reflection, which is a continuation of her former *sententia* of 14-15: now Medea learned through her misfortune what it means to leave behind one's fatherland.

νῦν δ' <u>ἐχθρὰ</u> πάντα, καὶ νοσεῖ τὰ <u>φίλτατα</u>.
<u>προδοὺς</u> γὰρ αὐτοῦ τέκνα δεσπότιν τ' ἐμὴν
<u>γάμοις</u> Ἰάσων βασιλικοῖς <u>εὐνάζεται</u>,
<u>γήμας</u> Κρέοντος παῖδ', ὃς αἰσυμνᾷ χθονός·
Μήδεια δ' ἡ δύστηνος <u>ἠτιμασμένη</u>
βοᾷ μὲν ὅρκους, ἀνακαλεῖ δὲ δεξιᾶς
πίστιν μεγίστην, καὶ θεοὺς μαρτύρεται
οἵας ἀμοιβῆς ἐξ Ἰάσονος κυρεῖ.
<u>κεῖται δ' ἄσιτος</u>, σῶμ' ὑφεῖσ' ἀλγηδόσι,
τὸν πάντα <u>συντήκουσα δακρύοις</u> χρόνον,
ἐπεὶ πρὸς ἀνδρὸς ᾔσθετ' <u>ἠδικημένη</u>,
οὔτ' ὄμμ' ἐπαίρουσ' οὔτ' ἀπαλλάσσουσα γῆς
πρόσωπον· ὡς δὲ πέτρος ἢ θαλάσσιος
κλύδων ἀκούει νουθετουμένη φίλων·
ἢν μή ποτε στρέψασα πάλλευκον δέρην
αὐτὴ πρὸς αὑτὴν πατέρ' ἀποιμώξῃ φίλον
καὶ γαῖαν οἴκους θ', οὓς <u>προδοῦσ'</u> ἀφίκετο
μετ' ἀνδρὸς ὅς σφε νῦν <u>ἀτιμάσας ἔχει</u>.
ἔγνωκε δ' ἡ τάλαινα συμφορᾶς ὕπο
οἷον πατρῴας μὴ ἀπολείπεσθαι χθονός.

Medea 16-35

But now everything is in enmity [*ekhthra*] and what is dearest

96   Chapter 2

[*ta philtata*] is sick.[103] For Jason, having betrayed [*prodous*]
his children and my mistress, sleeps [*eunazetai*] in royal wedlock
[*gamois*], married [*gêmas*] to the daughter of Kreon, the ruler
of the land.[104] And unfortunate Medea, <u>dishonored [*êtimasmenê*]</u>
invokes their oaths, appeals to the pledges
in which she put her deepest trust, and calls the gods to witness
what recompense she gets from Jason.[105]
She <u>lies unfed [*keitai d'asitos*]</u> having surrendered her body to
pains, <u>melting in tears [*suntêkousa dakruois*]</u> the whole time, [106]
since she found that she was <u>wronged [*êdikêmenê*]</u> by her husband,
neither raising her eye, nor lifting her face from the earth,
[deaf] like a rock or a sea wave
she listens to friends who try to reason with her; [107]
if she ever turns her white neck,
she calls to herself, in lamentation, her dear father and her
country and the home that she <u>betrayed [*prodous(a)*]</u> to come here
with a husband who <u>has</u> now <u>dishonored [*atimasas ekhei*]</u> her.
Now she learned, the wretched one, by her misfortune
what it means not to leave behind one's fatherland. [108]

---

[103] According to McDermott 1989.33, *philtata* refers to her family. On the importance of the contrast *ekhthra ta philtata* (ἐχθρά / τὰ φίλτατα) 'in enmity/the dearest' see Bongie 1977.27-56, especially 28, and n6.

[104] Note the emphasis of Jason's betrayal (*prodous*, 17) underscored further with Medea's description as 'dishonored' (*êtimasmenê*, 20, and *atimasas ekhei*, 33) and 'wronged' (*êdikêmenê*, 26). In addition, the use of three consecutive words related to marriage *gamois, eunazetai, gêmas* (γάμοις, εὐνάζεται, γήμας) 'wedlock', 'sleeps', 'married' emphasizes Jason's betrayal but also her indirect disapproval. Her account provides her own commentary.

[105] On the religious importance of the oath in Medea's revenge, and on *Medea* as a tragedy of revenge, see Burnett 1973.

[106] Cf. the chorus' description of the similar condition of unfed Phaedra in *Hippolytus* 121-140 and the Nurse's comment in 275 (τριταίαν γ' οὖσ' ἄσιτος ἡμέραν). Cf. also Penelope in *Odyssey* iv 789 (κεῖτ' ἄρ' ἄσιτος, ἄπαστος ἐδητύος ἠδὲ ποτῆτος), and Achilles in *Iliad* XIX 346 (ὁ δ' ἄκμηνος καὶ ἄπαστος). Cf. further Ajax in *Ajax* 324-325 (νῦν δ' ἐν τοιᾷδε κείμενος κακῇ τύχῃ/ ἄσιτος ἀνήρ, ἄποτος). Medea, among the Euripidean heroes, "has a streak of Sophoclean heroic temper" (see Knox 1977.193ff., who discusses her similarities with Ajax). Cf. also here the similar description of Penelope melting in tears, like Medea, in *Odyssey* xix 136 (ἀλλ' Ὀδυσῆ ποθέουσα φίλον κατατήκομαι ἦτορ ὥς) and xix 208 (τῆς τήκετο καλὰ παρήϊα δάκρυ χεούσης).

[107] The interrupted flow of the Nurse's speech (26 interrupts the flow of 24-28) is due to her emotional participation in Medea's problems. On the Nurse's participation see also Pucci 1980.22 and 34-35. Pucci (41-42) observes that the rock simile indicates her cruelty, especially as she will kill her loved ones, i.e., her children.

[108] The Nurse uses in line 32 the same term for Medea's betrayal that she used on Jason in line 17 (*prodous* 'betrayed'), thus indirectly blaming Medea for betraying her

The Nurse's words echo the language of Medea. This shows that she is deeply affected by the grief of her mistress and that she experiences to some extent Medea's suffering. As Pucci remarks, she shares Medea's indignation at Jason's offense (17, 20, 26), and she gives a sympathetic picture of Medea's self-reproaches (30-35); "her language of love, pity and compassion implies that she feels as her own Medea's misfortunes and grieves, and therefore, she borrows, so to speak, Medea's language."[109]

At the same time, however, there is in her speech a voice of reproach and criticism of Medea's betrayal of her family in Colchis. Just as she blames Jason for betraying Medea, she blames Medea for betraying her family (especially killing her brother, a detail that the Athenian audience was certainly familiar with). Just as, by emphasizing Jason's betrayal, she expresses her indirect disapproval, so by using the same term for Medea's betrayal that she uses for Jason (*prodous* 'betrayed'), she indirectly blames Medea for betraying her family. The Nurse's account provides her own commentary. She pities Medea for the injustice she suffers from Jason but blames her for her crime: Medea is getting betrayal for betrayal. The Nurse's last sentence (34-35) verifies the same idea. Medea learned through her suffering like Agamemnon (see the chorus' words in *Agamemnon* 177: *pathei mathos* (πάθει μάθος) 'learning through suffering'. For Medea it is betrayal for betrayal, as for Agamemnon it was killing for killing.

The last part of the speech (36-48) can be subdivided into two smaller sections: 36-45 (the Nurse's fears) and 46-48 (the arrival of the children), both starting with a general statement and ending with a perceptive or a sententious observation.

---

family. Bongie 1977.28-29 remarks that the Nurse's account in the prologue presents from the very beginning "the paradox of Medea's masculine nature as she is shown reacting to a set of circumstances that could only happen to a woman." McDermott 1989.34 explains how in the Athenian society of Euripides' time a woman would turn for support first to her husband, next to her father, and finally to her male sons; Medea's thought follows this tripartite pattern, but she can find no hope with any, as even her children are hateful to her. And, as Williamson 1990.17-18 shows, Medea, having betrayed her family (by escaping with Jason without getting married and by killing her brother), now that her husband has abandoned her, unlike a divorced Athenian woman, has no home to return to.

[109] See Pucci 1980.38-40. Cf. the Nurse's use of the verb *atimazein* (ἀτιμάζειν) 'dishonor' (20 and 33) and Medea's direct reference to Jason (1354). On the Nurse's fear and concern for Jason's betrayal of Medea and of her excessively violent reaction cf. also Lesky 1983.218.

98 Chapter 2

The Nurse first expresses her fear for the children; she is afraid lest Medea plan something dreadful, she remarks ominously (37).[110] The Nurse continues expressing her fears at what Medea might also do to harm Kreon and her husband; she even fears lest Medea induce a greater misfortune. And she concludes with a perceptive observation: Medea is terrible to her enemies. The Nurse knows this well; she knows Medea's capacity for harm as she made clear with her observation on Pelias' example (9-10) and the 'betrayal' of her home (32). At that point, she sees the children coming with their Tutor, the *Paidagogos*, and she announces their arrival.[111] She concludes her speech with a new *sententia* about the children's innocent ignorance (48). The Nurse's words in 47-48 indicate Medea's plight, but also her potential for violence, and they come as a sharp contrast to the children's innocent games in 46:

---

[110] The foreshadowing refers to the children she mentioned in her previous sentence, but her fear may also refer to her next sentence (if we do not condemn 38-44). This ambiguity of the Nurse's fear is intentional; it allows surprise and suspense despite the foreshadowing; cf. Aphrodite's prologue in *Hippolytus* 21-50. In earlier versions of the legend, the children had died, but for other reasons. In one version by Eumelos (fr. 3), Medea unintentionally killed them while trying to make them immortal; in another, by Kreophylos, Medea killed Kreon, then left her children in the temple of Hera, where the Corinthians killed them and then spread the rumor that Medea was the murderer. But Euripides made Medea herself choose to murder them as part of her revenge against Jason; see Lesky 1983.220 and 457n22. March 1990.32-75 also remarks that Euripides' innovation was Medea's deliberate murder of her children. For a different interpretation see Michelini 1989.115-135. Michelini (130-134) contends that Euripides borrowed the dual voices of the 'conflict between Medea's ethic and her role as mother' from the play of Neophron; Euripides' innovation is that "he gave them a significance that was not in the original," she observes (134).

[111] The Nurse alone on stage announces the approach of the children. According to Halleran 1985.6-7, an entrance announcement with only one person on stage is rare. In addition, as Halleran notes, only the children, who do not have speaking roles but are only heard from inside (as they try to escape death at 1270-1279), are announced, and not the *Paidagogos* who accompanies them. This is because the children are the focus of attention, as they appear on stage after the Nurse has just finished expressing her fear of Medea's plotting against them; on the other hand, the *Paidagogos* is merely an extension of the children; "he exists just because they do." Euripides, Halleran concludes, breaks the convention to underscore the importance of the children and Medea's potential for violence. On the importance of the children theme in the play cf. also Conacher 1967.192 and McDermott 1989.5, who sees the drama centered around Medea's murder of the children and focuses her discussion on Medea, "the *teknophonos*," as the "incarnation of disorder."

στυγεῖ δὲ παῖδας οὐδ' ὁρῶσ' εὐφραίνεται.
δέδοικα δ' αὐτὴν μή τι βουλεύσῃ νέον·
(βαρεῖα γὰρ φρήν, οὐδ' ἀνέξεται κακῶς
πάσχουσ'· ἐγῴδα τήνδε, δειμαίνω τέ νιν,
μὴ θηκτὸν ὤσῃ φάσγανον δι' ἥπατος,
σιγῇ δόμους εἰσβᾶσ', ἵν' ἔστρωται λέχος,
ἢ καὶ τύραννον τόν τε γήμαντα κτάνῃ
κἄπειτα μείζω συμφορὰν λάβῃ τινά.)
δεινὴ γάρ· οὔτοι ῥᾳδίως γε συμβαλὼν
ἔχθραν τις αὐτῇ καλλίνικον οἴσεται.
ἀλλ' οἵδε παῖδες ἐκ τρόχων πεπαυμένοι
στείχουσι, μητρὸς οὐδὲν ἐννοούμενοι
κακῶν· νέα γὰρ φροντὶς οὐκ ἀλγεῖν φιλεῖ.

Medea 36-48

She hates her children and she is not pleased to see them.
I fear <u>lest she plot something new</u> [*mê ti bouleusêi neon*].[112]
For she has a dangerous <u>mind</u> [*phrên*] and she will not endure
to be injured.[113] <u>I know her</u> [*egôida tênde*], and I fear her,
lest she thrust a sword into her heart,
going silently into the house where her bed is made
or kill the <u>tyrant</u> [*turannon*],[114] and her husband,
and then induce a greater misfortune.[115]

---

[112] *Bouleuein* 'plot' (37); cf. Medea's similar wording *bouleumata* when she refers to her 'plans' to murder her children in 1044, 1048, and 1079. The Nurse not only echoes Medea; she foreshadows her. *Neon* 'new', sinister and euphemistic; cf. Page 1938.69, and McDermott 1989.18. Cf. also the Handmaid's words to Andromache in *Andromache* 60, bringing *neous logous* [bad] 'news' to her mistress (καὶ νῦν φέρουσά σοι <u>νέους</u> ἥκω <u>λόγους</u>).

[113] Cf. 9-10 and 32, where the Nurse hinted at Medea's previous murders. *Phrên* (φρήν) 'mind'; cf. also 103-104, where Medea's nature is variously described by the Nurse as *êthos* (ἦθος) 'character', *phusis* (φύσις) 'nature', *phrên* (φρήν) 'mind'. As Lesky 1983.218, notes, "Euripides probes through the vocabulary of the Nurse for concepts in a way characteristic of his time." Indeed, the Nurses in Euripides are sophisticated in language and philosophical thought, in line with Euripides' attaching importance to the characters of low birth; cf. also the Nurse in *Hippolytus*.

[114] The 'tyrant' could be Kreon, or most probably his daughter, as in 87. The name of his daughter does not occur in *Medea*; later writers vary between Glauke and Kreousa.

[115] Lines 37-44 have many textual problems; for a detailed discussion cf. Page 1938.68. Page, following Dindorf, condemns 38-43 and provides a full argumentation for the deletion. According to Page, three points seem beyond reasonable doubt: (1) 40-41 recur with a slight difference in 379-380, but repetition is only acceptable in case of commonplace or if it is dramatically effective; (2) *ê kai turannon* (ἢ καὶ τύραννον) 'or the tyrant' in 42 cannot be ascribed to Euripides because it should refer to Kreon's daughter, but, as it stands, it must refer to Kreon; (3) Euripides could not have written all the fear

100 *Chapter 2*

> For she is terrible. Whoever joins in enmity
> with her will not carry off the glory of victory easily.
> But here come the children now that their play is over.
> They understand nothing about their mother's evils,
> for a child's mind does not like sadness.

The speech of the Nurse in the prologue is both informative and foreshadowing. The Nurse 'knows' Medea well, as she claims in 39 *egôida tênde* (ἐγῷδα τήνδε). She followed her from Colchis and has witnessed her love for Jason from the very beginning; she also knows the crimes Medea committed in order to get what she wanted. From the past she can easily predict the future, especially as she is a witness of Medea's reactions to her present misfortune. Her foreshadowing is as accurate as a Euripidean prologue allows: it is revealing but at the same time ambiguous and confusing. It creates an atmosphere of foreboding for the impending danger and, at the same time, suspense as to whom Medea's dangerous nature will strike this time. The Nurse's words in 37 "I fear lest she plot something *neon* 'new'" (δέδοικα δ' αὐτὴν μή τι βουλεύσῃ νέον) sum up both the foreboding and the suspense.[116] The mentioning of Medea's feelings for her children, immediately preceding this utterance, raises a fear

---

expressions (δέδοικα δ' αὐτήν, δειμαίνω τέ νιν, βαρεῖα γὰρ φρήν, δεινὴ γάρ) quite so close together (37-44). I do not agree with Page on any of these three basic points. On the first point, I believe that the repetition is dramatically effective because by misleading the audience it creates suspense (in 41-42 Medea's death is implied, while in 379-380 Medea reveals different plans); on the second point, I suggest that the ambiguity of the identity of the *turannos* (τύραννος) 'tyrant' is intentional, again for the creation of dramatic suspense; on the third point, I believe that the repetition is dramatically effective in the creation of the atmosphere of foreboding. In general, the whole passage (37-44) is purposefully ambiguous—an interpolator would have been more accurate and less tricky. It is also in line with the Euripidean prologue, which provides foreshadowing but with enough ambiguity to maintain the suspense of the plot (see also my discussion on the prologue to *Hippolytus* in chapter 3). If 38-44 are deleted, another problem arises, as McDermott 1989.126 observes: the characterization in 44-45 (οὔτοι ῥᾳδίως γε συμβαλὼν / ἔχθραν τις αὐτῇ καλλίνικον οἴσεται) is not suited to Medea's children but to her enemies mentioned in 39-42. For an updated overview of the various problems surrounding 37-45, see Erbse 1984.107-110, who also accepts these lines as they follow completely naturally in the context of the play. As I pointed out, lines 37-44 should by no means be bracketed (the *OCT* brackets are left in the above extract to indicate more clearly the problematic text).

[116] Considering the Nurse's experience with Medea's previous crimes, 'something new' carries enough foreboding even in English, and there is in fact no need to translate 'something dreadful' or 'something horrible', as the general practice has been. For the different meanings of *neos* (νέος) see *LSJ* s.v.

for the children. Furthermore, the more explicit—but at the same time intentionally ambiguous—fears of the Nurse for the other characters in the play, Medea herself, Jason, and 'the tyrant'—Kreon or his daughter—immediately create suspense and even confusion.[117]

Indeed, the Nurse's fears are confirmed by Medea's first reactions: in 98 Medea considers suicide, "alas, alas, how could I perish" (ἰώ μοί μοι, πῶς ἂν ὀλοίμαν); in 112-114 she curses the children along with their father and the whole household, "O cursed children of a hateful mother, may you perish along with your father, and let the whole house crash" (ὦ κατάρατοι παῖδες ὄλοισθε στυγερᾶς ματρὸς / σὺν πατρί, καὶ πᾶς δόμος ἔρροι); in 143-147 she considers suicide again philosophizing on the meaning of her life: "what profit is there for me to keep on living?" (τί δέ μοι ζῆν ἔτι κέρδος; 145). The Nurse's foreshadowing is also confirmed by Medea's later pondering as to what course of revenge she should follow—in 261 on Jason: "pay my husband back for the evils he has done to me" (πόσιν δίκην τῶνδ' ἀντιτείσασθαι κακῶν); in 374-375 on Kreon, his daughter, and Jason: "three of my enemies I will make dead bodies, the father, the girl, and my husband" (τρεῖς τῶν ἐμῶν ἐχθρῶν νεκρούς / θήσω, πατέρα τε καὶ κόρην πόσιν τ' ἐμόν); and finally in 792-793 on the children, the worst of the Nurse's fears: "I will kill my children" (τέκνα γὰρ κατακτενῶ τἄμ').[118] In fact, as Medea elaborates on her revenge plans (376-385), she considers details almost identical with the Nurse's foreshadowings in 40-41.[119]

A dialogue with the Tutor follows the *rhesis* (49-95). The Tutor, like the Handmaid in the prologue to the *Andromache*, announces new evils. He brings the children and starts the dialogue with the Nurse, wondering what she is doing outside, away from her mistress,

---

[117] As McDermott 1989.37 accurately suggests, "Euripides is deliberately playing with the audience's expectations, teasing them, toying with them, in such a way as to heighten the feeling of suspense and their anxiety to know the resolution."

[118] For a detailed discussion on Medea's courses of revenge cf. McDermott 1989.37-38.

[119] Cf. especially 379-380: "or thrust a sword through their heart / getting quietly into the house, where their bridal bed is made" (ἢ θηκτὸν ὤσω φάσγανον δι' ἥπατος / σιγῇ δόμους εἰσβᾶσ', ἵν' ἔστρωται λέχος). This close similarity prompted the condemnation of 40-41 by Dindorf, Page, Diggle, et al., and along with these two lines the preceding 38-39 and the following 42-43, i.e., the whole passage 38-43. As I pointed out already, I strongly disagree with this condemnation, which deprives the play of the suspenseful ambiguity and foreshadowing of its prologue.

102 *Chapter 2*

muttering evils to herself (49-52).[120] His address of her, "old possession of the house of my mistress" (παλαιὸν οἴκων κτῆμα δεσποίνης ἐμῆς, 49), is not meant to be derogatory; it provides a postponed character identification of the Nurse: she is an old servant of Medea who came along with her mistress. Similarly, the Nurse's address of the Tutor, "aged escort of Jason's children" (τέκνων ὀπαδὲ πρέσβυ τῶν Ἰάσονος, 53), is a pompous response, matching the Tutor's long address and, like his, it provides a character identification of the Tutor. Similarly, he is an old servant of Jason, in charge of his children. Without hesitation, the Nurse expresses her loyalty and her concern for her mistress: when their masters' affairs are ill, she says, they become a misfortune for good servants and touch their heart.[121] She explains the urgency of her grief: her sorrow has become so great that a longing came over her to come out and tell the earth and the sky the story of the misfortunes of her mistress (53-58).[122]

The Tutor asks if Medea is not yet through with her weeping (59), and when the Nurse answers that her misfortune is only in the beginning (60), he exclaims: "foolish woman, *môros* (μῶρος), if one can say this of one's masters, for she knows nothing of the latest ills" (61-62).[123] The Nurse is curious to know: "what is it, old man, don't refuse to tell me" (τί δ' ἔστιν, ὦ γεραιέ; μὴ φθόνει φράσαι, 63). However, he refuses to speak, saying that he changed his mind even about what he said already (64). The Nurse insists: "I beg you by your

---

[120] The Nurse's place is inside with her mistress. Her presence alone outside is doubly strange for the curious Tutor.

[121] Servants are typically loyal to their masters, and in difficult times they assert their loyalty; cf. the old servant in *Iphighenia at Aulis* 867, the Handmaid in *Andromache* 59, and the Nurse in *Hippolytus* 698.

[122] These lines (57-58) were parodied by Philemon fr. 79. 1-2 K. Cf. also *Andromache* 93, where Andromache wants to fill the air with her lamentations. But, as Pucci 1980.22 observes, the Nurse's outburst of grief is not simply an expression of the pleasure of lamenting as a relief for her own pain (as in *Odyssey* xxii 500-501 and *Iliad* XXIV 514). The novelty of the Nurse's lament lies in the fact that it is out of pity for somebody else's misfortunes: "The Nurse's lament functions as a miniature Euripidean drama that tells us the story about somebody and persuasively invites us to feel pity for somebody else." Because of her pain for Medea, the Nurse can "erect herself, her wisdom and nobility, against the world. Furthermore, as the Nurse speaks aloud to Earth and Heaven she calls up the whole world to witness her noble feeling." Pucci 34-35.

[123] Tutors and Nurses are privileged servants and can criticize their masters openly, as Page 1938. 71 observes; cf. Sophocles' *Electra* 1326, where the Tutor calls both Orestes and Electra 'most stupid' (ὦ πλεῖστα μῶροι) to their faces.

beard, don't keep it secret from a fellow slave" (μή, πρὸς γενείου, κρύπτε σύνδουλον, 65), appealing to their similar status; two old slaves should trust and not keep secrets from each other. Moreover, she promises to keep the secret (66).

The use of the language of supplication and her promise of silence easily convince the Tutor.[124] Now he can speak: he heard, he says, without 'seeming to be listening' (67), somebody saying that Kreon was planning to expel the children with their mother from the land. "Whether the story is true, I do not know, but I wish it were not," he concludes, expressing his comment of displeasure (67-73). The Nurse also expresses her own criticism through her disbelief: "even so, will Jason ever allow his children to be treated in such a way, even if he is at variance with their mother?" (74-75). The Tutor answers cynically with a *sententia*: "old ties are weaker than new ties, and he is not a *philos* 'friend' to this household" (76-77). The Nurse, in a different tone, responds with a thoughtful and realistic observation: "we are lost if we add a new evil to the old, before we get rid of the first" (78-79). The Tutor wants to make sure that she will "keep quiet and keep the word secret" from Medea (80-81).[125]

The Nurse now turns to the children and, after openly blaming her master, she advises them to go inside: "O children, do you hear what kind of a father he is to you?" And she continues, responding to the Tutor's words in 77, "I can not curse him, for he is my master, but he is being caught evil to his *philoi* 'friends'" (82-84). The Tutor interrupts her with a cynical remark and continues with another *sententia*: "and who is not [evil] among mortals? Are you learning now that everyone loves himself more than his neighbor, as now, for the sake of a marriage-bed their father hates these children" (85-88).

The Nurse urges the children again to go inside for she fears their mother. And turning to the Tutor she expresses her fear more openly through her urgent request, to keep them as far from their mother as possible before "she does something harmful" (*ti draseiousan*, 93).[126] Medea will not stop her anger before she harms somebody, "I know

---

[124] The Nurse is not physically supplicating the Tutor (there is no dramatic need for such unusual supplication of a servant by another servant, and the text does not provide any support for such interpretation); her verbal expression of supplication is compelling enough to make him speak.

[125] The Nurse already promised silence, on her own accord, in 66. Still, the importance of her silence is emphasized by the redundancy in his request: "keep quiet and keep the word secret" (ἡσύχαζε καὶ σίγα λόγον, 81).

[126] Cf. 37 and 95, below.

well" (*saph' oida*, 93), the Nurse says.[127] She only wishes that it is her enemies and not her friends that Medea should harm (*draseie ti*, 95). She wishes according to the generally accepted ethical code that Medea should harm her enemies, not her friends, in this case, her children. The Nurse's thoughts in 91-95 reflect her fears expressed in 38-45; the conclusion of this dialogue (89-95) reflects the conclusion of her opening speech (36-48):

ἴτ', εὖ γὰρ ἔσται, δωμάτων ἔσω, τέκνα.
σὺ δ' ὡς μάλιστα τούσδ' ἐρημώσας ἔχε,
καὶ μὴ πέλαζε μητρὶ δυσθυμουμένῃ.
ἤδη γὰρ εἶδον ὄμμα νιν ταυρουμένην
τοῖσδ' ὥς τι δρασείουσαν· οὐδὲ παύσεται
χόλου, σάφ' οἶδα, πρὶν κατασκῆψαί τινα.
ἐχθρούς γε μέντοι, μὴ φίλους, δράσειέ τι.

Medea 89-95

Go children inside the house. It will be all right.
And you keep them as far from her as possible
and don't let them near their mother when she is in a bad temper.
For I have seen her casting an angry eye at them as if she were
to <u>do something [*ti draseiousan*]</u> to them; she will not stop
her anger, <u>I know clearly [*saph' oida*]</u>, before she has struck down
somebody. May it be her enemies, though, not her friends, that
she <u>should harm [*draseie ti*]</u>.

The Tutor and the Nurse are both very similar characters because of their duties, their social status, and their age.[128] Vellacott remarks that both the Tutor and the Nurse, as well as the Messenger, are the only characters in the play, other than the chorus, who are "humane and balanced in their judgement of Medea".[129] Page provides a character sketch of both these characters, and although I do not quite agree with his comment that the Nurse hardly understands her mistress, I agree with his description of the Tutor as "a pompous old cynic, self-important and sententious."[130] The Tutor truly "talks in proverbs," as Page remarks, while the Nurse talks in more thoughtful

---

[127] Another assertion of how well she knows Medea; cf. 39 *egôida tênde* 'I know her' (ἐγᾦδα τήνδε).
[128] Cf. *sundoulon* (65) 'fellow slave', the Nurse's address to the Tutor. Cf. also their similar ways of addressing each other emphasizing their old age (49, 63).
[129] Vellacott 1975.218.
[130] Page 1938.xiii.

reflections. Her *sententiae*, in contrast to the Tutor's cynicism, are more sensitive. Both the Tutor and the Nurse are critical of their masters. The Tutor calls Medea *môros* 'foolish' (61), although admitting that he should not speak this way of his masters; similarly, the Nurse hesitates to curse Jason, since he is her master (83), but she still strongly expresses her disapproval of his behavior and calls him *kakos* 'evil' to his friends (84). They both do not approve Jason's decision (cf. the Tutor's criticism in 73, and the Nurse's in 74-75 and 82-84); each, however, reacts in a different way. The Tutor reacts with a cynical understanding of human nature (76-77 and 85-88); the Nurse with covert or overt disapproval (74-75 and 82-84). The Tutor sympathizes with Jason as man to man, and also as tutor to *his* children, while the Nurse sympathizes with Medea as woman to woman, and as *her* mistress (cf. the Nurse's address of the Tutor at 53 and the Tutor's address of the Nurse at 49). In a way, the old Tutor, with his cynicism, explains his understanding for his master's behavior as an answer to the Nurse's open statement (in 54-58) of her loyalty and her sympathy for Medea in her misfortune.[131]

Their dialogue is almost equally balanced between the two; the Tutor has twenty-three lines (or twenty-two if we extrapolate 87), and the Nurse, twenty-four; he opens it, she closes it. This short dialogue, well balanced in number of lines and remarks, is like a micro-contest, an *agôn*, between the Tutor and the Nurse in which she practically has the last word and proves the winner. Although the Tutor's tone is more conceited, she has her way with him: she first convinces him to speak and share the information he happened to hear; then she gives him directions to keep the children away from their dangerous mother.

---

[131] Musurillo 1966.52-75, especially 53, remarks that the fundamental polarity of the play is established in the prologue by the characters of the Nurse and the Tutor, both of which Euripides manipulates cleverly. The Nurse reflects the woman's point of view and "acts as an emotional extension of Medea" while "the worldly wise self-important Tutor represents the calmly rational interests of Jason, the man." Thus the contrast between these two minor characters echoes the larger conflict between Jason and Medea. "For if it is given to the Nurse to portray the brooding unhappiness of Medea, the cynical comments of Jason's infidelity are put into the mouth of the Tutor." Similarly, Blaiklock 1952.24-25 remarks that if Medea and Jason were to bear any relation to life and reality, some preparation of the stage was required; Euripides provided this through the "racy conversation" of the Nurse and the cynical old *Paidagogos*, which "reveals their masters from the angle of the servant's hall."

Medea is now heard from inside trying in lamentation to think of a way to perish (ἰώ, ... ἰώ μοί μοι, πῶς ἂν ὀλοίμαν; 96-97), thus verifying the Nurse's fear in 39-43, especially 40 and 43. (Note also Medea's thoughts of death in 144-147). The Nurse repeats her advice to the children to go quickly inside (98-105).[132] She finishes her speech with accurate and ominous observations on Medea's imminent reaction (106-110). In the last part of her speech (106-110), she explains and expands further her first remark of 98-99:

> τόδ' ἐκεῖνο, φίλοι παῖδες· μήτηρ
> κινεῖ κραδίαν, κινεῖ δὲ χόλον.
> <u>σπεύδετε</u> θᾶσσον δώματος εἴσω,
> καὶ <u>μὴ πελάσητ</u>' ὄμματος ἐγγύς,
> <u>μηδὲ προσέλθητ</u>', ἀλλὰ <u>φυλάσσεσθ</u>'
> ἄγριον ἦθος στυγεράν τε φύσιν
> φρενὸς αὐθάδους.
> <u>ἴτε</u> νῦν <u>χωρεῖθ</u>' ὡς τάχος εἴσω.
> δῆλον δ' ἀρχῆς ἐξαιρόμενον
> <u>νέφος οἰμωγῆς</u> ὡς τάχ' ἀνάψει
> μείζονι θυμῷ· τί ποτ' ἐργάσεται
> μεγαλόσπλαγχνος δυσκατάπαυστος
> ψυχὴ δηχθεῖσα κακοῖσιν;

Medea 98-110

> Just as I said, dear children; your mother's
> heart is troubled, her anger is roused.
> <u>Hurry</u> quickly inside the house,
> and <u>do not come close</u> to her sight,
> and <u>do not go close</u> to her, but <u>beware</u>
> of her <u>fierce manner</u> and the <u>cruel nature</u>
> of her <u>defiant temper</u>.[133]
> <u>Go</u> now, <u>get</u> inside as quickly as possible.
> It is clear that the gathering
> <u>cloud of sorrow [nephos oimôgês]</u> will burst

---

[132] The urgency of her effort to remove the children is underscored by the six imperatives in 100-105, underlined in the text: 'hurry', 'do not come close', 'do not go close', 'beware', 'go', 'get' (σπεύδετε, μὴ πελάσητ', μηδὲ προσέλθητ', φυλάσσεσθ', ἴτε, χωρεῖθ'). Cf. Eurykleia's orders to the maids in the *Odyssey* (xx 147-156), also expressed through a series of imperatives (see chapter 1, pp. 34-35). In a sense, the Nurse here displays the same authority over the children as Eurykleia, the Nurse in the *Odyssey*, displays over the maids.

[133] On Medea's nature variously described by the Nurse as *êthos* (ἦθος) 'character', *phusis* (φύσις) 'nature', or *phrên* (φρήν) 'mind', cf. *Medea* 38, above, and n113.

in a major fury;[134] I wonder what
this impetuous, indomitable
heart will do, bitten by evils?

Medea is heard lamenting again, this time cursing her children, along with their father and the whole house (ὦ κατάρατοι / παῖδες ὄλοισθε στυγερᾶς ματρὸς / σὺν πατρί, καὶ πᾶς δόμος ἔρροι, 112-114), thus confirming the Nurse's comments in 36 and her fears in 37-45. The Nurse responds to Medea's lamentation and curses with a lamentation of concern for the children (115-118). She worries exceedingly lest something [evil] happen to them: *mê ti pathêth' hôs huperalgô* (μή τι πάθηθ' ὡς ὑπεραλγῶ, 118).[135] The rest of her lament is a chain of *sententiae* (119-130). First she comments on the anger of tyrants, referring to Medea this time (119-121).[136] She concludes with a modified maxim of the golden mean, "it is better to be used to living in equality" (τὸ γὰρ εἰθίσθαι ζῆν ἐπ' ἴσοισιν / κρεῖσσον, 122-123), which she applies to herself (123-124).[137] Then, generalizing again, she returns to her maxim and analyzes it, first in its positive and then in its negative form (125-130):[138]

ἰώ μοί μοι, ἰὼ τλήμων.
τί δέ σοι παῖδες πατρὸς ἀμπλακίας
μετέχουσι; τί τούσδ' ἔχθεις; οἴμοι,
τέκνα, μή τι πάθηθ' ὡς ὑπεραλγῶ.
δεινὰ τυράννων λήματα καί πως
ὀλίγ' ἀρχόμενοι, πολλὰ κρατοῦντες,
χαλεπῶς ὀργὰς μεταβάλλουσιν.
τὸ γὰρ εἰθίσθαι ζῆν ἐπ' ἴσοισιν

---

[134] For the 'cloud of sorrow' *nephos oimôgês* (νέφος οἰμωγῆς) cf. the gloomy cloud gathering on Phaedra's brows in *Hippolytus* 172: *stugnon d' ophruôn nephos auxanetai* (στυγνὸν δ' ὀφρύων νέφος αὐξάνεται).

[135] Cf. her anxious words to the children in 100-105 and her fears expressed once more in 106-110, as she hurried them inside. Cf. also the Nurse's worries for Phaedra in *Hippolytus* 259-260: *hôs kagô têsd' huperalgô* (ὡς κἀγὼ τῆσδ' ὑπεραλγῶ).

[136] Knox 1979.238 notices that Kreon later unconsciously echoes the "sociological reflections" of the Nurse on royal tempers. As a contrast to royal tempers hardly changing their minds, cf. Phaedra's Nurse, who believes in the advantage of second thoughts (κἀν βροτοῖς αἱ δεύτεραί πως φροντίδες σοφώτεραι, *Hippolytus* 435-436). Cf. also the Guard in *Antigone* 223-233.

[137] Cf. Phaedra's Nurse and her similar position on moderation in *Hippolytus* 264-265 (οὕτω τὸ λίαν ἧσσον ἐπαινῶ / τοῦ μηδὲν ἄγαν); cf. also Phaedra's Nurse philosophizing on old age and the applications of moderation in *Hippolytus* 60.

[138] 125-127 refer to moderation and its benefits; 127-130 to excess and its risks.

Chapter 2

<blockquote>
κρεῖσσον· ἐμοὶ γοῦν, εἰ μὴ μεγάλως,
ὀχυρῶς γ' εἴη καταγηράσκειν.
τῶν γὰρ <u>μετρίων</u> πρῶτα μὲν εἰπεῖν
τοὔνομα νικᾷ, χρῆσθαί τε μακρῷ
λῷστα βροτοῖσιν· τὰ δ' <u>ὑπερβάλλοντ'</u>
οὐδένα καιρὸν δύναται θνητοῖς·
μείζους δ' ἄτας, ὅταν ὀργισθῇ
δαίμων, οἴκοις ἀπέδωκεν.
</blockquote>

Medea 115-130

> Ah, me, unhappy me!
> Why do the children partake in their father's
> guilt? Why do you hate them? Alas,
> children, <u>how I worry too much lest something happen to you</u>.
> The dispositions of the tyrants are dreadful, and somehow
> being little under control but much in power,
> they hardly let go their anger.
> <u>It is better to be used to living in equality</u>;
> for myself, in any case, I wish, if not greatness,
> at least a safe old age.
> <u>Of moderation [metriôn]</u>, first the very name
> is a winner; to practice it is by far
> the best for mortals; but <u>excess [huperballont(a)]</u>
> has no power for profit for mortal men;
> for if a god is provoked, with major misfortunes
> he punishes your house.

The philosophizing Nurse of 119-130 resembles Phaedra's Nurse in *Hippolytus* 250-266. Medea's Nurse is worried about the children (115-118), as Phaedra's Nurse is worried about Phaedra (*Hippolytus* 258-260). Their worries make both philosophize on old age (*Medea* 123-124, *Hippolytus* 250-252), while their mistresses' excessive passions make both philosophize on moderation, as it applies to their own situation (*Medea* 122-124, *Hippolytus* 253-260) as well as on its value and merits in general (*Medea* 125-130, *Hippolytus* 261-266).

The reflections of the Nurse come to an end as the chorus women enter and ask her to tell them why Medea is lamenting (131-136); they want to know because they share the sorrows of the household, they explain (136-138). They first call her formally *geraia* 'old woman', as they seek information from her, acknowledging the judgement and the authority of her old age; later, though, in a more friendly and confidential tone, they call her *gunê* 'woman', in an effort to establish the tie of their common sex for mutual trust as they explain the

Nurse Characters in Aeschylus, Sophocles, and Euripides   109

motive for their curiosity. The Nurse, reassured that they are friendly to Medea, trusts the women of the chorus and speaks.[139] She tells them epigrammatically that there is no hope and gives them an accurate summary of the situation (139-143), which is, in fact, a summary of her previous account in her *rhesis* in the prologue (16-33):[140]

οὐκ εἰσὶ δόμοι· φροῦδα τάδ' ἤδη.
τὸν μὲν γὰρ ἔχει λέκτρα τυράννων,
ἡ δ' ἐν θαλάμοις τήκει βιοτὴν
δέσποινα, φίλων οὐδενὸς οὐδὲν
παραθαλπομένη φρένα μύθοις.

Medea 139-143

There is no home anymore. It is gone already.
The tyrant's bed possesses him,[141]
and she is melting away her life [*têkei biotên*] in the house,
my mistress, comforting [*parathalpomenê*] her heart
by the words of none of her friends [*philôn*].[142]

Medea is heard lamenting again (144-147) and questioning the purpose of life: "what is the good of living any longer" (τί δέ μοι ζῆν ἔτι κέρδος, 145), confirming the Nurse's fear in 40.[143] After the chorus' comments of sympathy (148-159), Medea is heard lamenting again (160-167). This time she calls upon Themis and Artemis to witness the injustice she suffers from Jason (160-165); then she calls upon her city and her father in regret for *aischrôs* 'wretchedly' killing her own brother (166-167).[144] In turn, the Nurse, judging from Medea's lamentations, predicts that she is not going to stop her

---

[139] Although native Corinthian, they sympathize with Medea, a foreigner; their ties are women's ties, as Medea's speech in 214-266 also emphasizes. The Nurse had indicated the friendly welcome of the Corinthians to Medea in 11-12.

[140] Cf. 138-139 and 16, 140 and 17-19, 141-143 and 20-33; and more specifically, 141-142 and 24-25, and 142-143 and 28-29.

[141] Tyrant here clearly refers to Kreon's daughter; cf. also 42.

[142] Cf. the similar wording in the Nurse's description of Medea's condition in the prologue: 25 *suntêkousa dakruois* 'melting in tears' (συντήκουσα δακρύοις), and 29 *nouthetêmenê philôn* 'listening to friends' (νουθετημένη φίλων).

[143] For Medea's words of despair at 145, cf. Andromache's similar wording in *Andromache* 404 (τί δῆτ' ἐμοὶ ζῆν κέρδος); cf. also *Alcestis* 960, and *Helen* 56, and 293.

[144] Cf. the Nurse's account in 30-33 and her reflection in 34-35. Medea has no home and no city to return to; the use of the adverb *aischrôs* 'wretchedly' indicates that she also reproaches herself, as the Nurse also reproached her for this action already, although indirectly, at 32.

110 Chapter 2

bitterness soon (168-172); for Medea now calls upon Themis of the Prayers and Zeus, who is believed to be the *horkôn tamias* (ὅρκων...ταμίας) the 'steward of oaths'.[145] There is no way that her mistress will stop her bitterness at a small cost.

The chorus women try to find a way to make Medea come outside and listen to them, lest they manage to make her stop her anger and her plans (173-179). They ask the Nurse to go inside and bring her out (180-183). Now they call her *phila* 'friend' (φίλα) as they ask for her help in their common purpose, to stop Medea from doing something foolish. The Nurse promises that she will do it, although she is afraid that she will not be able to convince her mistress (184-185); still, she will grant the chorus "the favor of her laborious effort" (*mokhthou kharin*, 186).[146] And in an effort to explain how difficult it is to convince Medea, she compares her to a lioness, and at the same time to a bull: like a lioness with cub *apotauroutai* "she casts the glare of a mad bull" (τοκάδος δέργμα λεαίνης / ἀποταυροῦται), when any of the servants attempts to speak to her (187-189).[147] She continues in a philosophizing mood with observations on the inadequacy of songs for Medea's case: previous mortal men have invented joyful hymns for feasts and banquets and dinner parties, but they have not discovered music and songs of different notes to cease the weary sorrows of men (190-203).[148]

---

[145] There is a difficulty here: Medea did not call upon Zeus; only the chorus mentioned his name in 157. Page 1938.79-80 summarizes the most important solutions propounded, and he offers his own, which I also adopt: the Nurse calls Medea's complaint about Jason's oaths in 161-163 an appeal to Zeus, whom she defines in 169-170 as the 'steward of oaths'.

[146] The word *mokhthos* (μόχθος) 'labor/laborious effort', emphasizes the difficulty of convincing Medea; cf. the Nurse's fear at 184.

[147] The double metaphor lioness/bull is confusing and misleading: it creates the illusion that Medea, like a lioness, will protect her children fiercely; at the same time, it also reflects the male attributes of Medea, as reflected in the bull image. On the combination of the images of bull and lioness, see also Pucci 1980.42. Blaiklock 1952.24-25 remarks that by the time Medea appears at 213, "her case, from the human point of view is stated, and the very necessary ground of sympathy for wronged womanhood is prepared. The only hint of the savage violence in her ... comes, quite significantly, in the words of the Nurse, Medea's loving and devoted champion."

[148] She is a connoisseur of the poetry of the 'previous mortal men' (*prosthe brotoi*, 191), just as Phaedra's Nurse is a connoisseur of the 'writings (or paintings) of older men' (*graphai palaiterôn*, *Hippolytus* 451). The target of her statement seems to involve both epic and lyric poetry, both sung in festivities or banquets; cf. Murray 1912.83-84. In his translation, however, Murray assigns these verses to the chorus for two reasons: first, the Nurse should not hesitate so long to go in, and, second, the following chorus stasimon

Despite her doubts, however, it seems that the Nurse is successful since, without delay, Medea comes out and addresses the Corinthian women (214). We do not see the Nurse again, except very briefly, and for the last time, later, some time after the exit of Aigeus, at 819-823, when Medea asks her to summon Jason. We can not be sure when exactly she returned to stage. She must be present, however, when the chorus criticize Medea's decision (811-818), since Medea sees her and sends her to fetch Jason.[149] The person Medea addresses in 820-823, in whom she is putting *ta pista* 'her confidence' (821), and who is a *gunê*, a 'woman', like her, well-disposed to her 'mistress' (*despotais* 823), and therefore her servant, cannot be anyone other than the Nurse:

> ἀλλ' εἶα χώρει καὶ κόμιζ' Ἰάσονα·
> ἐς πάντα γὰρ δὴ σοὶ <u>τὰ πιστὰ</u> χρώμεθα.
> λέξῃς δὲ μηδὲν τῶν ἐμοὶ δεδογμένων,
> εἴπερ φρονεῖς εὖ <u>δεσπόταις γυνή</u> τ' ἔφυς.
>
> *Medea* 820-823

> But go and bring Jason;
> I am putting all <u>my confidence [*ta pista*]</u> in you.
> You should speak none of my decisions, if you are well disposed to your <u>masters [*despotais*]</u> and you are born a <u>woman [*gunê*]</u>.[150]

Although the Nurse is used as a messenger by Medea to Jason, a separate messenger is used to give the long report of the deaths of Kreon's daughter and Kreon himself (1121-1230).[151] Medea's Nurse would have no place in the young bride's bedroom, in contrast to the

---

(204-212) does not allow enough time for the fetching of Medea. I do not agree especially with Murray's first point: the Nurse has the tendency for prolonged philosophizing (cf. 119-130, above); cf. also Phaedra's Nurse in *Hippolytus* 186-197. As Pucci 1980.25-26 comments, the Nurse understands the therapeutic notion of poetry (cf. Gorgias, *Apology of Helen* 14, where the action of the *logos* 'word' is explained as *pharmakon* 'drug' in the following analogy: as the *pharmakon* acts on the nature of the body, so the *logos* acts on the disposition of the soul). Cf. also the Nurse's words in *Hippolytus* 478-479, again referring to the power of words as drugs for Phaedra's disease: "there are soothing *logoi* 'words' / there will appear a *pharmakon* 'drug' for this disease" (εἰσὶν...λόγοι θελκτήριοι / φανήσεταί τι τῆσδε φάρμακον νόσου).

[149] Indeed, when Jason comes, he announces his arrival verifying that he came *keleustheis* 'invited' (866).

[150] In this case, 'masters' is her 'mistress', Medea. Notice also here the emphasis on the common bond of womanhood. Medea trusts the Nurse as her servant, but also as a fellow woman.

[151] Cf. the messenger in *Oedipus Tyrannus*.

112   Chapter 2

Women of Trachis, where Deianeira's Nurse has easy and natural access to her mistress' room and can also be used as the messenger.

This play can be performed with only two actors, although Euripides could easily have used three. In a performance with two actors, in this scene only, the Nurse, who does not have a speaking part, must be the deuteragonist, the second actor who just played, among others, the role of Aigeus. In all the other scenes, however, her role may be played by the protagonist, who also plays Medea. This may explain why, except for this brief occasion, during which she does not speak, she is never on stage with Medea. This interpretation differs from Pickard-Cambridge, who assigns the roles of Medea and the Tutor (49-91) to the first actor, and all the other characters including the Nurse, and also the Tutor in 1002-1018, to the second actor.[152] The distribution I suggest avoids the problem of the Tutor's speaking parts delivered by two different actors.

The importance of the Nurse in *Medea* lies not in her power to influence and direct her mistress, like the Nurses in the *Women of Trachis*, in *Andromache*, and especially in *Hippolytus*, but in her ability to understand deeply Medea's nature and predict her reactions. Her function is not to influence or avert Medea; she does not even attempt this. She knows Medea too well, and she knows how hard it is to change her 'royal temper'. Besides, the one who possesses the skill of *sophia* 'cleverness' in *Hippolytus*, as we will see, is the Nurse; in *Medea*, however, the one who possesses the skill of *sophia* is Medea herself, as she herself maintains in 384-385.[153] The Nurse's function, therefore, is, rather, to emphasize and underscore Medea's character, and she does this in a very thoughtful and insightful way. In fact, she identifies with Medea and her problems, and her presence on stage, if she is portrayed by the same actor as her mistress, makes this identification even more powerful.[154]

I suggest that the prologue in *Medea* is comparable to the prologue in *Hippolytus*, and that the Nurse's foreshadowing of the impending tragedy can be paralleled to Aphrodite's foreshadowing in *Hippolytus*. The Nurse, of course, has no power or influence in the action of the plot because what has happened in the past and what will happen

---

[152] See Pickard-Cambridge 1962.145.

[153] On Medea's 'cleverness', see Knox 1977.202, 221-222.

[154] This assumption raises a big question about the conventions of the play and whether such doubling of roles is dramatically significant. This important issue, however, is beyond the scope and the limitations of this book.

Nurse Characters in Aeschylus, Sophocles, and Euripides 113

later in the play is not her plan. Still, knowing Medea's past, she displays correct and accurate judgement of Medea's nature and reactions.[155] Therefore, the prologue, given by her instead of another servant or a messenger, is much more effective and powerful. What she fears and predicts happens almost as accurately as what Aphrodite plans and foreshadows in *Hippolytus*. Moreover, the Nurse in *Medea* exhibits many of the traits of the Nurse in *Hippolytus*. Indeed, as Page suggests, "it is but a step from the Nurse in *Medea* to the Nurse in *Hippolytus*".[156] As I have noted, her sententiousness and wisdom regarding human nature are no less than those of her most developed descendent.

The Nurse also cares and worries for the children and, by convincing the Tutor to keep them out of their mother's sight, she tries to save them. She is also successful in convincing the Tutor to reveal what he knows, in their micro-*agôn*, as I have discussed above. She is also successful in convincing Medea to come out of the palace, in the presence of the chorus of the Corinthian women. Perhaps, Medea's first words to them "Corinthian women, I have come out of the palace; do not criticize me" (214-215) reflect the Nurse's effort to convince her to come outside. At least, the Nurse's intervention informs Medea of their friendly disposal and triggers her entry. This is the only occasion in which Medea, the chorus, and the Nurse are all present together on stage. The Nurse does not, however, interact with Medea, except when she is asked to fetch Jason. Still, she has Medea's trust, due to her role as her servant and Nurse, but also due to their bond as women.

Her ties with the chorus are similar: ties that bind women together. Indeed, her interaction with the women of the chorus is based on the bond of friendship among women. They trust her knowledge and her power to convince Medea, and she trusts their feelings of sympathy and friendship for Medea. She is cooperative and listens to them; she becomes their messenger to Medea.

There is, indeed, a bond of friendship not only between the Nurse and Medea, but also between her and the women of the chorus, as

---

[155] In this, I take the opposite stand from Page 1938.xiii in his assessment of the Nurse, especially his comment that she "hardly understands her mistress at all." Neither do I agree with Blaiklock 1952.24-25, who, although he accepts that "her instinct was very sure," still remarks that "the old woman may not understand her mistress."
[156] Cf. Page 1938.x: Page remarks that the characters in *Medea* foreshadow the later development of Euripidean art.

114 Chapter 2

well as between them and Medea. This bond of women's friendship stresses once more the lyric 'background' of women's poetics in tragedy, as this is also the link among the members of the female aggregate that we find in archaic choral compositions like Alcman PMG 1.

3

The Nurse in Euripides' *Hippolytus*

1. Introduction

This chapter discusses the Nurse in *Hippolytus*. It suggests that beyond the traditional authority of a nurse that allows her to advise, praise, and blame her mistress—exhibited by all the nurses who interact with their mistresses—she displays extensive authority and power of speech that enable her to direct her mistress, and furthermore, to direct the action in the first part of the play.

Scholarly criticism on the *Hippolytus* has taken different directions. The theme of speech and silence, central to the play, has caught especially the attention of Bernard Knox,[1] Barbara Goff,[2] and Charles Segal.[3] Knox sees the contribution of the Nurse's speech in the play as more important, but he does not center his discussion around her. Goff concentrates on the central themes in the play, the paradoxes of speech and silence, revealing and concealing, outdoors and indoors, but she does not direct her emphasis toward the contribution of the Nurse. Segal concentrates more on the dichotomy between male and female speech, and the destructive effect of female speech in the play. In that sense, both Phaedra's speech and the Nurse's speech are central in his discussion. Segal also discusses the theme of confusion and concealment, central in the play, but also in the speech of Phaedra and the Nurse. My discussion is centered around Phaedra's Nurse, as part of my general discussion of the Nurse figure, and

---

[1] Knox 1952.1-31.
[2] Goff 1990.
[3] Segal 1993, 89-109 and 136-153.

suggests that her leading part in the action of the play is the result of her authority. This authority continues the poetic tradition of her Homeric predecessor, Eurykleia, and develops it further according to contemporary values and ideas. As to performative tradition, in the choral performative aspect, it may also be seen, stylistically at least, as a survival of an old model of female authority, as personified in the figure of the lyric *khorêgos* in dramatized compositions like Alcman's PMG 1.[4]

As Goff observes, although this play concerns itself with female silence, it is motivated by female speech. "The relation between speech and silence is set up by the play as an opposition analogous to that operating on a social and sexual level between male and female, on a spatial level between exterior and interior, and on a dramatic level between revelation and concealment." Goff considers exterior and interior in terms of the house, revelation and concealment in terms of sight and speech. She sees men functioning in the *polis*, outside of the house, while women's realm is the house, the *oikos*: women had no recognized existence in the public sphere of the *polis*, and their activities were confined to the private sphere of the *oikos*; therefore, Goff maintains, "Phaedra's exit from the house sets the play in motion"; similarly, "the loosening of her body (199) and of her veil (202) act as preludes to the 'loosening' of her language in the delirium."[5]

Still, although Phaedra's exit from the house, her speech, and the partial revelation of her secret—these three paradoxes—set the play in motion, it is only through the Nurse's pressure and the power of her speech that Phaedra breaks her silence meaningfully and totally reveals her secret. It is through the Nurse's force of persuasion that Phaedra reveals her love, along with her decision to die. Once the Nurse has succeeded to break Phaedra's silence with her power of speech, she devises a plan of action. She dissuades Phaedra from dying and persuades her that her plan of action is better: she reveals Phaedra's secret to Hippolytus, at the same time securing his silence.[6]

---

[4] On early lyric compositions, their performative character, and their survival in the Athenian drama cf. Calame 1977, esp. 367-372; Herington 1985.20-57, esp. 20-24 and 54-55; and Nagy 1990a. 344-381, esp. 377-379.

[5] Goff 1990.2-7.

[6] Thus, metaphorically speaking, she assumes first the playwright's role, and then she becomes both director and actor. She continues the role of the producer and director of the play, which, as Goff 1990.82 comments, were assumed by Aphrodite at the beginning of the play (cf. 21-22).

Her intervention, in turn, triggers Phaedra to initiate her own course of action—write the false letter, which eventually destroys Hippolytus, and put an end to her own life, maintaining her good reputation (as was Aphrodite's plan). Therefore, it is through the Nurse's persuasion, direction, and action that the plan of Aphrodite comes to fulfillment. Without the Nurse's authority, power, and skill, Phaedra would have died silently, and Hippolytus would not have been destroyed; Aphrodite's plan would not have been fulfilled.

The Nurse in *Hippolytus* is one of the main characters in the play. In fact, she has more lines than either Phaedra or Theseus.[7] Her role, far from being secondary, is the most instrumental in the development of the plot, revealing clear elements of a character of authority who, I suggest, acts as the agent of Aphrodite and her plans. As Knox has pointed out, the other central characters act according to a specific code of conduct or an ideal they believe in: reverence for Hippolytus, good reputation for Phaedra, action for Theseus. The Nurse, however, has a purpose that is specific and practical—to save Phaedra's life. Her ideal is expediency. Her objective is to convince Phaedra through *logos*—speech, reason, and argument—as used by the contemporary sophists, according to the doctrine of expediency. Therefore, she is flexible and she can come to second thoughts, even third and fourth thoughts.[8] Furthermore, I contend, she is the advocate of speech, speech that leads to action, and the advocate of action. Most important, her authority allows her to direct Phaedra, and she does this effectively through both speech and action.[9]

As the play develops we watch the flexibility with which the Nurse promotes speech and action. With her entrance on stage she makes clear that she is the advocate of action (177). Her action at this point is to make Phaedra speak. In order to achieve this, she uses her *logos* (her speech, her reason, and her arguments). When she manages to make Phaedra break her silence and speak, at least indirectly, of her love for Hippolytus, she speaks the words that Phaedra will not say. Once the secret is out, the Nurse starts directing Phaedra to act— to do something about her love. Since Phaedra is again unwilling to

---

[7] 223 lines, including 776-778, 780-781, and 786-787 (the voice inside the house announcing Phaedra's death).

[8] Knox 1952.18-19.

[9] The chorus' words in 282-283, which encourage her to exercise pressure on Phaedra to speak, suggest that they accept her authority.

act—as she was before unwilling to speak—the Nurse now undertakes the initiative and the responsibility for action, to reveal Phaedra's love to Hippolytus. Again, she promotes action through speech. And although she fails to gain Hippolytus' interest in Phaedra, still, through the persuasive power of her speech, she manages to secure his oath to keep his silence.[10]

Following the unfolding of the story, I discuss how the Nurse sets the action in motion, and actually directs the action in the first part of the play, through her interaction with Phaedra, Hippolytus, and the chorus. More specifically, I discuss how she uses her authority with each of these characters, in the form of advice or directions, praise or blame (approval or disapproval), and persuasion—employing devices of contemporary rhetoric.[11] I also suggest that her speech in her effort to persuade Phaedra in 373-524 acquires the form of the speech in a rhetorical contest, an *agôn*, and even resembles the performative character of a poetic contest in early Greek female choral compositions, with the chorus acting as the judges. I will attempt to show how the Nurse, as the director of the action through her skill and her authority, recalls a lyric *khorêgos*, who, as Nagy has suggested, in Attic drama develops into a leading character, the chorus-leader or another actor.[12]

The first two parts of this chapter discuss how the Nurse, first, proclaims her *sophia*, her cleverness, to the chorus and, second, how she applies this *sophia* to her *logos*, her speech, and how in full control of *logos* she becomes the advocate of speech and encourages Phaedra to speak. The third part discusses her interaction with Phaedra in 373-524 as a rhetorical *agôn* between the two women, looking also at its performative resemblance to a choral competition. The fourth and fifth parts follow first the Nurse in charge of action, directing the action in her attempt to win over Hippolytus, and then Phaedra trying to win independence from the Nurse and gain control of both speech and action. The final part of this chapter sums up my conclusions.

---

[10] Off stage; cf. 611, 657.

[11] Among other rhetorical devices, she uses examples, analogies, rhetorical questions, and even the Socratic dialectic method. Finally, in order to achieve her goal, the Nurse does not hesitate to use, as her last resource, the very act of supplication.

[12] Cf. Nagy 1990a.377-379.

2. The Nurse Among the *Sophoi*

In the prologue to *Hippolytus* (1-57), Aphrodite summarizes the plot of the tragedy.[13] Hippolytus has insulted her by totally rejecting her, and she will punish him "on this very day" (1-22).[14] She has prepared the path already: Phaedra saw him and fell in love with him. And now she wastes away "in silence" (*sigêi*), and none of the household knows her *nosos*, her 'disease' (39-40).[15] But she will reveal (*deixô*) the matter to Theseus, and he will kill her young foe with the curses Poseidon granted him (41-46), Aphrodite continues.[16] Then referring to Phaedra she concludes: "and she, though *eukleês* 'with a good reputation', still, she will perish" (ἡ δ' εὐκλεὴς μὲν ἀλλ' ὅμως ἀπόλλυται, 47).[17]

This summary does not reveal the innovations of this play, especially the order of events, with Phaedra's death preceding the death of Hippolytus. According to the traditional form of the legend, Phaedra, rebuffed by Hippolytus, accuses him to Theseus, and after Hippolytus is accursed and dies, she commits suicide in disgrace

---

[13] On the prologue to *Hippolytus*, see Erbse 1984.1-22.

[14] Euripides emphasizes that the action will take place "on this very day" (ἐν τῆδ' ἡμέρᾳ, 22). The repetition of this notion adds special emphasis in the continuation of the play: Phaedra later repeats the same words "this very day" (τῆδ' ἐν ἡμέρᾳ, 726) as she complies with Aphrodite's plans, and along with her death she sets in motion Hippolytus' destruction.

[15] The postponement of the word *sigê* 'silence' until the end of its clause and its position at the beginning of the next line creates special emphasis on this important detail: Phaedra's silence will dominate the first quarter of the play, and it is part of the importance in the play of the themes of speech and silence. Cf. Goff 1990.1-26. We may assume that in the first *Hippolytus* Phaedra's Nurse was already aware of her love at the beginning of the play, and she probably delivered the prologue speech itself. Euripides may have chosen this wording deliberately to indicate the different plot in this play. See Barrett 1964.163 and 34-35. On love as disease, cf. 477 and following discussion. On the importance of knowledge in the play, see Luschnig 1983.115-123.

[16] Not directly, but indirectly, through Phaedra's letter. Euripides is intentionally vague in an effort not to reveal the innovative plot of this play. On Euripides' deliberate silence about the confrontation between father and son, which depends on Hippolytus' oath to the Nurse, see Erbse 1984.38-39. The vocabulary of revelation and concealment is crucial to the play. On concealment cf. 243, 245, 250, 251, 279, 330, 394, and 1458; on revelation cf. 332, 368, 428, 479, 593, and 1452. On the importance of this motif see Goff 1990.12-20 and Segal 1993.136-153.

[17] Phaedra's concern with her good reputation is vital to the play. Cf. 329, 423, and especially 717, where her good reputation will be crucial to the further development of the play through her accusation of Hippolytus.

120   *Chapter 3*

(upon exposure or in remorse). Consequently, the word *eukleês* comes to the audience as a surprise and it creates curiosity and suspense as to the plot in this play.[18]

As Aphrodite retires, Hippolytus enters the stage returning from the hunt and followed by a band of attendants. He addresses Artemis with a speech of devotion and makes offerings to her statue while he ignores Aphrodite (73-87).[19] In a stichomythic dialogue an old attendant advises him that he should also pay respect to Aphrodite. Hippolytus, however, reveals his contempt for her, which comes as a sharp contrast after his reverence and devotion to Artemis, and he haughtily leaves the stage bidding Aphrodite a long farewell in open contempt (88-113).[20]

A chorus of Troizenian women now enter the scene, expressing their concern for the well-being of Phaedra (121-169).[21] They are discussing a rumor that their mistress is wasting away sick in her house. "For three days now she keeps her body *hagnon* 'pure' from Demeter's grain (138), because of some 'secret suffering', a 'secret passion' (*kruptôi pathei*, 139), yearning for the sad haven of death"

---

[18] Cf. Barrett 1964.164. Euripides used the *traditional* legend in his first *Hippolytus* (*Hippolytus Kaluptomenos*), a play that met with disfavor and led Euripides to produce his second *Hippolytus* (*Hippolytus Stephanias* or *Stephanêphoros*), which won one of the only four first places in Euripides' career. In the first *Hippolytus*, Phaedra makes a deliberate attempt to seduce him, and after he rebuffs her, she accuses him to Theseus of rape or attempted rape. Then, after Hippolytus, cursed by Theseus, is killed and her treachery is exposed, she kills herself. The prologue in this first play may have been delivered by Phaedra or her Nurse, and, in another scene, the Nurse perhaps attempted to restrain her. It appears that Phaedra, in person, made an approach to Hippolytus on stage, and he, in horror, reacted by veiling his head; hence the title *Kaluptomenos*. Euripides' first *Hippolytus* seems to be the model for Seneca's *Phaedra*, where the Nurse tries vainly to dissuade Phaedra, and only when Phaedra threatens suicide does she offer to help. Sophocles' *Phaedra* also follows the traditional legend, but it seems it did not offend the Athenian public as Euripides' "shameless and unprincipled" Phaedra in his first *Hippolytus* did (see Barrett 1964.6-15).

[19] Appropriately, Hippolytus, when we first meet him, comes from his characteristic activity, hunting, which he shares with Artemis (cf. Aphrodite's complaints in 15-19); accordingly, his speech reveals his devotion to chastity (cf. *aidôs*, 78, *sôphronein*, 80).

[20] This is not a surprise for the audience but in line with Aphrodite's complaints in 13-14. Note that the old servant criticizes the thoughtlessness of his young master and, alone on the stage after Hippolytus leaves, he asks Aphrodite to forgive him and pretend she did not hear (114-120). On Hippolytus' irony see among others Blaiklock 1952.40-42.

[21] The chorus from the very beginning sympathize with Phaedra, primarily as women with another woman (cf. the chorus in *Andromache, Medea, Women of Trachis*, and *Libation-Bearers*, and all tragedies with a female chorus and a female heroine).

The Nurse in Euripides' Hippolytus   121

(131-140).²² Having exposed Phaedra's condition, now the chorus women speculate about the cause of her disease. First, they speculate on divine causes: is she possessed by Pan or Hekate or the holy Korybantes or the mountain mother (141-144), or has she neglected sacrifice to Dictynna (145-147)? Next, they turn to the possibility of human causes: first, they suspect Theseus' unfaithfulness (151-154); or is it bad news from home (155-158)? Finally, they speculate on Phaedra's possible pregnancy and suffering from *aphrosunê* that affects pregnant women (161-164).²³ As they ponder about the reason of their mistress' distress, they see and announce the *trophos geraia* 'old Nurse' in front of the gates bringing Phaedra outside the palace (170-171).²⁴

Now, the focus of attention falls on the Nurse, who will dominate the action until Phaedra's suicide, and who, with the power of her speech, will direct the course of action according to Aphrodite's plans. The first words of Phaedra's Nurse are indicative of the plurality and of the complexity of her role. They express her sententiousness as well as her involvement with action. The first line, as she bewails the afflictions of human nature, reflects her tendency for sententiousness.²⁵ The second line indicates her function as the

---

²² In the light of Hippolytus' use of the word *hagnos* (ἁγνός) at 102 of his sexual purity, the word has a further significance: Phaedra's attempt to keep her body 'pure' from food derives from her wish to keep herself pure sexually (cf. 388ff.), that is, faithful to her husband (see Segal 1970.280). For the description of Phaedra's condition by the chorus cf. Aphrodite's description in 38-40. Also, notice the similarity of 131-140 with the description of wasting away in love in Sappho 31.

²³ It was a general belief (see Dodds 1951.87) that mental illness was due to possession by various gods. On women seen as "a model for possession," see Padel 1983.1-19; on Phaedra, see 12-13. Dictynna is a Cretan goddess identified with Artemis. On Theseus' unfaithfulness, cf. Orestes' questions regarding Hermione's distress in *Andromache* 904-905, and 907. A husband's unfaithfulness was always considered a serious cause of a woman's distress; in *Medea* and *Women of Trachis*, it is the central issue in the tragedy. *Aphrosunê* is the antonym of *sôphrosunê*; on the importance of *sôphrosunê* or the lack of it in Phaedra and Hippolytus, cf. especially 667 and 731. This speculation explains the previous speculation concerning possible neglect of sacrifice to Artemis. Artemis, although a virgin goddess of hunting, is also a goddess of childbirth.

²⁴ For the announcement of these new characters as a "moving tableau," see Halleran 1985.11. The presence outdoors of women, whose place is regularly inside the house, suggests that something is wrong. Among others see Shaw 1975.255-66, especially 255-256, opposed by Foley 1982.1-21, especially 1-3. For a recent discussion see Goff 1990.2-11. On the same perception in Modern Greece see Hirschon 1978.66-88, especially 71.

²⁵ For the Nurse's sententiousness, cf. also *Andromache*, *Medea*, and *Women of Trachis*. Such tendency for sententiousness is also typical of the chorus and of older servants, e.g.,

122 Chapter 3

person who has the responsibility for action: she has to do something or refrain from doing something:

> ὦ κακὰ θνητῶν στυγεραί τε νόσοι.
> τί σ' ἐγὼ <u>δράσω</u>; τί δὲ <u>μὴ δράσω</u>;
>
> Hippolytus 176-177

> O evils of mortals and hateful pains!
> What shall I <u>do</u> with you? What shall I <u>not do</u>?

The verb *draein/drân* 'do/act' is the verb that most strongly indicates action, especially action on stage (cf. the term 'drama').[26] The Nurse is setting the tone for her role: to give directions and direct the action in the play. She is the advocate of action, as she later makes clear in her advice to Phaedra, "better the deed...than the name" (κρεῖσσον δὲ τοὔργον...ἢ τοὔνομα, 501-502).[27]

In her first speech, the Nurse is critical of Phaedra and scolds her for her changing caprice. "Here is your daylight and your bright sky," she says. The bed of her sickness with its cushions is now out of the house. Yet, the cloud on her brows grows thicker (στυγνὸν δ' ὀφρύων νέφος αὐξάνεται, 172).[28] "For every word of yours was to come here; soon though, you will rush into the house again," she predicts and explains the basis of her judgement: "for quickly you find that you are wrong (*sphallein*, 183) and enjoy nothing; you do not like what you have but you prefer what you do not have" (178-185).[29]

She concludes her complaints with a general statement about her duties:

> κρεῖσσον δὲ νοσεῖν ἢ θεραπεύειν·

---

the old servant in *Iphighenia at Aulis* 31-32 and the old servant of Hippolytus above (88-120).

[26] See Nagy 1990a.387-388. For the performative meaning of this verb cf. also its special use in Aeschylus' *Libation-Bearers* 552-553, Sophocles' *Antigone* 69-70, Sophocles' *Electra* 465, 466, 467, Euripides' *Electra* 967.

[27] For a detailed analysis of this idea, see my discussion later on 501-502.

[28] Cf. Medea's "cloud of sorrow" in *Medea* 106-107. I agree with Barrett 1964.180, who, following Wilamowitz, transposes 172 from the chorus to the Nurse, after 180: Phaedra's ever changing mood explains the Nurse's impatience. I further suggest that without 172 here, the Nurse would only guess, without any indications or clues, that Phaedra will soon wish something else: to go inside again (182).

[29] The verb *sphallein* appears in this play eight times (more frequently than in any other play of Euripides) and is central to the meaning of the play, especially as it is emphasized in Aphrodite's prologue (see Knox 1952.25-26). Cf. also line 262 and discussion.

τὸ μέν ἐστιν ἁπλοῦν, τῷ δὲ συνάπτει
λύπη τε φρενῶν χερσίν τε πόνος.

Hippolytus 186-188

Better be sick than to care for the sick;
the one is simple, the other combines
worry of the mind with labor of the hands.

The first part of her speech (178-188) is reminiscent of Kilissa complaining of taking care of young Orestes and only guessing his desires; Phaedra needs similar attention, because she also does not know what she wants, and the Nurse treats her as a child.[30] Soon, though, she moves to depths of metaphysical thoughts. She philosophizes on the nature of human life, even on what comes after life. She starts, expressing the sad reality of human life; then she continues with more elaborated metaphysical thoughts:[31]

πᾶς δ' ὀδυνηρὸς βίος ἀνθρώπων,
κοὐκ ἔστι πόνων ἀνάπαυσις.
ἀλλ' ὅτι τοῦ ζῆν φίλτερον ἄλλο
σκότος ἀμπίσχων κρύπτει νεφέλαις.
δυσέρωτες δὴ φαινόμεθ' ὄντες
τοῦδ' ὅτι τοῦτο στίλβει κατὰ γῆν
δι' <u>ἀπειροσύνην</u> ἄλλου βιότου
<u>κοὐκ ἀπόδειξιν</u> τῶν ὑπὸ γαίας,
μύθοις δ' ἄλλως φερόμεσθα.

Hippolytus 189-197

The whole life of mortals is painful,
and there is no rest from sorrows.
But whatever is dearer than life,

---

[30] See *Libation-Bearers* 748-760 (cf. especially *Hippolytus* 186-188 and *Libation-Bearers* 760-762). The pains of nursing Phaedra in sickness make her look like the infant Orestes; therefore, the entrance of the Nurse may bring comic relief by association to similar scenes in other tragedies (see Michelini 1987.311-312).

[31] The sad reality of human life is a commonplace in Greek tragedy (cf., for example, *Oedipus Tyrannus* 1195-1196 and *Iphighenia at Aulis* 31-32), and a "typical" Greek attitude still today; in Modern Greek, this kind of sententiousness is called φιλοσοφίες 'philosophies' and is typical of older people, especially common folk. Her vocabulary in 191-197 shows familiarity with the Eleusinian or other Mysteries. The words *apeirosunê* 'no experience' and *apodeixis* 'proof' are philosophical terms; especially *apodeixis* is a technical term in mathematics, rhetoric, history, logic. The Nurse appears a connoisseur of current developments and expresses this in her vocabulary.

124 *Chapter 3*

> darkness covers and hides it with clouds.
> So we seem irrationally in love
> with whatever this is that shines on earth
> because of <u>no experience</u> [*apeirosunên*] of any other kind of life,
> and <u>no proof</u> [*k'ouk apodeixin*] of the things under the earth,
> and we are carried along by tales in other directions (in vain).

This speech serves two purposes: it adds to the picture of Phaedra's illness, but it also shows the Nurse's character. Rather than lack of sympathy and impatience with Phaedra's caprice, her involvement with Phaedra's health shows more than anything else that her primary concern is her mistress' well-being.[32] The Nurse's first speech is also indicative of her tendency for criticizing, and her tendency for philosophizing. This last tendency is common to elderly or secondary characters throughout Greek tragedy (chorus, older servants, messengers), but with this Nurse it is especially prominent, in light of the length and frequency of her *sententiae*.

Phaedra's voice puts an end to the Nurse's sententiousness and philosophizing. Phaedra cannot find any ease. She wants the maids, whom she calls *philai* 'friends' (199), emphasizing the bond of friendship among women, to lift up her body and hold her head upright, take her hands, loosen her hair (199-202).[33] The Nurse affectionately (she calls her *teknon* 'child', 203) tries to cheer her up and comfort her.[34] She advises her not to toss about painfully; she will bear her sickness easier with a quiet and brave attitude, she

---

[32] Cf. the Nurse's own statements on her concern for Phaedra to the chorus (285-287) and to Phaedra (698). A Nurse is traditionally concerned with her mistress' well-being; cf. the Nurses in *Women of Trachis*, *Andromache*, and *Medea*, especially 54-55. For different views see Barrett 1964.194-195, who sees the Nurse as deeply attached to Phaedra, but with no sympathy for her, "impatient, domineering, and with no moral scruple;" Kovacs 1987.39, who sees in her speech a combination of irritation and solicitude; and Michelini 1987.311, who remarks that "the *ethos* of the Nurse is suitable to her social role, which combines servile attention with parental moralizing and advice."

[33] The erotic connotations of Phaedra's loosening her limbs and especially her hair are clear to the informed audience but not the unsuspecting Nurse. Goldhill 1986.130 calls the whole play "a discourse of sexuality."

[34] Note the motherly tone in the way the Nurse addresses Phaedra: *teknon* (203, also 223, 299, 338, 340, 353, 517) and *pai* (212, 238, 348, 521). Although in most translations there is no differentiation between the two terms, I suggest for the more affectionate, *teknon*, 'my child,' and for the less affectionate *pai*, 'child' (cf. also *teknon* 'child' and *pai* 'girl' in Hadas and McLean 1960).

assures her.[35] She concludes her speech with a proverb, a *sententia*, which is a repetition of her longer thought in 189-190:

μοχθεῖν δὲ βροτοῖσιν ἀνάγκη

Hippolytus 207

It is necessary for mortals to toil.

Phaedra now bursts out in a delirium of unconventional and unrealistic wishes: she wishes to drink pure water from a fresh spring and to lie down and rest under poplars in a grassy meadow (208-211). Phaedra's wishes confuse and upset the Nurse, who is concerned with Phaedra's public image: "O child, what are you murmuring? (*ô pai, ti throeis?*) You will not say such things in front of people, a word riding upon madness" (212-214).[36]

Phaedra, not paying any attention, continues her delirium. Now she desires (*eramai*, 219) to be sent to the mountain and the forest and the pine trees, dreaming of hunting (215-222). The Nurse, now even more confused, is trying to be more gentle to Phaedra: "What in the world are you worrying your heart for, my child? What concern have you now for hunting? What is this longing (*erasai*) for mountain streams?" (223-225).[37] And she concludes with her practical advice: near the city walls there is a slope with cold water, where she can have a drink (226-227).

Now Phaedra calls upon Artemis, wishing to tame horses in her sanctuary (228-231), and the Nurse finally scolds her openly for being

---

[35] Cf. the Nurse's advice to Hermione in *Andromache* 851-852.

[36] Cf. the similar concerns of Hermione's Nurse in *Andromache* 832. Also cf. Phaedra's own concern for her image, her good name, her *eukleia*; both Phaedra and the Nurse are concerned with Phaedra's reputation, which, as Aphrodite predicts (84), Phaedra will maintain until the end. The Nurse is not only baffled, but concerned, with what people might say on hearing Phaedra's words, which are completely out of place for a respectful Greek woman whose place is at home, and not outdoors, especially on a grassy meadow, which, as Knox 1952.6n8, among others, notes, has strongly erotic associations. On the grassy meadow, see also Segal 1986.165-221. The verb *throein* that the Nurse uses on Phaedra's delirious speech is an onomatopoetic word referring primarily to the rustling noise of the leaves of trees with the wind; Phaedra is dreaming of trees, and the Nurse hears the sound of the leaves in her speech. Note also that now that the Nurse is upset with Phaedra's words, she calls her by the less affectionate term *pai*. She then interchanges to *teknon* in 223, and *pai* in 238.

[37] Cf. 119, used by Phaedra; this verb (cognate with *erôs*) primarily refers to sexual desire. The Nurse, who has no clue that Phaedra is in love with Hippolytus, does not understand this strange desire, but the audience makes the connection with Hippolytus, who, in the beginning of the play, came back from hunting.

126 *Chapter 3*

paraphrôn 'insane' to say such words again (232). A moment ago, she was bound for the mountain, yearning for hunting; now again she yearns for colts on the level sands (233-235).[38] And she concludes with a remark that reveals her perplexity at Phaedra's insanity:

> τάδε μαντείας ἄξια πολλῆς,
> ὅστις σε θεῶν ἀνασειράζει
> καὶ παρακόπτει φρένας, ὦ παῖ.
>
> *Hippolytus* 236-238
>
> It would take a deal of prophesy [*manteia*]
> to discover which of the gods is wrenching your reins
> and knocks you out of your mind, child [*pai*].[39]

Obviously, Phaedra's desires in her three outbursts (208-211, 215-222, 228-231) are incomprehensible to the Nurse's common sense: they require the skills of a seer, a *mantis* (236).[40] Especially after Phaedra's third outburst, the Nurse is clearly frustrated (notice the repeated use of the word 'again' in 232, 234). She now seriously suspects the sanity of her mistress (notice the repetition of the idea of madness in the first and last lines of her speech, 232, 238). At the very least, Phaedra's wishes are inappropriate for a noble woman, whose proper place is in the house, the *oikos*, and not outside.

Although Phaedra has kept secret her love for Hippolytus, she has still uncovered and exposed her desires. This causes her shame and the need actually to hide herself, as if she could hide the shame her words have caused her. She laments her situation (239 ff.). "Poor me, what have I done to myself," she exclaims, admitting her madness (*emanên*) and her fall (*epeson*), and she addresses the Nurse with

---

[38] Cf. *aphrosunê* (164) and *paraphrôn* (232). For references on the different interpretations of Phaedra's delirium see Kovacs 1987.41. For a psychoanalytic reading, see Glenn 1976.435-442. In her delirium, Phaedra wants to do what Hippolytus does and to be where he is; cf. Goldhill 1986.124-125. Zeitlin 1985.110 argues that Phaedra desires not only to be with Hippolytus, but even to be Hippolytus. Gill 1990.76-107, especially 87, further suggests that Phaedra "sees herself as an aspiring, and in the end a failed, version of Hippolytus as regards their shared objective of being—and being seen—*sôphrôn*."

[39] Note that the Nurse, clearly upset now, goes back to her less gentle and affectionate address, *pai* 'child', again (238).

[40] This hint prepares for the role of the Nurse as a *mantis* of Phaedra's love in 352, although in 346 she repeats the idea that she is not a *mantis*. On the connotations of poetic authority of the word *mantis* see below.

affection and respect as *maia* 'Nurse'.[41] She asks her to hide (cover) her head again (*krupson*, 243, *krupte*, 245), for she is ashamed of what she has said (243-245).[42] She continues commenting how painful it is to come to one's senses (consciousness), and she finishes her speech with thoughts of death: "to think straight is painful, and to be mad is bad; to perish unaware is best" (247-249).[43]

The Nurse grants Phaedra's wish and covers her. Echoing the wish of her mistress for covering and her thoughts of death (243-249), she now wonders when death will cover *her* body: "I cover you (*kruptô*); but when will death cover (*kalupsei*) my body?" (250-251).[44] Then, changing tone, she announces her wisdom, a wisdom that, as she declares, she has acquired through old age:[45]

πολλὰ διδάσκει μ' ὁ πολὺς βίοτος.

Hippolytus 252

Long life has taught me many things.

And now she offers her own maxims, the conclusions of a life-long wisdom. First, she wishes the rule of moderation could apply to friendship (253-257), for she has in her soul a double load of pain bearing too much anguish for Phaedra (258-260).[46] Then, continuing with another maxim, she expresses her disapproval of "life's strict unswerving practices" (βιότου ἀτρεκεῖς ἐπιτηδεύσεις), and she offers her open approval of moderation (261-263). She concludes with yet

---

[41] Cf. the use of this address in the *Odyssey*; in tragedy, the term is also used of one's own mother (cf. Euripides' *Alcestis* 393).

[42] The verb *kruptein* 'hide' is used here in its literal sense. On covering and concealment, cf. Goff 1990.12-20; for a list of occurrences of concealment vocabulary see n16. Also cf. the dialogue between Hermione and her Nurse in *Andromache* 832-835.

[43] On these choices, see the perceptive interpretation of Knox 1952.15.

[44] Not only her anxiety for Phaedra makes her life not worth living, but also the burden of her old age is implied, which she mentions in the next line (252).

[45] The Nurse's authority in wisdom is a result of her experience in life. The statement in 252 explains the common view of the Greeks on old age as a source of wisdom. It is a favorite Greek idea expressed as a maxim in both ancient and modern times. Cf. Solon's proverbial line "I am getting old always learning many things" (γηράσκω δ' αἰεὶ πολλὰ διδασκόμενος, 22. 7).

[46] I agree with Barrett 1964.209-210 that the Nurse's reflections on excessive friendships refer to her excessive affection for Phaedra and not to Phaedra's excessive love for Hippolytus, contrary to Wilamowitz who assumes that the Nurse has already realized that Phaedra is in love and that this maxim refers to Phaedra's love. Nevertheless, the audience, knowing Phaedra's excessive love for Hippolytus, would perceive the irony of the Nurse's words.

128   Chapter 3

another maxim: she has less praise for extremes than for *mêden agan* "nothing in excess" (μηδὲν ἄγαν), and the sages will agree with her: [47]

> βιότου δ' ἀτρεκεῖς ἐπιτηδεύσεις
> φασὶ σφάλλειν πλέον ἢ τέρπειν
> τῇ θ' ὑγιείᾳ μᾶλλον πολεμεῖν.
> οὕτω <u>τὸ λίαν ἧσσον ἐπαινῶ</u>
> <u>τοῦ μηδὲν ἄγαν·</u>
> <u>καὶ ξυμφήσουσι σοφοί μοι</u>.
>
> *Hippolytus* 261-266

life's strict unswerving ways lead astray,
they say, rather than bring joy,
and they are more at war with health.
So <u>I have less praise for extremes</u>
<u>than for 'nothing in excess' (*mêden agan*),</u>
<u>and the sages [*sophoi*] will agree with me</u>.

This maxim "nothing in excess" was a commonplace in Greek life and was closely associated with Apollo's shrine in Delphi. It is often ascribed to Chilon, one of the proverbial Seven Sages. After her preliminary statement on her authority in wisdom (as a result of her old age) and her following maxims, her *sententiae*, the Nurse counts herself among the *sophoi*.[48] Although in reality she agrees with the maxim, she is so confident of her wisdom that she presents it as if it were her maxim—and the *sophoi*, the Sages, would agree with her.

Now that the Nurse has proclaimed her wisdom, the chorus women address her in praise and respect as "old woman, faithful Nurse of the queen" (267).[49] They admit their ignorance, saying that they have 'no clue' (*a-sêma*) regarding Phaedra's disease. Phaedra does not provide clues to the chorus for the recognition of her disease, or it may be that they cannot recognize the given clues. They

---

[47] Cf. Medea's Nurse in *Medea* 119-130. Reflections on excess and moderation are also typically expressed by the chorus in many tragedies; see also below. The Nurse, with her life-long wisdom, has grasped the fact that excess is the cause of *sphallein* 'making mistakes' in life. This verb is central to the meaning of the play. It appears in critical moments in the play (6, 183, 671, 871, 1232, 1414). For an excellent discussion on the meaning of the word here and in the beginning of the play, see Knox 1952.25-26; see also Fowler. 1978.15-51.

[48] Cf. also Phaedra's fear later (in 519) that the Nurse will be too *sophê* for her, too 'wise', but also too 'clever'.

[49] The address 'old woman' from the very context of the line seems prestigious rather than derogatory (as in later comedy). Cf. the same address to Eurykleia in the *Odyssey* (see Table III in chapter 1).

recognize, however, the Nurse's superiority in this skill (cf. Eurykleia, who was able to interpret another *sêma*, Odysseus' scar in *Odyssey* xix 468). Therefore, they wish to 'learn' (*puthesthai*) and 'hear' (*kluein*) from her (270).[50] Thus, by taking for granted her knowledge of Phaedra's distress, they admit the superiority of the Nurse in the realm of knowledge, at least in this matter:

> γύναι γεραιά, βασιλίδος πιστὴ τροφέ,[51]
> Φαίδρας ὁρῶμεν τάσδε δυστήνους τύχας
> <u>ἄσημα</u> δ' ἡμῖν ἥτις ἐστὶν ἡ νόσος·
> σοῦ δ' ἂν <u>πυθέσθαι</u> καὶ <u>κλύειν</u> βουλοίμεθ' ἄν.
>
> <div align="right"><i>Hippolytus</i> 267-270</div>

> <u>old woman [*gunai geraia*]</u>, faithful Nurse of the queen,
> Phaedra, we see her wretched fortunes
> but we have <u>no clue [*a-sêma*]</u> as to what her sickness is;
> it is from you we wish to <u>learn [*puthesthai*]</u> and <u>hear [*kluein*]</u>.

In the following dialogue, the Nurse admits to the chorus that she does not know, despite her questioning (*ouk oid' elenkhousa*), for Phaedra does not want to tell (271-273).[52] The chorus comments on Phaedra's weakness (274), and the Nurse explains that this is no surprise since she has been without food for three days (275). The chorus women know this already (cf. 135-138), but they wonder whether she is mad or is trying to die (276). The Nurse verifies without hesitation that Phaedra is starving herself to death (277).[53] The chorus had expressed this suspicion already in 139-140; the Nurse readily verifies the chorus' suspicion of Phaedra's intent to die.

The chorus now wonders what her husband, Theseus, says about this, and the Nurse explains that she hides it from him (*kruptein*) and

---

[50] This is a *hysteron-proteron*: the verb *puthesthai* 'learn' should follow *kluein* 'hear'. The verb *kluein* emphasizes the importance of hearing the Nurse's speech: "we want to hear from your own lips."

[51] There is lack of agreement among the editors on the position of the comma before or after Phaedra's name. Either way, the position of Phaedra's name suggests reference to both: Phaedra's old nurse and Phaedra's unhappy fortunes.

[52] Expressions of ignorance, abundant in this tragedy, have a special importance in a play where the ignorance of the characters plays such a central role. See Knox 1952.3-31. The verb *elenkhein* (ἐλέγχειν) 'to question', 'to refute', is commonly used in rhetoric. It emphasizes the power of speech and the difficulty in determining the truth; cf. 298 below. Cf. also 1267 (Theseus on Hippolytus), 1310 (Artemis on Phaedra), and 1322 (Artemis on Theseus).

[53] Cf. the Nurse's description of Medea's abstinence from food in *Medea* 24.

130   Chapter 3

denies that she is sick (279); only when the chorus wonders why Theseus cannot guess by looking at her face, does she reveal that he is away from the land (278-281).[54] At this point, the chorus suggests that the Nurse use *anankê* 'pressure' (σὺ δ' οὐκ ἀνάγκην προσφέρεις) in an effort to find out Phaedra's illness and madness (282-283). Now the chorus accepts the superiority of the Nurse also in the realm of action by taking for granted her authority to exercise pressure on Phaedra, which she will actually apply soon (in 325).

It is important to note here that this suggestion comes after the information about Theseus' absence. Female authority that exceeds its conventional limitations is only possible with the absence of the male, the *kurios* of the house (cf. Eurykleia's excessive authority in the absence of Odysseus). It is also important to note that here the chorus offers advice that will be decisive for the development of the play: the pressure of the Nurse on Phaedra, which she will exercise by means of her speech and her supplication, will break Phaedra's silence. In this sense, the chorus, in particular the chorus-leader, displays a leading role, offering suggestions (cf. the chorus' urge to Kilissa to change the orders of Klytaimnestra in *Libation-Bearers* 770-772).

The Nurse has already tried to investigate Phaedra's sickness (cf. 271), and now that the chorus suggests that she should actually press Phaedra, she is willing to try again and invites the chorus to witness this; she invites the chorus women to be judges in her upcoming effort to exercise all the means she has for Phaedra's good:[55]

> εἰς πάντ' ἀφῖγμαι κοὐδὲν εἴργασμαι πλέον.
> οὐ μὴν ἀνήσω γ' οὐδὲ νῦν προθυμίας,
> ὡς ἂν παροῦσα καὶ σύ μοι ξυμμαρτυρῇς
> οἷα πέφυκα δυστυχοῦσι δεσπόταις.
>
> *Hippolytus* 284-287

> I have tried everything and I have no more resorts left.
> Still, I will not give up my efforts, even now,
> so that you too can <u>bear me witness [*xummarturêis*]</u>
> how [loyal] I am to my masters in distress.

---

[54] Theseus' absence is crucial for the development of the plot. His absence conforms to the pattern of the husband's absence, leaving his wife vulnerable to a male intruder (cf. Helen's affair with Paris during Menelaos' absence, Euripides' *Trojan Women* 937-944). On concealment cf. 40, 243, 245, and my previous references. On the face revealing the truth, cf. Phaedra's remarks later in 416.

[55] Conventionally, she addresses only the chorus-leader, who collectively represents all the chorus members.

The Nurse in Euripides' Hippolytus 131

The Nurse's efforts to make Phaedra speak have come to a dead end (cf. 284). Still, she has already made two significant announcements: (1) she has acquired much wisdom through her long life (πολλὰ διδάσκει μ' ὁ πολὺς βίοτος, 252), and (2) by saying that the *sophoi* will agree with her (καὶ ξυμφήσουσι σοφοί μοι, 266), she has counted herself among them. Moreover, the chorus admits her superiority in the realm of knowledge, as they want to learn and hear from her (σοῦ δ' ἂν πυθέσθαι καὶ κλύειν βουλοίμεθ' ἄν, 270), and in the realm of action, as they suggest that she should use pressure on Phaedra (σὺ δ' οὐκ ἀνάγκην προσφέρεις, 282). The Nurse will accept the challenge and force her power of speech on Phaedra, with the chorus members as witnesses and judges of her effort.

3. The Nurse as the Advocate of Speech

Now that the Nurse has announced to the chorus her new effort at persuading Phaedra to speak, she is ready for a new start, admitting the weakness of her first effort (cf. 284). She urges Phaedra to change her mood and reveal her problem. In her effort to make her break her silence she uses all her skill with persuasive speech:[56]

> ἄγ', ὦ φίλη παῖ, τῶν πάροιθε μὲν λόγων
> λαθώμεθ' ἄμφω, καὶ σύ θ' ἡδίων γενοῦ
> στυγνὴν ὀφρὺν λύσασα καὶ γνώμης ὁδόν,
> ἐγώ θ' ὅπῃ σοι μὴ καλῶς τόθ' εἱπόμην
> μεθεῖσ' ἐπ' ἄλλον εἶμι βελτίω λόγον.
> κεἰ μὲν νοσεῖς τι τῶν ἀπορρήτων κακῶν,
> γυναῖκες αἵδε συγκαθιστάναι νόσον·
> εἰ δ' ἔκφορός σοι συμφορὰ πρὸς ἄρσενας,
> λέγ', ὡς ἰατροῖς πρᾶγμα μηνυθῇ τόδε.
> εἶεν· τί σιγᾷς; οὐκ ἐχρῆν σιγᾶν, τέκνον,
> ἀλλ' ἤ μ' ἐλέγχειν, εἴ τι μὴ καλῶς λέγω,
> ἢ τοῖσιν εὖ λεχθεῖσι συγχωρεῖν λόγοις.
> φθέγξαι τι, δεῦρ' ἄθρησον· ὦ τάλαιν' ἐγώ.
>
> *Hippolytus* 288-300

Come on, dear child (*philê pai*), let us both forget
our earlier words, and you become more pleasant,
loosening your gloomy brow and trend of thought [*gnômês hodon*];

---

[56] On the Nurse's second thoughts see Knox 1952 and 1979.240-241.

132   Chapter 3

> and where I did not follow you well before,
> I am leaving that and <u>I am getting to a better suggestion</u>.
> If you are sick with any of the <u>unmentionable</u> ills,
> here are women to help you out with the disease;
> but if your misfortune can be <u>brought out</u> to men,
> <u>speak</u>, so that this matter can be <u>mentioned</u> to doctors. [57]
> Well; why are you <u>silent</u>? You should not be <u>silent, child [*teknon*]</u>,
> but either <u>disprove me [*elenkhein*]</u> if I do not <u>say</u> something right,
> or give in to my <u>well-spoken words/reasonable pleas</u>. [58]
> <u>Say</u> something. Here, <u>look up/speak [*athrêson*]</u>.[59] Poor me.

The Nurse is clearly the advocate of speech. Note that vocabulary referring to speech (or absence of speech) rings in every sentence she makes (λόγων 288, λόγον 292, ἀπορρήτων 293, ἔκφορος 295, λέγε, μηνυθῇ 296, σιγᾷς, σιγᾶν 297, ἐλέγχειν, λέγω 298, λεχθεῖσι, λόγοις 299, φθέγξαι 300, λόγοις 303). With such strong emphasis on words of speaking, this is the most representative passage of the Nurse's verbal effort to break Phaedra's silence. And the Nurse clearly masters the skill of speech. Her speech is rhetorically artistic, and her method of persuasion is organized and skillful. She opens and closes her speech calling Phaedra affectionately 'dear child'.[60] She admits that so far both she and Phaedra were wrong. Moving from the general to the specific, she suggests that both of them take a step for the better: Phaedra should loosen up and change her *gnômês hodos* 'trend of thought', and she should make better suggestions. Then, becoming even more specific, she encourages Phaedra to reveal what the Nurse thinks is a woman's problem. But since Phaedra does not respond and remains silent, she speaks in general terms again. At the

---

[57] Cf. 161ff., where the chorus discusses the possibility of Phaedra's pregnancy. This passage (293-296) is central in Charles Segal's discussion of the dichotomies of male versus female speech (see Segal 1993.89-109). On the oppositions in these lines, see also Goff 1990.1.

[58] Now she suggests that it is Phaedra's turn to disprove her, to refute her with questions (ἐλέγχειν). Cf. also 271 (οὐκ οἶδ' ἐλέγχουσα) referring to the Nurse's unsuccessful questioning of Phaedra.

[59] For the manuscripts' ἄθρησον (*athrêson*) 'look up', I would suggest that the reading ἄρθρωσον (*arthrôson*) 'articulate' is what the audience would expect to hear. I see here a deliberate confusion between the two verbs speak/look.

[60] Notice the endearing address *philê pai* 'dear child', as the Nurse is now trying a new approach in order to encourage Phaedra to speak. Cf. also her synonymous address *teknon* (τέκνον) in her peroration at the conclusion of her appeal (297). Cf. the final speech of Hermione's Nurse, who is also trying to advise her mistress for her own good, in *Andromache* 866-880.

same time, she narrows down to only two the options available to Phaedra; she reduces her practical suggestion (of a change of course for both, 288-292) to the most clear and simplified terms: "either you prove me wrong, or be convinced by my words." In fact, the Nurse suggests here a debate, an *agôn*, which in the fifth century was appealing to the Athenian audiences and to Euripides, in particular.[61]

Still, despite the clarity of the Nurse's argument, Phaedra maintains her silence. Exasperated, the Nurse turns to the chorus and expresses her frustration that Phaedra is no more persuaded now than before (301-303). Both her first effort *tote* 'before' (the one off-stage, to which she also referred in 271) and her second *nun* 'now' (in 288-300) have failed. By calling the chorus *gunaikes* (γυναῖκες) 'women', an indication of their equal-to-equal relationship, she appeals to their bond and understanding as women.[62]

γυναῖκες, ἄλλως τούσδε μοχθοῦμεν πόνους,
ἴσον δ' ἄπεσμεν τῷ πρίν· οὔτε γὰρ <u>τότε</u>
λόγοις ἐτέγγεθ' ἥδε <u>νῦν</u> τ' οὐ πείθεται.

Hippolytus 301-303

Women, we are giving ourselves all this trouble for no use.
We are as far off as before. For she was not touched by my words
<u>before [*tote*]</u>, and she is not persuaded <u>now [*nun*]</u>, either.

Then, turning back to Phaedra, she tries her last resources of persuasion: to argue on behalf of the interests of Phaedra's children against those of Hippolytus (304-310). At the sound of Hippolytus' name, Phaedra finally breaks her silence and, with a dramatic cry, she interrupts the Nurse. The Nurse thinks it was the thought of the children that touched her (310), but Phaedra protests that the Nurse destroyed her with her words and passionately asks her to be silent (*sigan*) about this man (311-312).[63]

The Nurse does not suspect the truth yet. As her next sentence shows, she thinks that Phaedra's concern is for her children. She is sane, then, she concludes (since she finally spoke, she has her senses), but, as she points out, it makes no sense to die and betray her children (313-314). Phaedra assures her that she loves her children, but she is troubled by another misfortune (315). The Nurse, in an

---

[61] On the *agôn* in Greek tragedy and in Euripides see Duchemin 1969.247-275; Collard 1975.58-71, especially 59-64; and Lloyd 1992, especially 1-18.
[62] They also call Phaedra *gunê* 'woman' later, in 572.
[63] For *sigan* cf. 273, 297.

134 Chapter 3

effort to exclude the impossible and encourage Phaedra to speak further, wants to be assured that Phaedra's hands are pure of blood (316). Phaedra immediately replies that her hands are pure but her heart is defiled (χεῖρες μὲν ἀγναί, φρὴν δ' ἔχει μίασμά τι, 317).[64] The Nurse asks if an enemy has wronged her (318), but Phaedra replies in riddles that a *philos* 'friend' unwillingly destroys her, though unwilling.[65]

The Nurse thinks that the 'friend' who has wronged her, who committed a *hamartia* against her, is Theseus (Θησεύς τιν' ἡμάρτηκεν εἴς σ' ἁμαρτίαν; 320).[66] Phaedra, however, strongly denies it: "may I not be seen doing him harm" (321), and, as the Nurse wonders why she wants to die (322), she bursts out: "O let me *hamartein* 'err'. It is not against you I *hamartanô* 'err'" (ἔα μ' ἁμαρτεῖν·οὐ γὰρ εἰς σ' ἁμαρτάνω, 323).

It is important to notice that Phaedra uses the same verb that the Nurse used in questioning Theseus' fidelity in 320: *hamartanô* (ἁμαρτάνω). The Nurse now has more clues about Phaedra's problem. She realizes that Phaedra is on the verge of revealing her secret, a secret that she suspects may have to do with infidelity; yet Phaedra is unwilling to speak any further. The Nurse will not let the opportunity slip away. She realizes the difficulty that Phaedra has in revealing such a crucial secret; she fervently protests that if she fails, the fault will be Phaedra's (324), and at the same time she clasps her hand in supplication. Now that the Nurse has succeeded with the force of her speech to make Phaedra speak, at least partially, and reveal a part of her secret, she is adding the force of her supplication to make her speak further and reveal her secret completely. It is the combination of speech and supplication that makes Phaedra speak—the pressure and power of speech reinforced by supplication.

This interpretation departs from the general view that the Nurse uses supplication because of her frustration at her failure to make

---

[64] On the dichotomy of body and mind cf. Hippolytus' statement in 612: "my tongue has sworn but my mind is unsworn" (ἡ γλῶσσ' ὀμώμοχ', ἡ δὲ φρὴν ἀνώμοτος). See also Avery 1968.19-35 and Kovacs 1987.45.

[65] The Nurse's question is according to the Greek notion "help your friends and harm your enemies." On this notion, see Blundell 1989. Note that, at this point, Phaedra considers Hippolytus as a *philos* 'one near and dear'. For an extended discussion on *philos*, see Goldhill 1986.76-106.

[66] The Nurse naturally thinks of the closest and nearest person to Phaedra—her husband, Theseus. Ironically, she suspects that Theseus is unfaithful to Phaedra. Cf. the chorus' speculations at 151-154.

Phaedra speak.[67] In this sense, I only partly agree with the view that Phaedra yields because she wants to relieve her soul with the disclosure of her secret.[68] Furthermore, I suggest, the Nurse uses supplication at a weak moment in Phaedra's confession, when, denying Theseus' *hamartia* against her, she starts talking of her own *hamartia*. The Nurse, in other words, helps Phaedra—with the act of supplication added to her verbal pressure—to reveal finally her secret, which she had indirectly started uncovering at the beginning of the play in her delirium.

As the Nurse clasps her hand in supplication, Phaedra protests that the Nurse is using force on her (*biazein*) by clasping her hand (τί δρᾷς; βιάζει χειρὸς ἐξαρτωμένη; 325).[69] The Nurse, however, assures her that she will not let go of her hand or her knees (326). Phaedra warns her that her woes will become the Nurse's too when she hears them (327). The Nurse protests that there is nothing worse than not succeeding with Phaedra (328), clarifying her response of 324. "You will be destroyed," Phaedra repeats, "but my death brings me honor" (329). With a series of Socratic questions, the Nurse now turns Phaedra's concern with honor around on her and encourages Phaedra—since she is so concerned with honor—to speak.[70] At the same time she is adding verbal emphasis to the physical act of her supplication: "why hide it then (*kruptein*), when I am supplicating you (*hiknoumenês*) for your own good?" (κἄπειτα κρύπτεις, χρῆσθ' ἱκνουμένης ἐμοῦ; 330).[71] Phaedra assures her that she is contriving good out of the evil—her death (331)—but the Nurse, not understanding, repeats her point of 330: "why then not speak and appear more honorable?" (οὔκουν λέγουσα τιμιωτέρα φανῇ; 332).[72]

---

[67] Mastronarde 1979.83-84 sees the supplication as a result of the complete breakdown of communication, while Goff 1990.16, in her discussion of the Nurse's persuasion of Phaedra to confess her passion, makes no mention of the act of supplication.

[68] Cf. Winnington-Ingram 1960.179, and Barrett 1964.222.

[69] Cf. 325 and 282, the chorus' suggestion that the Nurse should use pressure on Phaedra (σὺ δ' οὐκ ἀνάγκην προσφέρεις).

[70] As Knox 1952.8 pointedly remarks, the Nurse uses her persuasive skill "in a dialectic maneuver worthy of Socrates himself."

[71] Notice at this crucial point how the Nurse emphasizes the contrast between concealment (*kruptein*, 330) and the opposite idea of revelation through speech in her next sentence (*legein*, 332).

[72] Cf. 319. On the paradox of good coming out of evil see Loraux 1979.51-57, especially 57. On 331-332 see further Barrett 1964.220-221. The Socratic method of the questions that the Nurse uses here (330, 332) to bring Phaedra where she wants

136 Chapter 3

Phaedra, cornered by the questions of the Nurse, asks her to let her hand go (333), but the Nurse does not give up her supplication, as Phaedra does not give her the gift that she owes her—her secret (334). Finally Phaedra promises to give in for she respects the reverence of the Nurse's suppliant hand (δώσω· σέβας γὰρ χειρὸς αἰδοῦμαι τὸ σόν, 335).[73] The Nurse, relieved finally, lets go and yields the prerogative of speech to Phaedra:

σιγῶμ' ἄν ἤδη· <u>σὸς γὰρ οὑντεῦθεν λόγος</u>.

Hippolytus 336

I am silent already. <u>From now on, you speak</u>.

All this while the main concern of the Nurse was to induce Phaedra to speak. The Nurse has succeeded with her pressure, insistence, and amazing persuasive skill, through appeals combined with supplication, to induce Phaedra to speak; now, she can be silent and listen.[74] As the roles are reversed, from now on, the prerogative of speech belongs to Phaedra.

I suggest that the Phaedra/Nurse episode, in the context of the presence of the chorus, is comparable, as a performance, in form and style, to similar choral performances in early compositions of Greek lyric poetry. Specifically, the Phaedra/Nurse episode can be compared with Alcman PMG 1, where two leading figures of choral poetry, the older, Hagesikhora, and the younger, Agido, compete in grace and skill as they perform in the presence of a female choral aggregate acting as the judges of their skills. On the performative level of choral conventions of hierarchy, the Nurse is presented as the older performer who initiates the younger performer, Phaedra, in her art; as the younger performer assumes the skill of speech, the older performer relinquishes her power to the younger performer.

Indeed, Phaedra speaks, but she is still unable to tell the truth directly. She laments her mother's and her sister's love afflictions (337, 339), and she adds that she is the third to perish (341). The Nurse is worried with her words (340); she is confounded as to where

---

resembles the old servant's speech in the prologue (88-107), as he skillfully tries to convince Hippolytus to show respect to Aphrodite.

[73] On *aidôs* in supplication cf. Barrett 1964.222. On the importance of supplication in general see Burnett 1971.76ff., 119-22, 131ff., 157ff. On the supplication in this scene see references in Kovacs 1987.130; see also Gould 1973.74-103, especially 85-90, and Taplin 1978.69-70.

[74] For a thorough discussion of the Nurse's rhetorical skills, see Knox 1952.7-10.

The Nurse in Euripides' Hippolytus 137

Phaedra's words will lead (342); she knows now nothing of what she had expected and wished to hear (344). Moreover, she feels shaken after Phaedra's references to her mother's and her sister's strange love afflictions (337, 339).

Phaedra now wants to speak but she cannot; she wishes that the Nurse could speak the words for her (345). "I am not a *mantis* 'seer'," the Nurse protests (346).[75] Phaedra responds with an unexpected question, indirectly hinting that she is in love: she wants to know what it is to fall in love (347). "Sweet and painful," the Nurse replies in wisdom (348), and Phaedra reveals that she has only known the latter (349).[76] The Nurse is now startled: "What are you saying? You are in love, my dear child? With what man?" (350). "Whoever he is, the Amazon's—" Phaedra starts (351), and the Nurse interrupts her, horrified: "Hippolytus, are you saying?" (351). Phaedra is now relieved; the Nurse, not she, speaks Hippolytus' name (352). Her wish of 345 that the Nurse would say it for her is now fulfilled. Indeed, the Nurse first puts into words Phaedra's love and then speaks Hippolytus' name for her. The responsibility and blame for such words now belong to the Nurse, not to her:

ΦΑΙΔΡΑ φεῦ·
πῶς ἄν σύ μοι λέξειας ἁμὲ χρὴ λέγειν;
ΤΡΟΦΟΣ οὐ μάντις εἰμὶ τἀφανῆ γνῶναι σαφῶς.
ΦΑΙΔΡΑ τί τοῦθ', ὃ δὴ λέγουσιν ἀθρώπους, ἐρᾶν;
ΤΡΟΦΟΣ ἥδιστον, ὦ παῖ, ταὐτὸν ἀλγεινόν θ' ἅμα.
ΦΑΙΔΡΑ ἡμεῖς ἄρ' ἦμεν θατέρῳ κεχρημένοι.
ΤΡΟΦΟΣ τί φῇς; ἐρᾷς ὦ τέκνον, ἀνθρώπων τίνος;
ΦΑΙΔΡΑ ὅστις ποθ' οὗτός ἐσθ', ὁ τῆς Ἀμαζόνος...
ΤΡΟΦΟΣ Ἱππόλυτον αὐδᾷς; ΦΑΙΔΡΑ σοῦ τάδ', οὐκ ἐμοῦ κλύεις.

Hippolytus 344-352

PHAEDRA Alas! How can you say for me what I should say?[77]
NURSE I am not a seer [*mantis*] to know clearly vague things.

---

[75] Cf. 236 (τάδε μαντείας ἄξια πολλῆς), the Nurse's words on the need of a seer during Phaedra's delirium.

[76] Although this was a commonplace, still the comparison between the Nurse's definition of love and Sappho's famous description of bitter-sweet love (fr. 130) is unavoidable:

Ἔρος δηὖτέ μ' ὁ λυσιμέλης δόνει,
γλυκύπικρον ἀμάχανον ὄρπετον.

[77] Note the emphasis on speaking (*legein*), used twice in the same line (345), and also in 350 and 352.

138 *Chapter 3*

> PHAEDRA What is this that people call falling in love?
> NURSE Most sweet, my child, and painful, at the same time.
> PHAEDRA Well, we have known only the latter.
> NURSE What are you saying? Are you in love, my child? With which man?
> PHAEDRA Whoever he is, the Amazon's—
> NURSE Hippolytus, are you saying? PHAIDRA You heard it from yourself, not from me.

At this point, the Nurse is again in full control of speech. Phaedra started talking but could not spell it out that she was in love; the Nurse had to put it into words for her. The competence of the Nurse in the realm of speech and in the realm of knowledge has reached its maximum. Phaedra's words in 345, like her incomprehensible language in her delirium (236), required a *mantis*. As the Nurse verbalizes first Phaedra's love (350) and then her love for Hippolytus (352), she actually now becomes the *mantis*, although she said before that she was not (346). In terms of conventional reference to poetic authority, she is now presented as the seer/poet, especially as she has just described love in terms that recall the poetry of Sappho (348).[78]

The Nurse, however, is, at first, overwhelmed by Phaedra's secret, which she, so eagerly, insisted to hear. She reacts with a dramatic outburst identifying with her mistress in her plight: "*oimoi* 'alas', what will you say, my child. How you have destroyed me!" (οἴμοι, τί λέξεις, τέκνον; ὥς μ' ἀπώλεσας, 353). The Nurse's reaction is, indeed, described in identical terms as that of Phaedra at the sound of Hippolytus' name in 310-311: "alas...you have destroyed me, Nurse" (οἴμοι....ἀπώλεσάς με, μαῖα). She, who was trying to avert Phaedra from dying, now cannot endure living anymore. Phaedra's warning in 327, 329, that her secret would destroy the Nurse, is now verified. The identity of the Nurse with her mistress can be observed here in its most dramatic manifestation. Indeed, early in the play, the Nurse was bound with the problems of her mistress (186-188, 253-260, 324, 328), and Phaedra sees this inescapable bond too (327 and 329).[79]

---

[78] On the poet as seer, see Nagy 1989.23-24.

[79] The Nurse is bound with the problems of her mistress and identified with her, just as Medea's Nurse is bound with the problems of Medea and identified with her mistress. As Gill 1990.85-88 observes, the Nurse sees herself as an adjunct of Phaedra's existence, although her view of *sôphrosunê* is an inversion of that of her mistress, and although their characteristic styles are sharply contrasted.

The Nurse in Euripides' Hippolytus 139

Turning to the chorus she exclaims in dramatic tones that, were this not such a dramatic moment, could seem almost comic:[80] "Women, this is intolerable. I will not endure living. Hateful is the light I see. I shall fling, I shall hurl my body, I shall quit this life and die. Farewell. I no longer exist" (353-357).[81] Then, in a more sober tone, admitting Phaedra's *sôphrosunê*, she expresses her criticism of Phaedra's love, but blames it on Aphrodite (358). And assuming her philosophical mood once more, she acknowledges the destructive force of Aphrodite's power (358-361).[82]

οἱ σώφρονες γὰρ οὐχ ἑκόντες, ἀλλ' ὅμως
κακῶν ἐρῶσι. Κύπρις οὐκ ἄρ' ἦν θεός,
ἀλλ' εἴ τι μεῖζον ἄλλο γίγνεται θεοῦ,
ἣ τήνδε κἀμὲ καὶ δόμους ἀπώλεσεν.

Hippolytus 358-361

The moderate [*sôphrones*], although unwillingly, still
fall in love with evil. Kypris is not a god, then,
but something greater than a god,
who has ruined her and me and the whole house.

The women of the chorus are equally shocked at Phaedra's unheard of passion (362-363). They also partake in Phaedra's ruin. In a dramatic lament (362-372), they wish that they would rather perish than reach Phaedra's state of mind. They agree that Phaedra is ruined now that she has exposed her evils to the light (368).

It is important to note that the chorus address Phaedra as *phila* 'friend' (365). By doing so, they reveal to her their friendship, which she will later (419) return addressing them also as *philai* 'friends' (cf. also 351, where the Nurse addresses the chorus women as *philai*). At this dramatic moment, the two female characters and the chorus of female members identify with each other as they all participate in Phaedra's problem, a woman's problem, and establish their bond of common friendship. The bond of closeness and friendship is also essential among the female members of the choral aggregate of

---

[80] On the overdramatic tones of the Nurse that reach comic level see Michelini 1987.311.

[81] Her dramatic outburst, in contrast to Phaedra's sober tone in announcing her decision to die (391-402), recalls rather Hermione's uncontrolled reaction and even her chosen method of death, falling from a height (cf. *Andromache* 849-851). On the option of death by falling and its implications see Loraux 1987.19.

[82] On the super-power of Aphrodite, see also the Nurse's speech at 447-450 and the following discussion.

140 Chapter 3

Alcman's maiden songs, especially PMG 1, which is central in the discussion of this play.

4. The *Agôn* or the 'Contest of Words'

So far, Phaedra was only indirectly able to hint that she is in love with Hippolytus, and it was the Nurse who put it down in precise words for her, as Phaedra had wished (cf. 345). Now, however, that her destructive secret is out, Phaedra finally resumes completely the power of speech, and, being in control of speech, she accepts the invitation of the Nurse at 298-300 for an open debate, an *agôn*.

The *agôn* starts with Phaedra's long speech addressed formally to the members of the chorus, the Troizenian women (373-430).[83] In this speech, she thoroughly explains her case and announces her decisions. There are two main readings of this difficult and ambiguous speech. According to the first, Phaedra is apologizing, explaining why she failed to do what was right; according to the second, Phaedra is explaining not her moral failure, but her moral standards which require her decision to commit suicide. I concur with this second reading, as I see here an effort by Phaedra to refute the Nurse (accepting her challenge at 298-300), and to persuade the chorus, her judges, of the rightness of her decision to die.[84]

Phaedra argues that the shame of adultery is so great that in order to avoid it, she will take her own life; she knows this is the right thing to do and will not let anything keep her from doing it. As an introduction to her speech, she announces her reflections, which led to her decision (375-390). As an answer to the Nurse's comment on

---

[83] Cf. Medea's address to the Corinthian women (*Medea* 214) in a similar speech where she also announces her plan to a chorus of foreign women. Notice also that a formal address to the chorus is a signal for the beginning of an *agôn*: e.g., in *Andromache* 154. On the elements of an *agôn* in the speeches of Phaedra and the Nurse, as well as their similarity to a lyric poetic contest, see my discussion below.

[84] For the first reading cf. Dodds 1925.102-104, Winnington-Ingram 1960.171-197, Barrett 1964.227-238, and Segal 1970.278-299; for the second reading cf. Kovacs 1980.287-303 and Halleran 1995.180-181, who also gives a comprehensive summary of the arguments. For a detailed analysis of Phaedra's arguments, see also Sommerstein 1988.23-41, especially 23-28. In many respects, Phaedra's speech can be seen as a second prologue. Like Aphrodite, Phaedra explains her plans, going back to the beginning, and, like Aphrodite, she intends to make revelations (cf. 9 and 391). The two speeches are almost identical in length (58 and 57 lines). On the prologue characteristics of this speech, see Luschnig 1988.107.

The Nurse in Euripides' Hippolytus 141

her wisdom as a result of her long life (in 252), Phaedra explains that she has come up with some serious thoughts after long hours of sleepless nights; she has also concluded, like the Nurse in 189-190, that human life is wrecked (375-376). We know what is right, she says, but we do not strive to accomplish it because some of us are lazy while others prefer pleasure over the good. There are many pleasures, long talks, idleness, and *aidôs* 'shame'; and there are two kinds, one not bad, but the other, a burden on a house (377-386). These are her views, and there is no *pharmakon* 'drug' that can make her change her mind (389-390). She says, in short, that she cannot prove false to her beliefs, knowing the good and not striving for it— which, however, is exactly what the Nurse will urge her to do; the *pharmakon* that will make her change her mind is the Nurse's speech.[85]

Now that she has explained her ethical views to the chorus (373-390), she turns and addresses specifically the Nurse, who had begged and challenged her to speak, and announces pointedly her 'course thought' (*gnômês hodos*). She uses, on purpose, I suggest, the same words the Nurse uses in 290; this is Phaedra's answer to the Nurse's challenge for an *agôn*, her challenge to refute her words or to comply with them (288-299). She reveals the three stages of her reaction to her passion for Hippolytus—first, to keep quiet, then to bear it with moderation, and finally, to die (391-402); this is her best decision, and "none will oppose it" (*oudeis anterei*, 402). This specific comment is again addressed to the Nurse, the one who is in the habit of debating. I believe that Phaedra at this point, as in 391, looks directly at the Nurse before she turns to the chorus again for the conclusion of her speech.

λέξω δὲ καὶ σοὶ τῆς ἐμῆς γνώμης ὁδόν·
ἐπεί μ' ἔρως ἔτρωσεν, ἐσκόπουν ὅπως
κάλλιστ' ἐνέγκαιμ' αὐτόν. ἠρξάμην μὲν οὖν
ἐκ τοῦδε, σιγᾶν τήνδε καὶ κρύπτειν νόσον.
γλώσσῃ γὰρ οὐδὲν πιστόν, ἣ θυραῖα μὲν

---

[85] On the *pharmakon* cf. Goff 1992.49. Phaedra's philosophy, like Hippolytus', echoes Socratic ideas, while, as we will see, the Nurse's answer to Phaedra's speech echoes sophistic ideas and sophistic methodology (cf. Michelini 1987.313). The passage on *aidôs* (377-386), and specifically line 385, has caused problems in interpretation and translation. Some scholars speak of two kinds of shame, others of two kinds of pleasure. This is probably another purposeful ambiguity of Euripides and, either way it is understood, the emphasis on Phaedra's *aidôs* is clear. For the different interpretations see Solmsen 1973.420-425, Kovacs 1980a.287-303, and Halleran 1995.182-183.

φρονήματ' ἀνδρῶν νουθετεῖν ἐπίσταται,
αὐτὴ δ' ὑφ' αὑτῆς πλεῖστα κέκτηται κακά.
τὸ <u>δεύτερον</u> δὲ τὴν ἄνοιαν <u>εὖ φέρειν</u>
τῷ σωφρονεῖν νικῶσα προὐνοησάμην.
<u>τρίτον</u> δ', ἐπειδὴ τοισίδ' οὐκ ἐξήνυτον
Κύπριν κρατῆσαι, <u>κατθανεῖν</u> ἔδοξέ μοι
κράτιστον, <u>οὐδεὶς ἀντερεῖ</u>, βουλευμάτων.

Hippolytus 391-402

<u>I will tell you too [lexô de kai soi]</u> <u>my course of thought
   [gnômês hodon]</u>.[86]
When love wounded me I was considering
how I might best bear it. So <u>I started [êrxamên]</u> from this:
<u>keeping quiet (sigan)</u> and <u>hiding (kruptein)</u> my disease.
For nothing can be trusted to the tongue, which knows
how to school the thoughts of other men,
yet possesses too many evils of its own.[87]
<u>Second [deuteron]</u>, I took thought <u>to bear with an easy mind
   [eu pherein]</u>
my folly by subduing it with moderation.
And <u>third [triton]</u>, when I could not manage by these means
to master Kypris, I thought it the best plan,
<u>to die [katthanein]</u>, and <u>none will oppose me [oudeis anterei]</u>.

After explaining her general principles (373-390) and the three stages of her course of action culminating in her decision to die (391-402), she articulates the motivation for her decision: her good name, and the benefit it will bring to her children (403-430). She first prays for witnesses to her good actions, and not to her bad ones (403-404). She knows that not only the *ergon* 'deed/act', but even the mere *nosos* 'sickness' (her love for Hippolytus) brings a bad name (405). Besides, she is a woman, *misêma pasin* 'an object of hatred for all' (407).[88] Then

---

[86] Note the contrast between her present resolution to speak (*lexô*, 391) and her former wish for silence (*sigan* and *kruptein*, 394).

[87] This is another answer to the Nurse, who prompted her to break her silence and speak (297-299). Phaedra's statement, however, is ironic: although she holds the belief that the tongue is not to be trusted, she has already revealed her secret. On the unreliability of speech with women see Goff 1990.1-20. According to the norm, women should keep silent; speech is unreliable, not to be trusted; and this is what Phaedra believes. The Nurse, however, contrary to this norm, believes in the power of speech and reasoning, as she declared already, and as she will prove later on with her action.

[88] For misogynistic ideas in the play see Hippolytus' speech at 616 ff.; cf. also Jason's speech in *Medea* 569-575, and Andromache's comments in *Andromache* 269-273. On the concept of misogyny in Euripides and in Athenian drama in general, see Foley

The Nurse in Euripides' Hippolytus 143

she curses adulterous women, especially from noble homes, since they give a bad example (407-412). She also hates adulterous women who are *sôphrones en logois* 'chaste in words' only (414); and she wonders how they can look their husbands in the face (415-416) and why they are not afraid that the timbers of their house will betray them (417-418).[89] And, turning to the chorus again, whom she addresses again as *philai* 'friends', she concludes with the motivation for her suicide—her good name: so that she may never be caught shaming her husband and her children, and that they may live *eukleeis* 'with a good reputation' because of their mother (419-425). She finishes her speech emphasizing the importance of a just and good mind (426-430) and wishing that she may never be found among those who have a base mind. Phaedra's concluding thoughts (419-430) emphasize her obsession with good reputation, echoing her words in 321.[90]

Phaedra's speech is rhetorically organized; it contains a proem (373-390), narration (393-402), argument (403-425), and epilogue (426-430). Following a ring composition geometric pattern, it moves from the general (her principles), to the specific (her decisions), and back to the general (her principles again). It starts with her general principles and moves to their application to her own situation (373-390). Then, she reveals the three stages of her course of action (first, to conceal her passion, hoping that it would die down by itself, second, to fight against it, and third, after this failed, to die, 391-402), with lines 401-402, the climax of the speech, culminating in her decision to die. Finally, she returns to her principles again, explaining her motivation for her decision to die and finishing her speech with a wish—to be consistent with her ideals and her principles (403-430).[91]

1982.164n5. For a defense of Euripides seen as sympathetic and interested in women, although not a feminist, see Vellacott 1975 throughout and especially 125-126.

[89] Cf. the chorus' words at 280 (how come her husband does not read her face?). On the idea that a house may have voice cf. *Agamemnon* 37 and *Andromache* 124-125.

[90] On her *eukleia* 'good name', cf. also her wish for herself later, in 717, and the prophecy of Aphrodite in 47. For a discussion on the dualism between inner goodness and outer appearance, see Avery 1968.25-35 and especially on Phaedra, 29-31.

[91] The fact, however, that she has broken her silence, although she declared that "the tongue is not to be trusted," reveals that she has already deviated from her beliefs and that she is prompt to yield to more pressure from the Nurse.

144   Chapter 3

The chorus women, acting as judges of Phaedra's speech, comment on its merits. They sadly approve of Phaedra's speech and her *sôphrosunê*: [92]

φεῦ φεῦ, τὸ σῶφρον ὡς ἁπανταχοῦ καλὸν
καὶ δόξαν ἐσθλὴν ἐν βροτοῖς καρπίζεται.

Hippolytus 431-432

Alas, alas, how virtue is considered good everywhere
and harvests a noble reputation among mortals.

As I have already suggested sporadically, I contend that the central and most important part of Phaedra's speech, and the only part where she announces clearly and methodically her course of action (391-402), is addressed specifically to the Nurse (who by now must have either recovered on stage from her shock or returned on stage, if she left before shocked by Phaedra's revelation). The verbal clues in the beginning (*lexô de kai soi*, 391) and in the end of this part of the speech (*oudeis anterei*, 402) suggest this interpretation. Again, as more verbal clues suggest (*gnômês hodos*, 391; *glôssêi gar ouden piston*, 395), this is a direct response to the Nurse's invitation and challenge for an open discussion, an *agôn*, in 298-300. I also suggest that the clarity and organization of Phaedra's speech in the part pointedly addressed to the Nurse (391-402) is due to the fact that it is intended as an answer to the Nurse's clear and organized speech at 288-300.

In her speech at 288-300, the Nurse gives Phaedra a series of two choices: change your mind and I will turn to a better course; tell of your disease either to women or to a doctor; do not keep silent but speak; refute me or comply with me. Phaedra's answer is likewise clearly and methodically organized as she explains the three stages of her 'course of thought'. Although the style and the considerations of her speech are philosophical in her first and last part, which are both addressed to the chorus, the middle part, addressed to the Nurse, is highly rhetorical. It contains an enumeration of arguments (first, second, third) like the best examples of formal *agones*.[93]

---

[92] The chorus judges first Phaedra's speech and then the Nurse's speech (482-485), acting as judges in a rhetorical contest, an *agôn*, or even a poetic contest of early women's lyric compositions like Alcman PMG 1 (see following discussion).

[93] E.g., Menelaos' attack of Agamemnon (334-375) during their *agôn* in *Iphighenia at Aulis* 317-414, and especially Helen's defense against Hecuba (914-965) during their *agôn* in *Trojan Women* 895-1059.

The Nurse in Euripides' Hippolytus 145

These are clear indications that Phaedra has entered a formal debate, an *agôn*, on the best *gnômês hodon* 'course of thought' for the chorus to judge. An *agôn* presupposes hostility, conflict, or disagreement.[94] Indeed, although the verbal exchanges between Phaedra and her Nurse (373-524) do not involve hostility, they certainly contain disagreement and conflict of ideas; the issue is Phaedra's life: is it to be wasted or rather to be saved.[95]

From this point on, this *agôn*, although generally not seen as such, follows the rules of formal *agones*.[96] The first long speech is followed by brief comments by the chorus (431-432), then the second speech follows at similar length: Phaedra's speech (58 lines) is followed by the Nurse's speech (49 lines); and, although it does not answer Phaedra's points one by one, it answers almost all of them; most important, it offers, as a counter-suggestion, an alternative to Phaedra's decision to die. The Nurse's long speech is also followed by the comments of the chorus—this time double in length, and also with double evaluation of both speeches (482-485). A dialogue between Phaedra and the Nurse follows. It starts with longer parts—Phaedra's not exceeding four lines (4-2-4), the Nurse's considerably longer (8-4-9)—and it ends in a stichomythia (typical in an *agôn*), which concludes with the Nurse's longer and final speech.[97]

The existence of two *agones* in the same tragedy is not unique in Euripides. In *Andromache* there are also two *agones*, the first (147-273) between the two main female characters, Hermione and Andromache, in the presence of a female chorus (as in the Phaedra/Nurse episode); the second (547-746) between the two main male characters, Peleus and Menelaos (as in the *agôn* between Theseus and Hippolytus in *Hippolytus* 902-1089). There are many similarities between the *agôn* of Andromache and Hermione, and that of Phaedra and the Nurse: female contestants in the presence of a female chorus, formal address of the first speaker (Hermione,

---

[94] Cf. Duchemin 1968.41, Collard 1975.58-71, especially 61, and Lloyd 1992.1.

[95] Similarly, in another Euripidean tragedy, *Iphighenia at Aulis* 317-414, Iphighenia's life or sacrifice is the conflict issue in the formal *agôn* between the two brothers, Agamemnon and Menelaos.

[96] None of the scholars who have studied at length the *agones* in Euripides and in Greek tragedy in general (Duchemin 1968, Collard 1975, Lloyd 1992) has included *Hippolytus* 373-524 among the formal or even informal *agones*, while Halleran 1995.180 recognizes similarities with an *agôn*.

[97] She literally has the last word, after which she leaves the stage (see below). Cf. also Theseus' final speech and exit (1088-1089) in his formal *agôn* with Hippolytus.

146 *Chapter 3*

Phaedra) to the chorus, short comments by the chorus following both initial long speeches, a stichomythia concluding in a longer and decisive speech of the character who has the last word and leaves the stage (Hermione, the Nurse).

We should keep in mind that the essential purpose of an *agôn*, a debate or even a lawsuit, is persuasion. An *agôn* should therefore be seen primarily as a debate of opposing or conflicting ideas, rather than as a debate or conflict of enemies or opponents. Accordingly, the speech between Phaedra and her Nurse should be seen as an *agôn* in its purest form, since it is a debate of ideas (for the purpose of choosing the best *gnômês hodos* 'course of thought') through persuasion, and not a verbal attack between angry opponents or enemies. It is, rather, an *agôn* of conflicting ideas and attitudes, like the *agôn* between Electra and Chrysothemis in Sophocles' *Electra* 957-1057, which Duchemin calls one of the most authentic *agônes* ("un agon des plus authentiques").[98]

At the same time, an *agôn* in tragedy between two leading female personalities, an older and a younger one, recalls, in diction and in choral conventions of hierarchy, performances of early lyric choral compositions, such as Alcman's maiden songs. In particular, the episode between Phaedra and her Nurse, in which the old Nurse is trying to influence and convince her younger mistress, recalls Alcman's PMG 1, where an older leading personality, Hagesikhora (literally 'the one who leads the *khoros* 'song and dances'), competes in skill and grace with a presumably younger, literally, 'leading' personality, Agido, while a circle of young women act as judges in their contest. In these early choral compositions, Calame and Nagy see analogues of the dramatic chorus; and as early choral compositions, like PMG 1, were performed and re-performed, Herington also sees in them the beginnings of Greek drama.[99] Concurring with them I also see in these early lyric choral compositions the connections with Athenian drama, and I suggest that the Phaedra/Nurse episode provides an illustration of such connections. Moreover, the *agôn* itself, as Nagy convincingly argues,

---

[98] See Duchemin 1968.58.

[99] On the resemblances of early lyric compositions to tragic performances and a discussion on their connection with Attic drama see Calame 1977.367-372 [=Calame 1997.255-258] and Nagy 1990a.377-379; cf. also Herington 1985.20-24, and 54-55.

has its roots in archaic poetic contests.[100] This women's contest in the presence of a female chorus of judges provides an example of both a rhetorical and, at the same time, of a poetic contest in style, form, and language, as it contains the language of both agonistic rhetoric and poetic authority.[101]

After the chorus women judge Phaedra's speech, the Nurse gives her own speech, which they will also judge. During Phaedra's long speech, the Nurse has time to recover from her first shock and to prepare her own arguments. She will now be able to rebut Phaedra's 'course of thought' with her own and convince her with her arguments. She responds to Phaedra's speech addressing her as 'mistress', in contrast to the previous 'child' (288, 340, 353), thus signaling her change of tone from motherly, protective, affectionate, addressed to a sick daughter, to a more formal and sophisticated tone, addressed to a reasonable adult, her mistress.

As an introduction to her speech she first explains her immediate reaction to Phaedra's revelation. It took her unawares and caused her a terrible fear, but now she realizes that she was foolish. In a deliberate effort at a *captatio benevolentiae*, instead of blaming Phaedra, she blames her own reaction; she has now come to second, better thoughts:[102]

> δέσποιν', ἐμοί τοι συμφορὰ μὲν ἀρτίως
> ἡ σὴ παρέσχε δεινὸν ἐξαίφνης φόβον·
> νῦν δ' ἐννοοῦμαι φαῦλος οὖσα· κἀν βροτοῖς
> <u>αἱ δεύτεραί πως φροντίδες σοφώτεραι.</u>
>
> *Hippolytus* 433-436

---

[100] Nagy explores the pastoral background of the *agôn* and provides convincing arguments: In *Bacchae* 714-16, a herdsman is telling how he and his companions had come together for a *logôn erin* 'contest of words' (λόγων ἔριν) in describing the wondrous things performed by the devotees of Bacchus. This passage, according to Nagy, "provides the definition" and "reenacts the very etymology" of the crucial word *agôn* (see Nagy 1990a.386). The idea that the agonistic character of tragedy and its formal debates are not due entirely to the influence of sophistry, and that they are in part "natural inheritance from a long popular or pastoral tradition of dramatic poetry," has also been suggested by Duchemin 1969.247-275.

[101] Such words as *sophos, mantis, philos, ainos/ainein*, used as "marked" speech, have a special connotation in poetry and refer, in particular, to poetic authority. On the language of poetic authority see Nagy 1989.8-16 and 23-24. See also below.

[102] The Nurse has second thoughts like all the other characters in the tragedy, Hippolytus, Phaedra, Theseus; in fact, she changes her mind more often than any of them. See Knox 1952.5ff. and 1979.241.

148 Chapter 3

> Mistress, a while ago, your trouble
> suddenly gave me a terrible fear;
> but now I realize that I was foolish; among mortals
> <u>second thoughts are somehow wiser.</u>

The Nurse's concern is to save Phaedra's life, and, therefore, she will try anything. She has the necessary flexibility to achieve this goal. She already stated her philosophical position against life's 'unswerving/inflexible practices' (*atrekeis epitêdeuseis*) before the revelation of Phaedra's secret (261). Like contemporary sophists, she can turn every argument around to achieve expediency. As Knox observes, each character in the play is obsessed with an ideal: Hippolytus with *eusebeia* 'reverence', Phaedra with *eukleia* 'good name', Theseus with action; the Nurse, however, has no ideal: her purpose is to save Phaedra, and she will do this with expediency.[103]

After this short introduction (433-436), she explains her second thoughts. Turning everything around, she tries to convince Phaedra that falling in love is quite natural. She dismisses for the moment the fact that Phaedra is married and that the object of her love is her stepson—only later (at 462-466) she will hint at these two facts. Her first argument is an answer to Phaedra's decision to die after fighting her love and being unable to overcome it (cf. 391-402). There is nothing extraordinary or unreasonable, literally 'out of reason' but also 'out of argumentation' (*exô logou*), in what happened to her, she explains calmly: the anger of the goddess struck against her (437-438).[104] "You are in love—what is wondrous about it? —like everybody else. And then you will throw your life away because of love?" she remarks plainly but vividly through a storm of rhetorical questions (439-440); and she adds cynically, "it is of little profit for those who are in love if they have to die" (437-442).[105]

---

[103] Knox 1952.17-19.

[104] In expressing this common belief, the Nurse has accurately guessed Aphrodite's anger, although she does not know that her anger was caused by Hippolytus. The choice 'out of *logos*' (*exô logou*) has a double meaning: Phaedra's passion is not beyond 'reasoning', but also it is not out of the power of the Nurse's *logos*, her skill with 'speech', as Goldhill 1986.127-128 pointedly remarks.

[105] Rhetorical questions are abundant in this speech (cf. 439, 446, 459, especially 462-463, 464-465, 470). The Nurse's tone is in sharp contrast to the seriousness of Phaedra's decision to die (401-402). On the cynicism of the Nurse in contrast to Phaedra's idealism here and in general, see Knox 1952.19-21; also Kovacs 1987.49-50, and Michelini 1987.310-314.

The Nurse in Euripides' Hippolytus 149

She expands on the power of Aphrodite, first over mortals (443-446), and then in the universe (447-450). She warns Phaedra how the goddess goes gently to those who yield, "but if she finds somebody too high and haughty—what do you think?—she knocks his pride out of him" (445-446). Then she raises a hymn to the all-encompassing life-giving cosmic power of Aphrodite: she roves through the air, she is in the surge of the sea, Kupris, and all things are born from her. She is the one who sows and gives desire from which all who live upon the earth are born (443-450).[106]

To support her point on the power of Aphrodite, the Nurse uses mythological examples from the realm of the gods, which reveal her sophistic artistry of persuasion. These examples come from 'writings of the ancestors' (*graphas palaiterôn*, 451), and from poetry (*en mousais*, 452).[107] Even Zeus and Eos, she says, were overcome by Aphrodite (453-458). And she concludes with a powerful rhetorical question that leaves no doubt; Phaedra will certainly not be so hubristic as to think that she is stronger than the gods: the gods are overcome by this *sumphora* 'affliction', and she will not bear it? (458-459)[108] Then she continues with a down-to-earth cynical and ironic argument which

---

[106] Cf. her acknowledgment of the power of Aphrodite in 359-360. As Vellacott 1975.215-216 points out, the Nurse, like the Old Servant in the beginning of this play, recognizes the existence and the power of Aphrodite, but she knows her nature better and her perception of her "flows from her lips in poetry." Indeed, the Nurse's hymn resembles the Homeric *Hymn to Aphrodite* 2-5. Cf. also the choral odes at 525ff. and 1276ff.

[107] The word *graphai* is ambiguous and could refer to 'writings' or 'paintings' (see Barrett 1964.41-42 and Halleran 1995.188-189; also cf. Segal 1993.102). However, *palaiteroi* 'the ancestors' is more appropriate to poets; therefore, although it would be strange if the old Nurse should speak of written works as a source of popular knowledge (cf. Barrett, 1964.41), the reading 'writings' is preferable. Moreover, in the next line the Nurse speaks of poets again, and by her description of the cosmic power of Aphrodite she shows familiarity with the Homeric hymn, or, at least, with its story. Her skillful use of sophistic methods, her knowledgeable statements and sententious maxims, portray her as an informed member of the Athenian society. Despite her social status as a servant, she is intellectually sophisticated.

[108] Another rhetorical question (for a list of the rhetorical questions in this speech see above, n105), instead of a negative statement, meaning "certainly you cannot resist Aphrodite, if even the gods cannot." This *exemplum a fortiori* is her compelling answer to Phaedra's statements on her efforts to overcome Aphrodite in 391-402. Cf. the reference to Phaedra's *sumphora* 'affliction' in 433: the Nurse used this word in the beginning of her speech to describe Phaedra's affliction, and now she uses the same word on the gods' passions to make her point more compelling. Cf. also the same argument (*exemplum a fortiori*) on the power of Aphrodite in Helen's speech, in *Trojan Women* 948-950.

150 Chapter 3

resembles Hippolytus' extreme ideas (618-623) in his angry speech to the Nurse. "Your father, then," she says, "must have begotten you by special arrangement or with other gods as masters, if you will not put up with these laws" (459-461).[109]

So far the Nurse has been very methodical in presenting the power of Aphrodite and the way she punishes those who resist her (437-450). After proving to Phaedra how not even the gods can resist the goddess (451-466)—an *exemplum a fortiori*—she moves on to more examples in the world of humans, choosing them specifically to match Phaedra's case. How many men, does she think, among those who are really sensible, seeing their marriage bed sick, pretend they do not see? And how many fathers help their amorous sons in their escapades? These two successive rhetorical questions fit Theseus' case as both husband and father. Though based on a hypothetical syllogism, clearly and forcefully, they hint at Theseus' imaginary and even expected reaction to the possible discovery of his wife's infidelity and his son's affair (462-464). Because, she continues with a commonsense maxim, "it is the practice 'among the sensible' (*en sophoisi*) not to notice what is not good" (ἐν σοφοῖσι γὰρ / τάδ' ἐστὶ θνητῶν, λανθάνειν τὰ μὴ καλά, 465-466), an answer to Phaedra's concern for good things going unnoticed (403).[110] And, as a direct answer to Phaedra's ideas on struggling for perfection at 380-381 ("we know the good things but we do not *ekponoumen* 'toil' for them"), she adds another maxim, opposing Phaedra's argument, and reinforcing her previous point at 261 (that "life should not be too exacting"): "surely men should not *ekponein* 'toil' too much over their lives" (οὐδ' ἐκπονεῖν τοι χρῆν βίον λίαν βροτούς, 467). She supports her

---

[109] The Nurse's arguments represent Euripides' iconoclastic ideas (cf. Michelini 1987.313). Her practical, down-to-earth reasoning is dressed in the sophistic ideas in fashion at the time (cf. Knox 1952.18). On the sophistic artistry of the Nurse in her long speech, see further Knox 1952.18-21 and Goldhill 1986.128-130.

[110] There is an ambiguity in *en sophoisi* (465). It could be either masculine, 'sensible men', or neuter, 'sensible things': "wise men have this trait" or "this is one of the wise things among men" (cf. Barrett 1964.243). For a Greek-speaking audience, the ambiguity adds to the force of the argument by making at the same time a double point on sensible men and the sensible thing to do. This may be a maxim that the Nurse creates here for the occasion, but most probably it was a generally accepted commonsense proverb; there is a similar deeply rooted expression of common sense in Modern Greek: *kanô ta strava matia* (κάνω τά στραβά μάτια) "pretend not to see." Also cf. Phaedra's identical words in 403 'not notice the good things' (μήτε λανθάνειν καλά). The Nurse is using Phaedra's words as an answer to Phaedra's concern for what goes noticed or unnoticed; she is assuring her that only the good things will be noticed, the bad things will be unnoticed.

argument with an example from architecture—the imperfection of the roof (468-469), an analogy matching Phaedra's metaphor and her concern for the house acquiring a voice in 418. And she concludes by rewording her thought of 467 into a new maxim: "If you have more good than evil in your character, being only human, you will be doing well enough" (471-472). This is her ethical and philosophical position as a final answer to Phaedra's ethical and philosophical position that, when we know what is good, we should accomplish it. She answers Phaedra's philosophizing with generally accepted commonsense maxims and observations.

Her speech ends with a peroration to Phaedra, in which she addresses her as 'dear child', as she is trying smoothly to regain her motherly influence over her. In her peroration, she appeals to Phaedra to stop her *hubris*, trying to be better than the gods, for her love was a god's will (473-475): she should 'overcome' (*katastrephein*) her sickness with an easy mind (476-477).[111] There are *epôidai* 'incantations' and *logoi thelktêrioi* 'beguiling words', she continues; there will be some *pharmakon nosou* 'drug for the sickness' (478-479). Moreover, she concludes, being women, they will contrive *mêkhanai* 'devices' (480-481):[112]

ἀλλ', ὦ φίλη παῖ, λῆγε μὲν κακῶν φρενῶν,
λῆξον δ' ὑβρίζουσ'· οὐ γὰρ ἄλλο πλὴν ὕβρις

---

[111] The Nurse guessed very accurately Aphrodite's games, although without knowing why. The emphasis on the idea that Phaedra's resistance to Aphrodite is a *hubris* is emphasized by the epexegesis in 474-475 and by the repetition of the word twice in the same line (474). Cf. Helen's words in *Trojan Women* 948-950. The verb *katastrephein* 'overcome' has a double meaning: 'subdue' or 'turn around', 'direct'; the Nurse's advice is somewhat ambiguous from the beginning.

[112] This is an answer to Phaedra's declaration that there is no *pharmakon* that can make her change her mind (389). *Pharmakon nosou* also has a double meaning: a drug against her disease or a love charm. In fact, *pharmakon* has a double function: as a love charm it will also be the drug to cure the disease, her physical sickness, but, especially after 476 (τόλμα δ' ἐρῶσα) we have to assume that the drug would not fight her love, but rather help her consummate it. Moreover, the word *nosos* also has a double meaning: her actual physical sickness due to her love and her love itself. Both *pharmakon* (φάρμακον) and *mêkhanai* (μηχαναί) 'remedy' and 'devices', I suggest, refer to speech: *epôidai* 'incantations' and *logoi thelktêrioi* 'beguiling words' (ἐπῳδαὶ καὶ λόγοι θελκτήριοι, 479), as the continuation of the plot will show. On women's devices cf. Andromache's words in *Andromache* 85, and Medea's words in *Medea* 407-409. On the deceptive power of speech and action in women exemplified by the Nurse's words here and in Phaedra's letter later, see Goldhill 1986.128, and the challenging discussion in Segal 1993.89-109. On the *pharmakon nosou* see also Segal 1993.102.

152   Chapter 3

τάδ' ἐστί, κρείσσω δαιμόνων εἶναι θέλειν·
τόλμα δ' ἐρῶσα· θεὸς ἐβουλήθη τάδε.
νοσοῦσα δ' εὖ πως τὴν <u>νόσον</u> καταστρέφου.
εἰσὶν δ' <u>ἐπῳδαὶ</u> καὶ λόγοι θελκτήριοι·
φανήσεταί τι τῆσδε <u>φάρμακον νόσου</u>.
ἦ τἄρ' ἂν ὀψέ γ' ἄνδρες ἐξεύροιεν ἄν,
εἰ μὴ γυναῖκες <u>μηχανὰς</u> εὑρήσομεν.

Hippolytus 473-481

But, dear child, give up your bad mood,
stop your <u>hubris</u>; for these things are nothing else but <u>hubris</u>,
trying to be better than the gods.
Have the courage to be in love; it was a god's will.
And, being sick, overcome your <u>disease [noson]</u> easily somehow.
There are <u>incantations [epôidai]</u> and <u>beguiling words [logoi thelktêrioi]</u>;
there will be some <u>drug for this sickness [pharmakon nosou]</u>.
In the long run, surely men would discover <u>devices [mêkhanai]</u>
if we women are not going to contrive them first.

 The Nurse's long speech (433-481) is an answer to Phaedra's long speech (373-430). It is pointed and organized with rhetorical skill and symmetry. It starts with a *captatio benevolentiae*, announcing that she changed her mind for the better (433-436); then, in answer to Phaedra's decision to die, she juxtaposes that it is natural to be in love (437-442); in support of her statement, first, she speaks of the omnipotence of Aphrodite (443-450) and strengthens her argument by bringing examples from the realm of the gods as *exempla a fortiori* (451-462); then, she further strengthens her argument with examples among the mortals and more specifically examples that match Phaedra's case (463-466). In the continuation of her speech, as an answer to Phaedra's belief in perfection, she provides examples from the material world (467-472). Finally, in a peroration (473-481), she summarizes her main points and suggests practical solutions. She appeals to Phaedra to stop her evil thoughts (her thoughts of death) and her *hubris* trying to resist Aphrodite (473-476), and she advises her instead to have the courage to be in love and to overcome her disease (477-478). At the end of her speech, she suggests practical solutions: incantations, beguiling words, a *pharmakon*, women's devices (479-481). The Nurse has an answer for all of Phaedra's concerns. She has counter-suggestions and practical solutions for all her concerns, even the most crucial one—Phaedra's concern for *eukleia* 'good reputation'. For, although the Nurse does not openly provide a suggestion for Phaedra's *eukleia* in her speech, nevertheless, her 'devices' include a solution for it (the oath which secures Hippolytus' silence, as we will see further). As a whole, her speech is an answer to Phaedra's speech, and both speeches have the form of the initial long speeches of an *agôn*.

The chorus women, acting as the judges in an *agôn*, find the arguments of the Nurse *khrêsimôtera* 'more expedient', but they offer their *ainos* 'praise' to Phaedra; they admit, however, that their *ainos* will be harsher and more painful to bear than Phaedra's words:

Φαίδρα, λέγει μὲν ἥδε χρησιμώτερα
πρὸς τὴν παροῦσαν συμφοράν, αἰνῶ δὲ σέ.
ὁ δ' αἶνος οὗτος δυσχερέστερος λόγων
τῶν τῆσδε καὶ σοὶ μᾶλλον ἀλγίων κλύειν.

Hippolytus 482-485

Phaedra, indeed, she speaks *[legei]* more usefully
as to the present trouble, but it is you I praise *[ainô]*.
Yet, this praise *[ainos]* is harder to bear than her words *[logôn]*,
and for you more painful to listen to.

The dramatized occasion of the two women competing in words and the chorus offering their judgement also recalls a poetic choral contest, as I suggested already in my discussion at the end of Phaedra's speech. In particular, they recall the *khoros* of younger women in Alcman PMG 1, where the two leading personalities, Agido and Hagesikhora, compete in grace and poetic talent in the presence of the *khoros* of Spartan girls serving as the judges. In this maiden song, the *khoros* jokingly complains that their glorious *khorêgos*, "the one who 'leads' *[agein]* the *khoros*" (as the very name *Hagesikhora* suggests), does not allow them in any way either to praise or blame Agido:

ἐμὲ δ' οὔτ' ἐπαινῆν
οὔτε μωμῆσθαι νιν ἁ κλεννὰ χοραγὸς
οὐδ' ἁμῶς ἐῆι·

Alcman PMG 1 43-45

neither to praise *[epainein]*
nor to blame her the famous *khorêgos*
allows me in any way.

Note here the use of the verb *epainein* (ἐπαινεῖν) similar to *ainein* and *ainos* (αἰνεῖν/αἶνος) in *Hippolytus* 484, 485. The repetition of these two cognate forms by the tragic chorus in *Hippolytus* suggests an allusion to the choral model. At the same time, the split judgement of the chorus, underscored by the chiastic construction *legei...ainô/ ainos...logôn* (λέγει...αἰνῶ/αἶνος...λόγων), suggests that, although they offer their praise to Phaedra, they judge the Nurse superior in the context of a rhetorical contest, as the cognate forms *legei/logôn* imply.[113]

Encouraged by the praise of the chorus, Phaedra rebuffs the Nurse in a tone of mild outrage. Her sense of virtue is offended; the Nurse's beautiful speech, her rhetorical skills, in other words, are of no value, especially in regard to her concern with good reputation—which the Nurse's speech fails to answer. "This is what destroys cities and home—'very fine speeches' (οἱ καλοὶ λίαν λόγοι)," she remarks; "for one should not speak things pleasant to the ear, but those from which one will become *eukleês* 'renowned'" (486-489).[114]

The agonistic character of the first two speeches continues with Phaedra's speech. Phaedra has indeed discovered a weakness in the Nurse's speech: her neglect to answer her concern for *eukleia* 'good reputation'. Phaedra makes her point clear in her short speech (486-489): she is interested in being *eukleês*, in having a good reputation—this is her objective; for this, she is ready to sacrifice her life, as she pointed out already at 423 (cf. also Aphrodite's prophecy at 47).

At Phaedra's criticism, the Nurse immediately changes her tone; she also speaks in open disapproval, without keeping up any pretense. Phaedra approved the skill of her speech but not its content; she answers back in the same terms. She also approves the appearance of Phaedra's speech, but this is not what Phaedra needs now. She needs something more essential—the man she loves. Using her pragmatism she tries to put some reasoning into Phaedra and bring her to her senses. They must find a solution quickly; she would never have pushed her so far if Phaedra were not sensible. Now, however, there is an *agôn megas*, a 'great contest' for her life, and this is not worthy of blame (496-497).

---

[113] As Nagy 1989.10f notes, the word *ainos* or *epainos*, used as a "marked" term, is concerned more with the function of poetry and song, rather than the form; it stresses the occasion for which a given form is used. Nagy further refers to "Pindar's traditional diction," in which the term alludes to "praise poetry." *Logos*, on the other hand, is the "unmarked" word used in everyday speech, in prose, and therefore in rhetoric.

[114] Many Euripidean characters express suspicion about the power of speech, cf. Phaedra's words in 505, and Kreon's in *Medea* 316-317. Phaedra's words clearly refer to the skill of the Nurse's speech rather than to its content.

This *agôn* is literally and metaphorically for Phaedra's life. I do not believe that the use of the word *agôn* is unintentional: it is a self-reference to the rhetorical *agôn* in process, as it is used in Aristophanes' *Frogs* (785, 867, 813, 882).[115]

τί σεμνομυθεῖς; οὐ λόγων εὐσχημόνων
δεῖ σ', ἀλλὰ τἀνδρός---ὡς τάχος διοιστέον,
τὸν εὐθὺς ἐξειπόντας ἀμφὶ σοῦ λόγον.
εἰ μὲν γὰρ ἦν σοι μὴ 'πὶ συμφοραῖς βίος
τοιαῖσδε, σώφρων δ' οὖσ' ἐτύγχανες γυνή,
οὐκ ἄν ποτ' εὐνῆς εἵνεχ' ἡδονῆς τε σῆς
προσῆγον ἄν σε δεῦρο· νῦν δ' ἀγὼν μέγας
σῶσαι βίον σόν, κοὐκ ἐπίφθονον τόδε.

Hippolytus 490-497

What is this preaching? It is not fair words
that you need, but the man.[116] As fast as possible,
we must find out, speaking out frankly about you.[117]
For if your life were not in such a deep trouble,
and if you did not happen to be moderate/sensible [*sôphrôn*],
I would never, for the sake of your bed and your pleasure,
bring you to this point; but now, there is a big contest [*agôn*]
to save your life, and this is not worthy of blame [*(k)ouk epiphthonon*].

The Nurse says bluntly that the only way to save Phaedra's life is to get Hippolytus, but at the same time she expresses her moral values. She accepts that her words are not fair, as she accepted that Phaedra's love was bad (see 358-359). However, this is best for Phaedra; after all, she would not help her if her very life were not in danger and if she were not *sôphrôn* 'chaste/moderate/sensible' (494).[118]

In my translation, departing from the generally accepted "if you were chaste, sensible" I take the negative particle μή as referring to both verbs of the hypothesis (εἰ μὲν μὴ ἦν/ἐτύγχανες δέ): "if your

---

[115] On the self-referential use of the word *agôn* in the *Frogs*, see Nagy 1990a.402. On the etymology and the definition of the word *agôn*, see also above, n100.

[116] Indeed, this is what her own speech, at this point, is not—fair. Many Euripidean scholars have characterized the Nurse's direct speech as brutal (cf. Conacher 1967.39).

[117] There is disagreement in the interpretation of this difficult passage, due partly to the textual problems (see Barrett 1964.248-250) and partly to the intentional ambiguity of the Nurse's words.

[118] Chaste, moderate, sensible: the word *sôphrôn* has a variety of meanings, and it is central in this play, as all Euripidean scholars agree.

life were not in such deep trouble, and if you did not happen to be chaste/moderate/sensible." The Nurse had already included Phaedra among the *sôphrones* in 358 above, and she is not denying Phaedra's *sôphrosunê* here; on the contrary, she emphasizes it even more and she explains that her suggestion is based on it. I also depart from the general consensus that the Nurse does not have moral values and that her priority is expediency (expressed best by Knox).[119] I suggest, instead, that she does have moral values, of which she gives evidence here (493-496), but, in a matter of life and death, her priority is, indeed, expediency.

Phaedra, however, is disgusted at the Nurse's 'wicked' suggestions (498-499). The Nurse agrees that they are 'wicked' (*aiskhra*) but still better than Phaedra's fine principles. She rewords her point of 490-491, which offended Phaedra's sense of modesty, less bluntly and directly this time, but with equal emphasis. She explains to her that the deed is better than the good name if it will save her life; it is, indeed, a matter of choice between life and death (501-502):

κρεῖσσον δὲ τοὔργον, εἴπερ ἐκσώσει γέ σε,
ἢ τοὔνομ' ᾧ σὺ κατθανεῖ γαυρουμένη.

Hippolytus 501-502

the deed is better [*kreisson tourgon=to ergon*], if it will save you,
than the name [*ê tounoma=to onoma*] in which you will die
   exulting.

The Nurse is clearly the advocate of action: the *ergon* 'deed/action' (τοὔργον) is either the consummation of the affair or just doing something about it—action, in general; it is preferable to the *onoma*, her 'reputation', her 'good name' (τοὔνομα).[120] But the Nurse is also the advocate of speech, and speech is her talent. Phaedra feels her ground shaken and is afraid that she will be overcome by the Nurse's skillful speech, her convincing words. She admits again that she speaks fairly/well/effectively but wickedly: (εὖ λέγεις γάρ, αἰσχρὰ δέ, 503), and asks her not to go any further, for her soul is softened by desire. "If you speak wicked things beautifully" (τὰ αἰσχρὰ δ' ἢν λέγῃς

---

[119] Knox 1952.19.
[120] The contrast of word vs. deed is a commonplace in Greek literature. The Nurse uses this commonplace here without explaining what deed or action she means; by 'the name', however, she clearly refers to Phaedra's reputation.

καλῶς, 505), she repeats, "I will be consumed in what I am now trying to escape" (503-506).[121]

By pleading with the Nurse to stop pressing her with her arguments, because she will yield and will be consumed by what she is trying to escape (her love for Hippolytus), Phaedra acknowledges the superiority and power of the Nurse's speech and already admits her defeat in this contest of words and arguments.

Phaedra's confession that she is ready to yield encourages the Nurse to pursue Phaedra's persuasion to the very end and secure her approval in the specifics of her plan. At the end of her next speech (507-515), she gets to the practical details of what she suggested in her previous long speech (477-482)—the methods by which she will act in order to fulfill her plan. She asks Phaedra to listen to her; this is the second favor she is asking (508).[122] She has at home philtres, love charms, she just remembered, which will relieve Phaedra of her disease (509-512). They need to get some sign from Hippolytus, either a word or something from his clothes, and join the two together to get one favor (513-515).[123]

> εἴ τοι δοκεῖ σοι, χρῆν μὲν οὔ σ' ἁμαρτάνειν·
> εἰ δ' οὖν, πιθοῦ μοι· δευτέρα γὰρ ἡ χάρις.
> ἔστιν κατ' οἴκους <u>φίλτρα</u> μοι <u>θελκτήρια</u>
> <u>ἔρωτος</u>, ἦλθε δ' ἄρτι μοι γνώμης ἔσω,
> ἅ σ' οὔτ' ἐπ' αἰσχροῖς οὔτ' ἐπὶ βλάβῃ φρενῶν
> <u>παύσει νόσου</u> τῆσδ', ἢν σὺ μὴ γένῃ κακή.
> δεῖ δ' ἐξ ἐκείνου δή τι τοῦ ποθουμένου

---

[121] The same paradox of well-spoken words with wicked content that Phaedra criticized in 486-489 is criticized twice by Phaedra again in these lines (503 and 505).

[122] I suggest that the second favor she asks from Phaedra is to listen to her, the first being that Phaedra granted her the gift of her speech. For other interpretations, see Conacher 1961.37-44 and Halleran 1995.192-193.

[123] The Nurse's schemes recall her previous reference in 481 to women's devices (μηχανάς). Concurring with Goff 1990.52 for 514, I prefer the reading λόγον (word) to the OCT reading πλόκον (a lock of hair) because only λόγος explains Phaedra's fear in 520. A word and a touch of his dress, these two would weave a favor. I do not believe the Nurse means magic relics, but rather speech and supplication, so that she will weave from the two one favor to gain Hippolytus' response to Phaedra's love. This interpretation is based on the Nurse's words in 478-481, and the events that will follow later in the play, i.e., her effort in 603-615 to win Hippolytus through speech and supplication. For a different interpretation see Barrett 1964.255 (followed by most other Euripidean scholars). Barrett considers the two things that will give the desired result are the *philtra*, her 'drugs', and the *sêmeion*, the 'token', i.e., the lock of hair or a relic from his clothes—a personal relic of Hippolytus to direct the effect of her magic on to him.

158 Chapter 3

> σημεῖον, ἢ λόγον τιν' ἢ πέπλων ἄπο
> λαβεῖν, συνάψαι τ' ἐκ δυοῖν μίαν χάριν.
>
> *Hippolytus* 507-515
>
> If this is what you think, you should not err;
> if so, listen to me; this is the second favor I am asking.
> I have at home philtres, love charms [*philtra thelktêria erôtos*],[124]
> I have just remembered,
> that will make, neither harming your honor nor your mind,
> your disease cease [*pausei nosou*],[125] if you do not turn cowardly.
> We need to get something from the one you long for,
> a sign [*sêmeion*], or a word [*logon*], or something from his clothes,
> and join the two together to get one favor.

The speech of the Nurse is ambiguous and confusing. I believe that Euripides leaves the Nurse's message purposefully ambiguous both for the audience (so that it is held in suspense) and for Phaedra (so that she will not react to it); at the same time, the Nurse is portrayed as a skillful manipulator of speech to suit her purpose—to be able to act freely without Phaedra's further objections or resistance.[126] Therefore, she describes the philtres, the love charms she has at home, in such a way that Phaedra cannot tell if they are to charm love or charm love away, if they are to cure her love or to help her consummate it. Moreover, she assures Phaedra that these philtres will put an end to her disease, another ambiguity, since she does not make it clear again whether this will be through cure or through consummation (512).

Especially difficult and ambiguous is the continuation of her speech: she needs a sign from Hippolytus, a word or something from his clothes, and she will join the two together to get one favor (513-515). As I suggested, I prefer the reading λόγον (*logon*) 'speech' to πλόκον (*plokon*) 'a lock of hair'. This reading, on the one hand, maintains the vagueness and the ambiguity of the Nurse's speech, and so leaves both Phaedra and the audience in uncertainty as to her suggested course of action; on the other hand, it is an accurate account of what she is really going to do later in 601-615, namely, to try to convince Hippolytus with her speech, and when this fails, to try supplication, touching his robe (as she did successfully with

---

[124] Cf. her reference in 478 to *logoi thelktêrioi* (λόγοι θελκτήριοι).

[125] Cf. her reference in 479 to *pharmakon nosou* (φάρμακον νόσου).

[126] Cf. Conacher 1967.59, Kovacs 1987.53, and Segal 1993.96-97. Segal convincingly discusses this speech as an example of female communication by means of signs.

Phaedra). The speech and the touch of his robe—these two—would weave a favor: she hopes that Hippolytus will grant her the favor she seeks, either convinced by her words or moved by her supplication.[127] Still, considering the intentional ambiguity of this passage, when the audience sees the Nurse touching Hippolytus' robe, it was surely Euripides' intention to create the suspicion that the Nurse was probably going to tear a piece of it so that she could use it as a love charm.

The Nurse's ambiguous speech indeed weakens Phaedra's resistance and makes her reconsider her previous thoughts at 389-390. At that time she did not believe that there would be a *pharmakon* 'drug' to make her change her mind, but now Phaedra wants some more information about the Nurse's drug, the *pharmakon*, which would put an end to her disease—is it a salve or a potion? (πότερα δὲ χριστὸν ἢ ποτὸν τὸ φάρμακον; 516).[128] The Nurse, however, avoids an answer and tells Phaedra not to wish to know (μὴ μαθεῖν βούλου, τέκνον, 517). The Nurse addresses and treats Phaedra, again, as a child, not as her 'mistress' as before (433); she is trying to direct her again, controlling even her wish for knowledge.[129]

The Nurse's answer is not reassuring but raises suspicions in Phaedra as to her intended course of action. Phaedra admits that she is afraid that the Nurse is too clever, too *sophê*, for her (δέδοιχ' ὅπως μοι μὴ λίαν φανῇς σοφή, 518).[130] The Nurse encourages her to be brave and to articulate her fears (519). Phaedra now openly admits that she is afraid lest the Nurse reveal anything to Theseus' son (μή μοί τι Θησέως τῶνδε μηνύσῃς τόκῳ, 520), still not daring to speak Hippolytus' name. Phaedra fears that the Nurse will approach and speak to Hippolytus, as her last words in 520 reveal. And, overcome by the Nurse's skill with words, as she had feared she would be (504-

---

[127] As we will see, neither her words nor her supplication on stage (603-615) will convince Hippolytus, but the oath that she made him take previously will. She certainly convinced him with her words to take that crucial oath, and it is possible that she also touched his robe to make her plea stronger; see below.

[128] The drug *pharmakon* (φάρμακον) is another source of ambiguity. Is it an aphrodisiac for Hippolytus or a drug to help Phaedra cure her disease? The wording of her question probably suggests that Phaedra thinks it is for her. Cf. Kovacs 1987.53 and n63.

[129] Notice also the imperative in 517.

[130] Cf. Kreon's fear in *Medea* 282-285. As Knox 1977.222 suggests, Kreon is afraid of Medea's cleverness, her intellectual accomplishment in sophistry. I suggest that it is the same fear that Phaedra expresses here concerning the Nurse's cleverness.

160 Chapter 3

506), she follows the Nurse's advice of 517 and does not investigate her suspicion any further, although she has difficulty understanding clearly what exactly the Nurse plans to do.[131]

By expressing her fear that the Nurse is too clever for her (518), Phaedra accepts the superiority of the Nurse in this contest of words and arguments, in this *agôn*. At the same time, by expressing her fear that she would be overcome by the Nurse's skill (504-506), in the performative aspect of a dramatized poetic competition, she is afraid that she will prove inferior and lose in this quasi-poetic contest. The Nurse, on the other hand, certain of her superiority, will give Phaedra no chances. With uncontested *sophia* and unrestrained authority, after depriving Phaedra even of the desire for further questions (517), she will now undertake action according to her own plans without waiting for Phaedra's approval; she only needs Aphrodite as her accomplice. As for the rest, she will tell friends within, she says vaguely.[132] With these words, as she leaves the stage, the Nurse literally has the last word, and the *agôn* is over:[133]

ἔασον, ὦ παῖ· ταῦτ' ἐγὼ θήσω καλῶς.
μόνον σύ μοι, δέσποινα ποτνία Κύπρι,
συνεργὸς εἴης· τἄλλα δ' οἷ' ἐγὼ φρονῶ
τοῖς ἔνδον ἥμιν ἀρκέσει λέξαι φίλοις.

Hippolytus 521-524

---

[131] For the different interpretations as to what Phaedra imagines of the Nurse's plans see Halleran 1995.193: Winnington-Ingram maintains that Phaedra knows what the Nurse plans to do; Wilamowitz, that she has some suspicion; Barrett, that she believes the Nurse's assurance. Halleran concludes that what exactly Phaedra knows or does not know is uncertain; like the spectators, she wonders what the Nurse will do; she makes clear that she does not want the Nurse to tell Hippolytus, but she lets the Nurse go on with her plan.

[132] She is vague again. Who are her friends within? Is it a real plural (the other servants whom she called *philai* 'friends' in 199) or is she speaking in general, implying Hippolytus, as the audience would suspect? Phaedra should also suspect what friend the Nurse means since she herself has already mentioned Hippolytus as a friend in 319. Hippolytus is the only 'friend within' since her husband, Theseus, who is also a friend, is far away; as for the chorus women who are also her friends, they are outside, and the other servants are unimportant in the play. As she speaks these last ambiguous words, the Nurse has started for the door into the house, while briefly stopping at Aphrodite's statue, whom she addresses in her crucial prayer, giving Phaedra no chance to respond. For a different interpretation see Bain 1977.22-29.

[133] Cf. Theseus' final speech and exit (1088-1089) in his formal *agôn* with Hippolytus; cf. especially the Nurse's decisive words in 521 (ταῦτ' ἐγὼ θήσω καλῶς) with Theseus' words in 1088 (δράσω τάδε).

Leave it (to me), child. <u>I will arrange these things well</u>.
Only may you, revered lady Kypris,
be my <u>accomplice [*sunergos*]</u>. As to the rest I have in mind,
it will suffice for me to tell to <u>friends [*philois*]</u> within.

The Nurse's speech echoes Sappho's poetry; in particular, fr. 1 27-28 where Sappho, in her prayer to Aphrodite, calls upon the goddess to be her ally:

σὺ δ' αὐτα
<u>σύμμαχος</u> ἔσσο

Sappho fr.1 27-28

and you yourself
be my <u>ally [*summakhos*]</u>.

The Nurse here also recalls Sappho (fr. 160), about to sing to delight her companions, her *hetairai* (ἑταῖραι), like the Nurse, about to present her plan to her *philoi* 'friends':

τάδε νῦν <u>ἑταίραις</u>
ταὶς ἔμαις τέρπνα κάλως ἀείσω.

Sappho fr.160

now for my <u>companions [*hetairai*]</u>
delightfully I will sing these pleasant songs.

At this point, the authority of the Nurse reaches its climax, as she calls upon Aphrodite as her ally, like Sappho in fr. 1 27-28. As the Nurse had said before, referring to Phaedra's delirium, Phaedra's incomprehensible words required a *mantis* (236). By putting into words Phaedra's love for Hippolytus (345 and 350-351), the Nurse now becomes the *mantis*. Moreover, she is the *sophos* (cf. 252, 266, and 519) who will transmit her *sophia* to her *philoi* (524).[134] On the other hand, Phaedra is completely defeated; her worst fear—that the Nurse would speak to Hippolytus—is now going to be realized, and she will do nothing to prevent it. The Nurse's skill in persuasion has proved superior. The power of her speech has won her unrestricted authority for action.

---

[134] On the use of the words *mantis*, *sophos*, and the transmission of *sophia* in the conventional language of poetry see Nagy 1989.23-48; Hesiod (*Theogony* 22-35) presents himself as *mantis*, and Theognis (367-370) as *sophos*. See also below, n186.

5. The Nurse as the Advocate of Action

As we are waiting to see what the Nurse will do, how she will exercise her authority and her prerogative of action, the chorus, in the next stasimon, sings of the power of love (525-564), thus testifying to the victory of the Nurse in this contest with Phaedra.[135] With the persuasion of her speech she defeated Phaedra's resistance, as Phaedra was already afraid she would (503-506). The ode of the chorus is interrupted by Phaedra's plea for silence.[136]

"Quiet women, we are lost" (565), she pleads in despair; and when the chorus wonders whether there is something wrong in the house (566), she asks for their silence again, for she wants to listen to the discussion inside (567).[137] As the chorus observes that Hippolytus' shouting is a bad prelude and grants her their silence (568), Phaedra bursts into lamentation. The chorus, or, more precisely, the chorus leader, addresses her as *gunê* 'woman' (γύναι) and encourages her to explain her fear (571-573).[138]

Phaedra invites the chorus to come close to the doors and listen, but they refuse and urge that she should listen and tell them (577-580).[139] Phaedra hears Hippolytus' voice. For the first time, she dares to speak Hippolytus' name. Now that her secret is revealed to him, she has no reason to fear speaking his name. Hippolytus is shouting, saying dreadful things to her maid (581-582), she tells the chorus, who admit that Phaedra is betrayed, her secrets are revealed, she is destroyed.[140] The chorus sympathizes with Phaedra, calling her *phila*

---

[135] For a thoughtful interpretation of this ode and its significance for the play's discourse on marriage, see Halleran 1991.109-121.

[136] With Phaedra's plea for silence, the second episode starts: it consists of three parts. In the first, Phaedra overhears the Nurse's revelation to Hippolytus (565-600); in the second, Hippolytus curses Phaedra and her Nurse and the whole of womankind (601-668); in the third, Phaedra denounces the Nurse and announces to the chorus her final plans (669-731).

[137] As Kovacs 1987.53 remarks, there is no need to think of Phaedra as eavesdropping. Being closer to the palace door she can hear better than the chorus; she only wants to listen more attentively.

[138] Cf. the Nurse's address to the chorus in 301; in contrast, the Nurse's address to Phaedra is 'child'.

[139] Stage conventions do not allow the chorus to leave the orchestra. The response of the chorus heightens the suspense and the impatience of the audience to hear the news along with the women.

[140] Revelation of Phaedra's secret means betrayal and destruction: what was to be concealed has now been revealed.

'friend' this time (591), instead of the previous address *gunê* 'woman' (572).

Phaedra laments in despair, and the chorus repeats that she has been betrayed by her friends (*prodotos ek philôn*, 595). Phaedra blames her Nurse for revealing her secrets, although in good intention, she admits, trying to cure her disease (596-597). She recognizes that the Nurse acted as a friend, although without success (*philôs, kalôs d'ou*, 597).[141]

Now that the Nurse's attempt has failed, the chorus—or, more precisely, the chorus leader—assumes the Nurse's advisory role and encourages Phaedra to act: "How then? What 'will you do' (*draseis*) having suffered plights that take 'no remedy' (*amêkhana*)—literally 'no devices'?" (πῶς οὖν; τί δράσεις, ὦ παθοῦσ' ἀμήχανα; 598).[142] Since the course of action of the Nurse has failed, Phaedra now has to undertake her own course of action. She does not hesitate to say that she has only one choice: to die as soon as possible (599-600). She already announced that she was resolved to die in her long speech (401-402); now she will expedite it.

At this point, Hippolytus and the Nurse enter the stage. Hippolytus is rushing into the daylight, shocked at the unspeakable words he heard from the Nurse. Now the Nurse, so far the advocate of speech for Phaedra, beseeches Hippolytus to be silent (603). At his refusal (604), she attempts supplication; first she touches his right hand (605), then his knees (607). Then she appeals to the confidentiality of the matter (609). At his ironic refusal (610), she appeals to the oath he took (611), thus revealing that before exposing Phaedra's love, she had asked him to swear an oath that he would keep his silence. At Hippolytus' response that his tongue has sworn but not his mind (612), she appeals to his love for his 'friends', implying Phaedra (613).[143] Finally, at Hippolytus' disgust and strong rejection of Phaedra as a friend ("Pah, no villain is my friend," 614), she urges him to show forgiveness, and she finishes her speech with a maxim: "It is natural for human beings to err" (615):

---

[141] Cf. the Nurse's self-defense later, in 698-701.

[142] The paradox of *draseis/amêkhana* (δράσεις/ἀμήχανα) indicates the dead end of Phaedra's situation. Cf. the Nurse's suggestion of using *mêkhanas* (μηχανάς) 'female devices' in 481. The chorus believes that there are no devices for Phaedra's plight.

[143] For an extensive treatment of this line (612), see Avery 1968.19-35. *Philoi* here (613) refers rather to 'those near' than to 'those dear'; in this case, to Phaedra as a member of his family.

164   Chapter 3

ΙΠΠ   ὦ γαῖα μῆτερ ἡλίου τ' ἀναπτυχαί,
       οἵων λόγων ἄρρητον εἰσήκουσ' ὄπα.
ΤΡΟΦ   σίγησον, ὦ παῖ, πρίν τιν' αἰσθέσθαι βοῆς.
ΙΠΠ   οὐκ ἔστ' ἀκούσας δείν' ὅπως σιγήσομαι.
ΤΡΟΦ   ναί, πρός σε τῆς σῆς δεξιᾶς εὐωλένου.
ΙΠΠ   οὐ μὴ προσοίσεις χεῖρα μηδ' ἅψῃ πέπλων;
ΤΡΟΦ   ὦ πρός σε γονάτων, μηδαμῶς μ' ἐξεργάσῃ.
ΙΠΠ   τί δ', εἴπερ ὡς φῂς μηδὲν εἴρηκας κακόν;
ΤΡΟΦ   ὁ μῦθος, ὦ παῖ, κοινὸς οὐδαμῶς ὅδε.
ΙΠΠ   τά τοι κάλ' ἐν πολλοῖσι κάλλιον λέγειν.
ΤΡΟΦ   ὦ τέκνον, ὅρκους μηδαμῶς ἀτιμάσῃς.
ΙΠΠ   ἡ γλῶσσ' ὀμώμοχ', ἡ δὲ φρὴν ἀνώμοτος.
ΤΡΟΦ   ὦ παῖ, τί δράσεις; σοὺς φίλους διεργάσῃ;
ΙΠΠ   ἀπέπτυσ'· οὐδεὶς ἄδικός ἐστί μοι φίλος.
ΤΡΟΦ   σύγγνωθ'· ἁμαρτεῖν εἰκὸς ἀνθρώπους, τέκνον.

                                        Hippolytus 601-615

HIPP   O mother earth, and unveilings of the sun!
        What an <u>unspeakable word</u> <u>I heard</u>![144]
NURSE   <u>Silence, son,</u> before somebody <u>hears</u> you <u>shouting</u>.
HIPP   There is no way <u>having heard</u> terrible things, that
        <u>I will be silent</u>.[145]
NURSE   I beg you, by your fair right hand.
HIPP   Do not come near my hand! Do not touch my cloak!
NURSE   O by your knees, <u>by no means</u> destroy me.
HIPP   Why, if as you say you have not said anything bad?
NURSE   This story, <u>son</u>, should <u>by no means</u> become public.
HIPP   But good things are better to be spoken in public.
NURSE   <u>My boy</u>, <u>by no means</u> dishonor your oaths.[146]
HIPP   My tongue has sworn, but my mind is unsworn.
NURSE   <u>Son, what will you do?</u> Will you destroy your <u>friends</u>?
HIPP   Pah! No villain is my <u>friend</u>.
NURSE   Show forgiveness; it is natural for men to err, <u>my boy.</u>

---

[144] Note the paradox: 'words'/'unspeakable' (λόγων/ἄρρητον).

[145] Note that Phaedra wanted to keep her shameful secret in silence but eventually it was revealed. Hippolytus, in contrast, cannot keep a shameful secret in silence. He wants to bring it out, but eventually he will not. Also note here the chiastic construction: silence...hears—having heard...I will be quiet (σίγησον... αἰσθέσθαι–ἀκούσας... σιγήσομαι, 603-604), which emphasizes even more the paradox of silence and revelation.

[146] The Nurse's effort to persuade Hippolytus to keep his silence is underscored by the use of the emphatic negative adverb 'by no means', in its two different forms μηδαμῶς/οὐδαμῶς, in three successive lines (607, 609, 611).

We see how the Nurse, after failing to gain Hippolytus for Phaedra's cause, uses all her means. Since her arguments (which we did not hear) failed, now she is using her old age to move Hippolytus. Starting with a polite request (σίγησον),[147] she calls him in a maternal tone *pai* 'my son' (603). Seeing that this has failed, she uses supplication, touching first his right hand (605), then his robe (606), and finally his knees (607).[148]

The fact that the Nurse—after her persuasive power of speech has failed—is actually touching Hippolytus' robe in supplication suggests that her enigmatic words in 514-515, in their purposefully ambiguous message, alluded to her plan to obtain his favor through both speech and supplication. The Nurse, of course, meant to use speech and supplication 'within' the house, as she announced in 524, but since Hippolytus rushed out in disgust, she is continuing her effort outside. Moreover, in order to secure his oath, she certainly used the persuasion of her speech and maybe, already, even supplication.

However, her supplication does not move Hippolytus to keep silent—in contrast to Phaedra, who yielded at her supplication and broke her silence (cf. 335). There is a reason for this: Hippolytus, a man, is more prompt to speak; keeping silence is against the norm for men. Still, further on, with her double question of disapproval, "What will you do? Will you destroy your friends?" (τί δράσεις; σοὺς φίλους διεργάσει; 613), she tries to dissuade him also from action— just as in a reverse way, she had tried to persuade Phaedra into action. Again, Hippolytus, as a man, is more prompt to action; abstinence from action would be against the norm.[149] The Nurse is trying with her speech to reverse these norms. An exception to the norm herself (by being the advocate of both speech and action), she is so successful with her speech that she manages to reverse the norm with Phaedra—i.e., to make her break her silence and speak.

---

[147] Aorist imperative expresses a polite request.

[148] The Nurse, in this dialogue, keeps addressing Hippolytus *pai* (παῖ) and *teknon* (τέκνον), 'son' and 'boy', alternately (παῖ in 603, 609, 613; τέκνον in 611, 615): she is using a motherly tone, trying to use indirectly, for her purpose, the authority that her old age gives her. In the only two lines she is not using this address (605, 607), she attempts the force of supplication.

[149] This is a crucial point of the play. Hippolytus is destroyed every time he acts against the norm. He has already fatally acted against the norm of Aphrodite's laws. Now, despite his strong protests, in order to honor his oath, he will have to eventually act against the norm of speech and action and do nothing but keep silent.

Momentarily, she seems to have failed with Hippolytus.[150] However, in the long run, she proves successful with him too, as he does not reveal the truth to his father, respecting the oath she had convinced him to take before she revealed Phaedra's love to him (see his words later, at 665-668).

Hippolytus is disgusted and enraged at this outrage and reveals his contempt and disgust for the whole female sex in his long tirade (616-667). After his general denunciation of the whole of womankind, culminating in the idea that life would be better if there were no female sex and men could get their children from the gods (616-639), he narrows down his attack, focusing indirectly on Phaedra's mischief. He hates a clever woman (*sophên de misô*, 640);[151] in particular, he hates a clever woman for her mischief in Aphrodite's realm. An *amêkhanos gunê* 'un-resourceful woman' is safer (643-644).[152] He also hates women's handmaids as go-betweens. Women should only interact with speechless beasts. No maid ought to be allowed to come near women. Beasts that can bite but cannot talk should dwell with them so that they can neither address one nor receive speech in return (645-648).[153] But as things are, he concludes,

---

[150] Hippolytus' refusal to keep silent is crucial to the further development of the plot: Phaedra, who has been present in this episode—for the first and last time in this play, together with Hippolytus—believes that her secret will be further betrayed, especially to Theseus, and is therefore prompted to commit suicide without further delay. The Nurse's attempt at persuasion in the next confrontation with Phaedra (695-709) will be totally ineffective. There is also another possibility, suggested by Smith 1960.162-178 and Østerud 1970.307-320 and supported by Kovacs 1987.54: Phaedra exits after the announcement of her decision to die as soon as possible, at 599, and re-enters the stage just before 680. This interpretation has been rejected by Taplin 1978. 191n7 and largely ignored by critics; it may be an answer to many questions (as Kovacs argues), but it deprives the scene of its dramatic tension.

[151] We cannot but think of the Nurse's references to cleverness (cf. 266, 436, 465), and especially Phaedra's fear lest she, the Nurse, prove too *sophê* 'clever' (δέδοιχ' ὅπως μοι μὴ λίαν φανῇς σοφή, 518). Cf. also *Medea* 282-285. In addition, cf. Eurykleia's epithets referring to her cleverness (see Table II for the summary of Eurykleia's epithets).

[152] Compared to the Nurse's statement in 481 that being women, they will find *mêkhanas* 'ways/resourses/devices' (γυναῖκες μηχανὰς εὑρήσομεν), this sounds like an oxymoron.

[153] This passage (640-650) represents the worst of male fear of female intellect and speech. See the emphasis on speech vocabulary (ἄφθογγα, 646, προσφωνεῖν, 647, φθέγμα, 648.)

The Nurse in Euripides' Hippolytus   167

"the wicked women sit inside and make wicked plans, and their servants bring them outside (649-650)."[154]

Hippolytus in 649-650 refers directly to Phaedra and her Nurse. He accurately blames female cleverness for this outrage but fails to see who the clever woman really is. He regards Phaedra as the instigator and the Nurse as her accomplice and go-between, and he fails to see that the clever woman he says he hates (640) is, in fact, the Nurse and not Phaedra. Now he angrily addresses the Nurse directly, telling her that she came to traffic in the sanctity of his father's marriage bed (651-652). Even to hear such things makes him feel unclean (655).[155] Despite his previous threats, however, that he would reveal everything, he promises now not to tell his father out of reverence to his oath, and to leave until his father returns. This is the oath to which the Nurse was referring in 611, the oath that she asked him to take before she revealed anything:

εὖ δ' ἴσθι, τοὐμόν σ' εὐσεβὲς σῴζει, γύναι·
εἰ μὴ γὰρ ὅρκοις θεῶν ἄφρακτος ᾑρέθην,
οὐκ ἄν ποτ' ἔσχον μὴ οὐ τάδ' ἐξειπεῖν πατρί.
νῦν δ' ἐκ δόμων μέν, ἔστ' ἂν ἔκδημος χθονὸς
Θησεύς, ἄπειμι· σῖγα δ' ἕξομεν στόμα.

Hippolytus 656-660

Put this well in your mind, my piety [*eusebes*] saves you, woman;
for, if I were not caught bound with oaths [*horkois*] by the gods,
I would not refrain from telling these things to my father.
Now I am going out of this house until Theseus returns
from his travel abroad; and I will keep my mouth silent [*siga*].

Then, for the first time, he refers to Phaedra more directly and threatens her along with the Nurse: "but I shall watch, when I come along with my father, how you will look at him, you and that mistress of yours" (661-662).[156] And as he leaves the stage, he finishes his vehement speech, cursing all women (664-668). Somebody should teach women *sôphrosunê*: "now, either let someone teach them to be chaste (*sôphronein*), or let me trample on them forever" (... ἢ νῦν τις

---

[154] Notice the contrast: 'inside', 'outside' (ἔνδον, ἔξω), although the text in 649 is corrupt. Younger women stay inside and only older women can go freely outside the house. Among others see Pomeroy 1975.79-80.

[155] Cf. also 601-602.

[156] He accused her of such thoughts already indirectly in 650 above. Still, the effect of these words on Phaedra, the only words he addresses to her, must have been devastating.

168 *Chapter 3*

αὐτὰς σωφρονεῖν διδαξάτω, / ἢ κἄμ' ἐάτω ταῖσδ' ἐπεμβαίνειν ἀεί, 667-668).[157]

As he leaves the stage, his words are still echoing in the ears of Phaedra, who all this time must have been cowering on the stage and who will soon have the chance to respond appropriately. As we will see later (729-731), she will never forget his tirade, especially his last words.

6. Phaedra in Charge of Speech and Action

Phaedra is devastated by Hippolytus' speech, as her monody in 669-679 seveals.[158] She can find no way out: "what craft, what words do we have, now that we have failed, to loosen the noose of words" (τίν' αὖ νῦν τέχναν ἔχομεν ἢ λόγους / σφαλεῖσαι κάθαμμα λύειν

---

[157] After his last sentence, as he is about to go away, he pauses to deliver another malediction (664-668). Barrett seems to agree, with Valckenaer, that these lines are interpolated but does not bracket them (see Barrett 1964.286-287). They are, however, thematically and rhetorically necessary as they provide a balanced ending to his speech corresponding to his opening statement (616-617), also a curse on women.

[158] Barrett 1964.287, like most editors, considers the whole passage (669-679) to be spoken by Phaedra. He sees the manuscript assignment of 669-671 to the chorus as an error stemming from the plural σφαλεῖσαι 'we failed' that, he suggests, refers to Phaedra and not Phaedra and the Nurse. He also sees 669 as a lament of Phaedra, not merely for her own, but for the tragedy of her whole sex exemplified in her own tragedy. Kovacs 1987.58 and 134 supports the possibility that the speaker of these lines is neither the chorus nor Phaedra, but the Nurse. The main reason for this interpretation is, according to Kovacs, the meaning of the words in 670-671. It was the devices and the words of the Nurse that failed, and therefore, she should be the logical speaker. The main objection to this reading is that a person of the Nurse's social status is rarely given a singing part in tragedy. Still, Kovacs suggests, since the Nurse is an important character in the play, it is possible that she was given a singing part in this monody. Although the Nurse may be seen as a suitable speaker for these lines, nevertheless, Phaedra is much more suitable, assuming that she never left the stage (see also n150 above). She is the most affected by the failure of the words and the devices of the Nurse and the most suitable to lament their failure. In any event, these words either by Phaedra or by the chorus, or even by the Nurse, as Kovacs has suggested, are a direct response to Hippolytus' curse upon the whole of womankind, and they certainly refer to Phaedra and the Nurse. As I noted above, I agree with the assignment of the monody to Phaedra, who, I suggest, not only did not leave the stage, but also heard the last words of the Nurse in 251-254 as Phaedra's words in 670-677 reveal, especially the intentional repetition of the word *sunergos*, which the Nurse used in her appeal for help to Aphrodite in 523.

λόγου... 670-671).[159] Phaedra, nevertheless, accepts her punishment (ἐτύχομεν δίκας, 672). She wants to hide her misfortune again: "oh earth, oh sunlight! What way have I to escape my plight?" (672-673).[160] Now that the Nurse's scheme has failed, she turns to the chorus for help and calls them *philai* 'friends': "how can I conceal my calamity, my friends?" (πῶς δὲ πῆμα κρύψω, φίλαι, 672-674), she asks the chorus. She wonders which god could come *arôgos* 'to her aid', or which mortal could stand *paredros* 'at her side' and be *xunergos* 'accomplice' of unjust deeds (τίς ἂν θεῶν ἀρωγὸς ἢ τίς ἂν βροτῶν / πάρεδρος ἢ ξυνεργὸς ἀδίκων ἔργων / φανείη... 675-677).[161]

The chorus realistically tells her that whatever is done is done, and the *tekhnai* 'devices' of her maid cannot be straightened; they have failed (679-680).[162] At the remark of the chorus, which verifies that the scheme of the Nurse is over and has not succeeded, Phaedra's lament gives way to anger against her Nurse. She turns on her and damns her cruelly and mercilessly for her betrayal (682-694): "vile, destroyer of your friends, (look) how you have ruined me... Did I not tell you to keep quiet... but you could not forbear. We will no more die *eukleeis* 'with a good name' (684). Now I am in need of *kainôn logôn* 'new plans' (ἀλλὰ δεῖ με δὴ καινῶν λόγων, 686)... I curse you and everyone who is eager to offer evil service to his unwilling friends" (693-694).

Phaedra is now convinced that Hippolytus will betray her secret and thus her good name and reputation will be lost.[163] She has to

---

[159] These are direct references to the Nurse's *mêkhanai* 'devices' at 481, which just failed. Cf. also the remark of the chorus in 680 on the failure of the Nurse's *tekhnai* 'devices', which is a response to and a verification of Phaedra's words in 670. This passage inspired Goff to title her book *The Noose of Words* (Goff 1990). The same passage, with the image of binding and unbinding, knots and unraveling, has been the subject of an extensive discussion in Zeitlin 1985.58ff.

[160] Cf. Hippolytus reaction of shame in 601-602.

[161] With the succession of the similar words *arôgos, paredros, xunergos* (ἀρωγός, πάρεδρος, ξυνεργός), the audience can only think of Aphrodite and the Nurse as her aids, especially since the Nurse appealed to Aphrodite as her *sunergos* (523) and all this was Aphrodite's will.

[162] This is a direct response to Phaedra's lament in 670-671. See also n159 above.

[163] Phaedra thinks that Hippolytus will blame her before his father for the Nurse's mistake, and the scandal will be spread (689-692). If we accept that Phaedra never left the stage during Hippolytus' tirade, we must assume that she was too upset to pay attention to his words about his oath or that, even if she heard, she could not risk entrusting her reputation to an angry Hippolytus, referring to his oath one moment and threatening the next that he could not keep silent.

170   Chapter 3

find a way to prevent it. She was resolved to die for her good name and fame from the very beginning of the play. Now that she thinks that the Nurse's intervention has destroyed this, she must find a solution. She must think of a new plan (684) not to avoid death, but to die with a good reputation, as she was initially resolved. The Nurse, however, despite Phaedra's vehement denunciation, will not give up. She is ready to make up for her failed effort. She answers Phaedra's rejection with a formal apology.

For the second time, the Nurse calls Phaedra *despoina* 'mistress', not *pai* or *teknon* 'child'.[164] This formal address marks a formal apology with rhetorical and sophistic skill. She admits her failure, but still she faces Phaedra's rage with calmness. She first appeals to reason (695-697), then to her love for Phaedra (698), and then to reasoning again (699-701). She does not accept her defeat. She is unwilling even now to admit that she is to blame; she did her best, but things went wrong. If she had succeeded, she would be appreciated for her wits now:

> δέσποιν', ἔχεις μὲν τἀμὰ μέμψασθαι κακά·
> τὸ γὰρ δάκνον σου τὴν διάγνωσιν κρατεῖ·
> ἔχω δὲ κἀγὼ πρὸς τάδ', εἰ δέξει, λέγειν.
> ἔθρεψά σ' εὔνους τ' εἰμί· τῆς νόσου δέ σοι
> ζητοῦσα <u>φάρμαχ</u>' ηὗρον οὐχ ἀβουλόμην.
> εἰ δ' εὖ γ' ἔπραξα, κάρτ' ἂν <u>ἐν σοφοῖσιν</u> ἦ·
> πρὸς τὰς τύχας γὰρ τὰς φρένας κεκτήμεθα.
>
> *Hippolytus* 695-701
>
> Mistress, you may indeed blame my ill-doings,
> for the sting of your hurt takes hold of your judgement;
> but I can answer your charge if you will allow me.
> <u>I nursed you [*ethrepsa*]</u> and I care for you. For your sickness,
> I sought <u>remedies [*pharmak(a)*]</u>, but I did not find what I wanted.
> If I had, I would be now <u>among the clever [*en sophoisi*]</u>, no doubt.
> According to successes, our wits are measured.

The last words of the Nurse express her bitterness at Phaedra's rejection and lack of any appreciation for her efforts, even though unsuccessful. She emphasizes the fact that she brought her up, she is her nurse and therefore she acted out of her care for Phaedra. If her *pharmakon*—the fulfillment of Phaedra's love, which she did not achieve with her approach to Hippolytus—had worked, she would be among the *sophoi*. For the Nurse, intelligence, cleverness, expediency

---

[164] Cf. her formal address in 433, the beginning of the *agôn*.

are the qualifications required for one to be considered among the *sophoi* (700). These last words of the Nurse recapitulate the importance that expediency has for her.

Phaedra protests the Nurse's words and refutes her argument with a rhetorical question full of irony:

> ἦ γὰρ δίκαια ταῦτα κἀξαρκοῦντά μοι,
> τρώσασαν ἡμᾶς εἶτα συγχωρεῖν λόγοις;
>
> *Hippolytus* 702-703
>
> What—is this fair, is this good enough for me,
> to wound me and then to come to terms in words?

However, the Nurse does not give up. She makes one last effort to exercise her control over Phaedra. She, who was so concerned to make Phaedra speak, now expresses her disapproval of Phaedra's words. She plainly observes that they are talking too much, implying that this is no time for long arguments but for practical solutions. She admits that she was not *sôphrôn* 'wise', but, even as things are now, she is ready to offer a solution to save Phaedra. And as she regains her control, she calls her *teknon* 'child' again:

> μακρηγοροῦμεν· οὐκ ἐσωφρόνουν ἐγώ,
> ἀλλ' ἔστι κἀκ τῶνδ' ὥστε σωθῆναι, <u>τέκνον</u>.
>
> *Hippolytus* 704-705
>
> We talk too long; I was not wise then,
> but it is still possible to save yourself from this plight, <u>my child</u>.

Phaedra, however, does not trust her advice anymore; she does not even want her around anymore. She stops her abruptly and denies her the prerogative of speech, expressing openly her disapproval of both her advice and her actions, i.e., to tell Hippolytus her secret (706-707). She continues harshly, ordering her to go away and to mind her own business; at the same time, she announces that she will "manage her affairs well" (708-709). This is a direct answer to the Nurse's words in 521 when she asked Phaedra to leave it to her, as she would manage her affairs well. Ironically, Phaedra now is using the exact words that the Nurse used then:[165]

---

[165] Cf. 521 (ταῦτ' ἐγὼ θήσω καλῶς) and 709 (ἐγὼ δὲ τἀμὰ θήσομαι καλῶς). This intentional repetition provides further evidence that Phaedra heard the last words of the Nurse. At this point we may assume that the Nurse leaves the stage, and Phaedra, until the end of the episode, engages in a dialogue with the chorus.

172 Chapter 3

> παῦσαι λέγουσα· καὶ τὰ πρὶν γὰρ οὐ καλῶς
> παρῄνεσάς μοι κἀπεχείρησας κακά.
> ἀλλ' ἐκποδὼν ἄπελθε καὶ σαυτῆς πέρι
> φρόντιζ'· <u>ἐγὼ δὲ τἀμὰ θήσομαι καλῶς</u>.
>
> Hippolytus 706-709
>
> Stop talking; you did not give me good advice before
> and you also attempted evil deeds.
> Get out of here and mind your own
> business; <u>I will manage my affairs well</u>.

We have no way of knowing if the Nurse had any specific plan in mind or what it was.[166] We may assume, however, that just as the Nurse, with the same words, had turned her back to Phaedra and called upon Aphrodite as her accomplice, so now Phaedra turns her back to the Nurse and calls upon the chorus as her accomplice to keep silence:[167] "And you noble Troizenian children, this much grant to my supplication: cover with silence what you have heard here" (710-712).[168]

For the first time, Phaedra not only refuses to listen to the Nurse, but she deprives her completely of her prerogative of speech (706). To the Nurse's suggestion in 704-705, she fires back her resolve in 709. As she said already, she needs new plans (ἀλλὰ δεῖ με δὴ καινῶν λόγων, 688). Phaedra now regains total control. She is now in charge of both speech and action. Furthermore, by calling the Troizenian women 'children', Phaedra now assumes a leading role, taking charge of the chorus and for the first time seeing the chorus from a higher stance.

The chorus swears to Artemis that they will never bring to light Phaedra's plight (713-714). The goddess to whom they swear is very appropriately *semnê* Artemis, the goddess of virginity. Since the course of Aphrodite proved ruinous, the course of abstinence,

---

[166] Kovacs 1987.59 suggests that the Nurse might have some specific plan in mind since she was hoping that Hippolytus, under oath, would not reveal Phaedra's secret. Phaedra, however, has no reason to believe this. Therefore, she will not give the Nurse the chance to speak.

[167] The Nurse, however, is asking Aphrodite's active help as her *sunergos* 'accomplice' (523), in contrast to Phaedra, who can only secure the passive cooperation of the chorus' silence. Cf. Phaedra's words in 675-677.

[168] In Greek tragedy, no intrigue can take place without the complicity of the chorus; consequently it is a commonplace that a character should pledge them to secrecy. The chorus honors the pledge of silence. Cf. *Libation-Bearers* 555, *Medea* 259ff., Sophocles' *Electra* 468f. The chorus grants their silence, despite their disapproval, as in *Medea*.

advocated by Artemis, may prove better; so it is most suitable that they now call upon her. Phaedra approves of their response (καλῶς ἔλεξας, 715).

Having secured the silence of the chorus, Phaedra will now be able to put her plan into words. Her words, however, are not very clear. She has found, she says, a cure for her plight, so that she will provide a good name for her children (εὐκλεᾶ μὲν παισὶ προσθεῖναι βίον, 717) and will neither shame her Kretan family nor have to face Theseus (715-721).

The chorus members express their fear lest she commit suicide: " what irreversible ill are you going to do?" (722). Phaedra, without the least hesitation, spells it out clearly, 'to die'; and cutting short the chorus from questioning her decisions, she continues determined: "and how, I will decide myself" (θανεῖν· ὅπως δέ, τοῦτ' ἐγὼ βουλεύσομαι, 723). She needs no directions anymore. She will take care of her own affairs, she will die the way she chooses herself. She is completely in charge of her speech, of her plan of action, and of action. The chorus tries to advise her: "do not say such a thing" (724);[169] Phaedra, however, will take no more orders or advice from anybody, neither the Nurse nor the chorus. In her very last speech, she ironically rejects advice of the chorus and then announces how, along with her death, she will bring joy to Aphrodite on this very day; she will teach Hippolytus how to be *sôphrôn*:[170]

> καὶ σύ γ' εὖ με νουθέτει.
> ἐγὼ δὲ Κύπριν, ἥπερ ἐξόλλυσί με,
> ψυχῆς ἀπαλλαχθεῖσα τῆδ' ἐν ἡμέρᾳ
> τέρψω· πικροῦ δ' ἔρωτος ἡσσηθήσομαι.
> ἀτὰρ κακόν γε χἀτέρῳ γενήσομαι
> θανοῦσ', ἵν' εἰδῇ μὴ 'πὶ τοῖς ἐμοῖς κακοῖς
> ὑψηλὸς εἶναι· τῆς νόσου δὲ τῆσδέ μοι
> κοινῇ μετασχὼν σωφρονεῖν μαθήσεται.
>
> *Hippolytus* 725-731

You keep up with your good advice.

---

[169] Cf. their euphemism in 722.

[170] Echoing Aphrodite's words 'on this very day' (ἐν τῇδ' ἡμέρᾳ, 22), she now directs the action according to Aphrodite's plan. Ironically, Phaedra will really bring joy to Aphrodite since her lesson of *sôphrosunê* will completely destroy Hippolytus, as was the plan of the goddess.

174 *Chapter 3*

> But I shall make Kypris, who is destroying me,
> happy, abandoning my life <u>on this very day</u>.
> I will be defeated by a bitter love.
> But at least I will be a bane for the other too
> with my death, that he may learn to be arrogant
> at my misfortunes; having his share of this disease
> <u>he will learn how to be moderate [*sôphronein mathêsetai*]</u>.

Phaedra's last words echo the bitterness of Hippolytus' last words in his arrogant denunciation of Phaedra and the whole of womankind (666-667). Phaedra is going to teach Hippolytus a good lesson. It is not he who will teach women *sôphrosunê*, but she, a woman, who will teach him the reverse meaning of *sôphrosunê*.[171] The audience would at this point think that Phaedra is a true disciple of her Nurse in rhetorical skills, in employing cleverness and determination to reach her goal; in the end Phaedra also aims at expediency. Now, in the absence of the Nurse, independent from her, she applies what she learned from her.

Throughout the first Nurse/Phaedra episode, the Nurse was in charge of speech and action. She was directing the action according to the plans of Aphrodite, being at the same time, metaphorically speaking, the playwright, the director, and the actor. The revelation of Phaedra's love to Hippolytus, securing his silence, was her part of the scenario, which she directed and also acted out (playing the role of the messenger to Hippolytus). After that point, Phaedra takes over. Phaedra, who throughout the first part of the play was under the Nurse's influence and direction, gradually breaks her silence and regains the power of her speech, until finally she displaces the Nurse and takes over. By regaining complete authority of speech and action, displacing and replacing her older instructor, the Nurse, and by assuming a leading stance in front of the chorus, Phaedra now becomes the playwright, the director and the actor. At the beginning

---

[171]Barrett 1964.297 comments that when Hippolytus is so sure of his own *sôphrosunê* (80, 949f, 995, 1007, 1035, 1100, 1365) and of Phaedra's lack of it (667, 1034), Euripides may perhaps have intended a special point in Phaedra's words. Barrett doubts that the audience would have taken the point, but I believe they did before even watching the whole play. The idea of *sôphrosunê* in its different connotations is central to the play. Gill 1990.85-88 suggests that the three main figures—Phaedra, Hippolytus, and the Nurse—are closely interlocked in their articulation of *sôphrosune*. Phaedra, he suggests, "sees herself as a 'failed' version of Hippolytus as far as *sôphrosune* is concerned." But although this may have been true in the beginning of the play, I do not believe that she felt the same way at this point.

of the play, in the prologue, Aphrodite was the playwright and the director; as Aphrodite retired from the stage, the Nurse assumed, along with the role of the actor, both these roles which she exercised with exceptional skill, at the same time initiating her younger mistress, Phaedra. Therefore, when her *muthos*, her scenario, came to a dead end, Phaedra was already competent to undertake not only speech and action, but along with them, the roles of the playwright, the director, and the actor. The false letter she writes to Theseus, accusing Hippolytus is her contribution to the *muthos*. But she is not only the playwright; as she herself writes the letter, she directs and acts out her *muthos*; and finally, she brings it to its completion, thus bringing Aphrodite's plans to fulfillment.

Phaedra, indeed, leaves the stage to act out her plan, and, after a long chorus interval (732-775), we hear the Nurse (or a handmaid, a *therapaina*) calling for help and announcing Phaedra's suicide (776 ff.).[172] Until the last moment, the Nurse is giving directions and making judgements. Her last words, "stretch and straighten up the miserable corpse" (786), are followed by an accurate judgement: "a bitter housekeeping this is for my master" (787).[173] And, indeed, the comments of the chorus that follow reveal that her instructions are followed again and Phaedra's body is already laid out (789).

At first sight, it looks as if, although her aim was to save Phaedra, the Nurse ends up destroying her; Phaedra, however, was resolved to die before the intervention of the Nurse. This was, after all, Aphrodite's will, and the Nurse only precipitates it. Besides, she openly declared herself Aphrodite's advocate and *sunergos* 'ally' (623); therefore, although she is not successful in what she wants to do (save Phaedra), she is quite successful as Aphrodite's agent and ally. She precipitates Hippolytus' destruction, since Phaedra's deceptive letter is the result of the Nurse's approach to him. In fact, by securing Hippolytus' silence, the Nurse also succeeds in maintaining Phaedra's

---

[172] There is a confusion of various designations in the scholia and the *hupothesis*: *trophos* 'nurse' (τροφός), *therapaina* 'handmaid' (θεράπαινα), *exangelos* 'messenger' (ἐξάγγελος), and *angelos* 'messenger' (ἄγγελος). As Barrett 1964.312 notes, the last two are clearly false. Between the first two there is no real question since for the audience the speaker is simply a voice from the house, and a closer definition is neither necessary nor justifiable. But since convention calls for a designation, I prefer with Barrett *trophos*, as the lines are spoken by the actor who played the Nurse and the audience may perhaps have identified the voice. Moreover, I suggest that the tone of the voice, especially the imperatives "help...straighten up" (βοηδρομεῖτε . . . ὀρθώσατε), confirms this designation.

[173] This comment prepares the audience for the arrival of Theseus (790 ff.).

176 Chapter 3

eukleia 'good name'. This was Aphrodite's plan for Phaedra, as well as Phaedra's main consideration. In order to maintain her good name, Phaedra was resolved to die before the Nurse approached Hippolytus. Clearly, then, the intervention of the Nurse did not destroy Phaedra; it triggered and precipitated the action that led to Phaedra's destruction, which in turn triggered and precipitated along with it the destruction of Hippolytus, always according to the plan of Aphrodite.

7. Conclusions

The first consideration of the Nurse was to persuade Phaedra to break her silence and speak clearly. Even in the first part of the play, where the Nurse functions in the conventionally conservative way, advising Phaedra to be moderate, she urges her at the same time to speak clearly and reveal what she is trying to hide. Phaedra gradually proceeds from unclear utterances (212)[174] to inducements to the Nurse to say what she herself should, but could not, say (345);[175] and when the Nurse names Hippolytus (352),[176] Phaedra protests that she did not say anything, it was the Nurse's words (353).[177]

Clearly, it is the Nurse who has the active role, not only in the realm of speech, but also in the realm of action, as her first words indicate (177).[178] Later, she advises Phaedra that the deed is better than the name (501-502),[179] and as the advocate of action, she undertakes the responsibility for action and herself directs the action (cf. 521).[180]

The whole episode of the Nurse/Phaedra confrontation has the form of a rhetorical contest, an *agôn*, but also, as a performance, it has the form of a pseudo-rivalry between the older performer, the Nurse, and the younger performer, Phaedra. The chorus of the Troizenian women resembles the *khoros* of younger women in lyric poetry, in a

---

[174] τί θροεῖς; the Nurse asks Phaedra in 212.
[175] πῶς ἂν σύ μοι λέξειας ἁμὲ χρὴ λέγειν; (345)
[176] Ἱππόλυτον αὐδᾷς; (352)
[177] σοῦ τάδ', οὐκ ἐμοῦ κλύεις (353).
[178] τί σ' ἐγὼ δράσω; τί δὲ μὴ δράσω; (177)
[179] κρεῖσσον δὲ τοὔργον... ἢ τοὔνομ' (501-502).
[180] ἔασον, ὦ παῖ· ταῦτ' ἐγὼ θήσω καλῶς (521).

composition like the maiden song of Alcman (PMG 1). The Nurse in *Hippolytus* is presented on the performative level as a figure like Alcman's Hagesikhora, the most experienced choral personality and leader of the *khoros*; she is directing Phaedra, a younger leading personality like Agido; and the chorus of the Troizenian women act as the judges in their quasi-poetic contest, like the *khoros* of the Spartan girls.

After Phaedra indirectly reveals her secret (351-352), she soon resumes the power of speech and finally addresses the chorus, setting forth her plan of action—her decision to die—and its motivation (373-430). The chorus sadly approves her decision (431-432). The Nurse, in turn, gives her long speech, suggesting a different course of action (433-481). In this speech she transmits the will of Aphrodite using all her persuasion. The chorus again comments on this speech and its merits. They find the arguments of the Nurse *khrêsimôtera* (χρησιμώτερα) 'more expedient', but they offer their *ainos* (αἶνος) 'praise' to Phaedra (482-483). The chorus women judge the speeches of Phaedra and the Nurse as judges in a poetic contest, like the *khoros* in Alcman PMG 1 judging the skills of Agido and Hagesikhora.

As Phaedra becomes more and more reluctant to be persuaded, the Nurse, making full use of her authority, now insists that Phaedra be persuaded (508).[181] Phaedra feels her ground shaken and expresses the fear that the Nurse will prove too *sophê* for her, which in the language of poetic authority implies that she is afraid she will be considered an inferior poet/performer.[182]

Phaedra is afraid that she will prove inferior and lose in this quasi-poetic contest. The Nurse, on the contrary, certain of her superiority, will give Phaedra no chances. She will manage the matter well; she only needs Aphrodite's cooperation; as for the rest, it will suffice to share her thoughts with her 'friends' (521-524). At this point, the authority of the Nurse reaches its climax, as now she, as the accomplice of Aphrodite, will transmit her *sophia* to her *philoi*.

The Nurse assumes the role of the older wise poet, who has divine inspiration and cooperation. Resemblances in diction suggest that we may view her as a figure like Sappho who stepped out of the chorus circle into monody.[183] The Nurse calls upon Aphrodite to be her

---

[181] πιθοῦ μοι (508).
[182] δέδοιχ' ὅπως μοι μὴ λίαν φανῇς σοφή (519).
[183] See Nagy 1990a.370.

sunergos (συνεργός) in *Hippolytus* 523, like Sappho who calls upon Aphrodite to come to her and be her ally, her *summakhos* (σύμμαχος) (fr. 1. 27-28). The Nurse herself has proclaimed her *sophia* early in the play: after her statement on her authority in wisdom as a result of her old age (252) and her maxims of wisdom, she actually counted herself among the *sophoi*, the sages (263-266).

After the Nurse has proclaimed her wisdom, her authority in the realm of knowledge is accepted by the chorus women, as they address her in respect and praise, and, admitting their ignorance, wish to hear and learn from her. Thus they admit the superiority of the Nurse in the realm of knowledge (267-270). Later Phaedra, pressured by the Nurse, wants to speak but cannot, and she wishes that the Nurse could speak the words for her (345). The Nurse comments that she is not a prophet, a *mantis* (346).[184] Soon, however, she verbalizes both Phaedra's love (350) and its object—Hippolytus (351). With the help of Phaedra's clues, she now becomes the *mantis* that she said she was not (in 346 and in 236, earlier in the play, when, puzzled at Phaedra's delirium, she noticed that Phaedra's words needed a *mantis* to interpret).[185] Actually, at this point, the authority of the Nurse in the realm of knowledge reaches its zenith. She becomes the seer and the poet, especially after she has described love in Sappho's language. The Nurse, like Sappho, understands the paradox of love: when Phaedra asks what love is like, she answers by recalling the 'bitter-sweet' description of love by Sappho (fr. 130).

The language of poetic inspiration and authority is abundant throughout the Phaedra/Nurse episode. The idea of the poet as *mantis* (236, 346) and as *sophos* (266, 436, 465, 518) who shares his/her wisdom with *philoi* 'friends' (318, 419, and especially 524), the select ones who can understand and partake of this wisdom and who offer their *ainos* 'praise and approval' (483, 484), is central in this play.[186]

The resemblances observed in the conventions of hierarchy between the dramatized performance of the choral contest and the

---

[184] οὐ μάντις εἰμὶ τἀφανῆ γνῶναι σαφῶς (346).

[185] τάδε μαντείας ἄξια πολλῆς (236).

[186] The word σοφός (*sophos*) has a wide range of connotations (see *LSJ*), but in the conventional language of poetry it bears the connotation of poetic authority; cf. Theognis 367-370. See Nagy 1989.48. The words σοφός, μάντις, φίλος, αἶνος, αἰνῶ used as "marked" speech have a special connotation in poetry and refer, in particular, to poetic authority. On the poet as seer and the language of poetic authority see Nagy 1989.8-16 and 23-24.

dramatic *agôn* between Phaedra and the Nurse and the resemblances in diction suggest that the Nurse may be seen diachronically as the development of the persona of the lyric *khorêgos*. Phaedra's Nurse, her confidante and advisor, is a figure of uncontested authority, who has the power to give directions to her mistress, and even to direct, to a great extent, the action in the play. In this sense, she is like a stylized *khorêgos* in early choral performances, who, as Nagy has suggested, survives in Athenian drama both in an undifferentiated form as the chorus-leader and in a differentiated form, as one of the actors— protagonist, deuteragonist, or tritagonist. This interpretation provides a diachronic continuity of the authority of the Nurse figure in fifth century Athenian drama from choral models of hierarchy, first attested in the earliest fully developed predecessor, the epic character of Eurykleia in the *Odyssey*.

At the same time this interpretation may be synchronically significant as the occasion of the play suggests. In the prologue, Aphrodite plans the destruction of Hippolytus and directs the action. Accordingly, the Nurse, acting as the agent of Aphrodite, succeeds in directing Phaedra, who in turn directs the action according to the plan of the goddess. It is possible that the connection of women's lyric poetry with the poetry of Phaedra and her Nurse is not coincidental in a tragedy that takes place in Troizen, around Hippolytus, a figure whose cult is attested in Troizen. As Artemis announces at the end of the play, the memory of Hippolytus will not die, but he will be the subject of bridal maiden songs.[187] It is possible, I suggest, that there is a connection between such women's songs and the Nurse/Phaedra episodes. These episodes are potentially women's poetry about women's poetry, and, subsequently, *Hippolytus* may be seen as a play about women's poetry.

Like Goff, I see the self-referential qualities of the ending of the play: "the play ends with a rite that includes a reference specifically to song." I concur with Goff that "both the song's content and the fact that it is a song justifies the consideration of it as a self-conscious comment on the play."[188] Furthermore, as the play institutes bridal

---

[187] On the play's ending and the establishment of the cult in honor of Hippolytus (1423-1430), see Goff 1990.105-129. As Halleran 1991.120 notes, "Unmarried maidens will offer up to him locks of their hair before their wedding and remember him and Phaedra's passion in song....The maidens' song about Hippolytus and about Phaedra's passion will commemorate the sad events of the play, but here the destruction will be only mimetic, safely sung by the maidens as they pass to a new stage of their lives."

[188] Goff 1990.111-125.

songs and bridal rites in memory of Phaedra and Hippolytus, it provides a self-conscious comment on the model of the play in maiden songs performed by younger women led by leading personalities, such as Phaedra and her Nurse as presented in the play.

Bibliography

Adams, S. M. 1957. *Sophocles the Playwright*. Toronto.

Andrews, N. 1989. *The Poetics of the Argonautica of Apollonius of Rhodes: a Process of Reorientation the Libyan Maidens*. Ph.D. diss., Harvard.

Ardener, S., ed. 1978. *Defining Females: The Nature of Women in Society*. London.

Arend, W. 1933. *Die typischen Szenen bei Homer*. Berlin.

Arnott, P. 1959. *Introduction to the Greek Theater*. London.

———. 1962. *Greek Scenic Conventions of the Fifth Century*. Oxford.

———. 1971. *The Ancient Greek and Roman Theater*. New York.

Auerbach, E. 1953. *Mimesis: The Representation of Reality in Western Literature*. Trans. by W. R. Trask. Princeton.

Austin, J. L. 1962. *How to do Things with Words*. Oxford.

Austin, N. 1975. *Archery at the Dark of the Moon*. Berkeley.

Avery, H. C. 1968. "My Tongue Swore but my Mind is Unsworn," *TAPA* 99: 19-35.

Bain, D. 1977. *Asides and Related Conventions in Ancient Drama*. Oxford.

Barrett, W. S., ed. 1964. *Euripides: Hippolytos*. Oxford.

Batchelder, A. G. 1995. *The Seal of Orestes: Self-Reference and Authority in Sophocles' Electra*. Lanham, Md.

Bates, W. N. 1930. *Euripides: A Student of Human Nature*. Philadelphia.

Bergren, A. L. T. 1985. "Language and the Female in Early Greek Thought," *Arethusa* 16: 69-96.

Beringer, W. 1982. "'Servile Status' in the Sources for Early Greek History," *Historia* 31: 13-32.

Blaiklock, E. M. 1952. *The Male Characters of Euripides: A Study in Realism*. Wellington.

Block, E. 1985. "Clothing Makes the Man: A Pattern in the *Odyssey*," *TAPA* 115: 1-11.

Blundell, M. Whitlock. 1989. *Helping Friends and Harming Enemies*. Cambridge.

Bongie, E. B. 1977. "Heroic Elements in the 'Medea' of Euripides," *TAPA* 107: 27-56.

182 Bibliography

Bowra, C. M. 1934. "The Occasion of Alcman's Partheneion," *CQ* 28: 35-44.

——. 1944. *Sophoclean Tragedy*. Oxford.

——. 1961. *Greek Lyric Poetry: From Alcman to Simonides*. Oxford.

Brockmeyer, N. 1979. *Antike Sklaverei*. Erträge der Forschung 116. Darmstadt.

Büchner, W. 1931. "Die Niptra in der Odyssee," *Rheinisches Museum*, LXXX: 129-36.

Burian, P., ed. 1985. *Directions in Euripidean Criticism*. Durham, N.C.

Burkert, W. 1983. *Homo Necans: The Anthropology of Ancient Greek Sacrificial Ritual and Myth*. Originally published 1972, Berlin. Trans. by P. Bing. Berkeley.

——. 1985. *Greek Religion*. Originally published 1977, Stuttgart. Trans. by J. Raffan. Cambridge, Mass.

Burn, A. R. 1960. *The Lyric Age of Greece*. New York.

Burnett, A. P. 1971. *Catastrophe Survived: Euripides' Plays of Mixed Reversals*. Oxford.

——. 1973. "*Medea* and the Tragedy of Revenge," *CP* 68: 1-24.

Calame, C. 1977. *Les choeurs de jeunes filles en Grèce archaique I: Morphologie, fonction religieuse et sociale*. Rome = Calame 1997. *Choruses of Young Women in Ancient Greece: Their Morphology, Religious Role, and Social Functions*. Trans. by D. Collins and J. Orion. Lanham, Md.

Cameron, A. and A. Kuhrt, eds. 1983. *Images of Women in Antiquity*. London and Melbourne.

Campbell, D. A. 1970. *Greek Lyric Poetry*. London and New York.

Chantraine, P. 1968, 1970, 1975, 1977, 1978. *Dictionnaire étymologique de la langue* grecque. vols: I-IV. Paris.

——. 1933. *La formation des noms en grec ancien*. Paris.

Clark, G. 1989. *Women in the Ancient World*. Greece and Rome: New Surveys in the Classics No. 21.

Collard, C. 1975. "Formal Debates in Euripides' Drama," *Greece & Rome*, xxii: 58-71.

Conacher D. J. 1961. "A Problem in Euripides' *Hippolytus*," *TAPA* xcii: 37-44.

——. 1967. *Euripidean Drama: Myth, Theme and Structure*. Toronto.

——. 1987. *Aeschylus' Oresteia: A Literary Commentary*. Toronto.

Davies, M., ed. 1991. *Sophocles' Trachiniae*. Oxford.

Devereux, G. 1976. *Dreams in Greek Tragedy: an Ethno-Psychoanalytic Study*. Berkeley.

Dimock, G. E. 1989. *The Unity of the Odyssey*. Amherst.

Dodds, E. R. 1925. "The αἰδώς of Phaedra and the Meaning of the Hippolytus," CR 39: 102-4.

———. 1951. *The Greeks and the Irrational*. Berkeley.

———. 1960. "Morals and Politics in the Oresteia," *PCPS* n.s. 6: 19-31.

Duchemin, J. 1968. *L' AΓΩN dans la Tragédie grecque*. 2nd ed. Paris.

———. 1969. "Les origines populaires et paysannes de l'agon tragique," *Dioniso* xliii: 247-275.

Ducrot O., and T. Todorov. 1972. *Dictionnaire Encyclopédique des sciences du language*. Paris. = *Encyclopedic Dictionary of the Sciences of Languages*. Trans. by C. Porter. Baltimore, 1979.

Easterling, P. E. 1977. "Character in Sophocles," *G & R* 24: 122-3.

———., ed. 1982. *Sophocles 'Trachiniae'*. Cambridge.

Edmonds, S. E. 1976. *Homeric ΝΗΠΙΟΣ*. Ph.D. diss., Harvard.

Ehrenberg, V. 1954. *Sophocles and Pericles*. Oxford.

Entretiens sur l'antiquité classique. 1960. *Euripide*, Vol VI. Fondation Hardt, Geneva.

Erbse, H. 1966. "Euripides' 'Andromache'," *Hermes* 94: 276-97.

———. 1984. *Studien zum Prolog der euripideischen Tragödie*. Berlin.

Falkner, T. M. 1985. "Euripides and the Stagecraft of Old Age." In Hartigan 1985: 41-9.

Falkner, T. M. and J. de Luce. 1989. *Old Age in Greek and Latin Literature*. New York.

Farnell, L. R. 1896-1909. *The Cults of the Greek States*. Oxford.

Fenik, B. 1974. *Studies in the Odyssey*, Hermes Einzelschriften. xxx. Wiesbaden.

Fernández-Galiano, M., ed. 1992. *A Commentary on Homer's "Odyssey,"* bks. 21-22. 2nd ed. Oxford. Originally published 1984 in Italian under the title *Omero, Odissea, libri xxi-xxii: Introduzione, testo e commento*. Fondazione Lorenzo Valla, Rome. In Russo, J. A., M. Fernández-Galiano, and A. Heubeck, eds. 1992.

Fine, J. V. A. 1983. *The Ancient Greeks: A Critical History*. Cambridge, Mass.

Finley, J. H., Jr. 1978. *Homer's Odyssey*. Cambridge, Mass.

Finley, M. I. 1965, 2nd ed. 1978. *The World of Odysseus*. New York.

———. 1981. "The Elderly in Classical Antiquity," *G&R* 28: 156-71.

Flacelière, R. 1959. *La vie quotidienne en Grèce au siècle de Pericles*. Paris.

———. 1962. *L'amour en Grèce*. Paris.

Foley, H. P., ed. 1981. *Reflections of Women in Antiquity*. New York, London, Paris.

———. 1982. "The 'Female Intruder' Revisited," *CPh* 77: 1-21.

———. 1985. *Ritual Irony: Poetry and Sacrifice in Euripides*. Ithaca NY, London.

———., ed. 1994. *The Homeric Hymn to Demeter*. Princeton.

Fowler, B. H. 1978. "Lyric Structures in Three Plays of Euripides," *Dioniso* 49: 15-51.

Friedrich, W. 1953. *Euripides und Diphilos: zur Dramaturgie der Spätformen*. Zetemata 5. Munich.

Garland, Y. 1988. *Slavery in Ancient Greece*. Ithaca and London.

Garvie, A. F., ed. 1986. *Aeschylus: Choephori*. Oxford.

Gill, C. 1990. "The Articulation of the Self in Euripides' *Hippolytus*." In Powell 1990: 76-107.

Glenn, J. 1976. "The Fantasies of Phaedra: A Psychoanalytical Reading," *CW* 69: 435-42.

Goff, B. 1990. *The Noose of Words*. Cambridge.

Goldhill, S. D. 1984. *Language, Sexuality, Narrative: the Oresteia*. Cambridge.

———. 1986. *Reading Greek Tragedy*. Cambridge.

Gomme, A. W. 1925. "The Position of Women in Athens in the Fifth and Fourth Centuries B.C.," *CP* 20: 1-25.

Gould, J. P. 1973. "Hiketeia," *JHS* xciii: 74-103.

Greenwood, L. H. G. 1953. *Aspects of Euripidean Tragedy*. Cambridge.

Hadas, M. 1936. "Observations on Athenian Women," *CW* 29: 97-100.

Hadas M. and J. McLean. 1960. *Ten Plays by Euripides*. Toronto.

Hall, E. 1989. *Inventing the Barbarian: Greek Self-Definition through Tragedy*. Oxford.

Halleran, M. R. 1985. *Stagecraft in Euripides*. Totowa, New Jersey.

———. 1991. "*Gamos* and Destruction in Euripides' *Hippolytus*," *TAPA* 121: 109-121.

———., ed. 1995. *Euripides: Hippolytus*. Warminster.

Hamilton R. 1978. "Prologue, Prophecy and Plot in Four Plays of Euripides," *AJP* 99:277-302.

Hartigan, K., ed. 1985.*The Many Forms of Drama*. Lanham, Md.

Henderson, J. 1987. "Older Women in Attic Old Comedy," *TAPA* 117: 105-129.

Herfst, P. 1922. *Le travail de la femme dans la Grèce ancienne*. Utrecht.

Herington, J. 1985. *Poetry into Drama: Early Tragedy and the Greek Poetic Tradition.* Berkeley and Los Angeles.

Heubeck, A., ed. 1992. *A Commentary on Homer's "Odyssey,"* bks. 23-24. 2nd ed. Oxford. Originally published 1986 in Italian under the title *Omero, Odissea, libri ix-xii; xxiii-xxiv: Introduzione, testo e commento.* Fondazione Lorenzo Valla, Rome. In Russo, J. A., M. Fernández-Galiano, and A. Heubeck, eds. 1992.

Heubeck, A. and A. Hoekstra, eds. 1989. *A Commentary on Homer's "Odyssey."* Vol. 2, bks. 9-16. Oxford.

Heubeck, A., S. West, and J. B. Hainsworth, eds. 1988. *A Commentary on Homer's "Odyssey"* Vol. 1, bks. 1-8. Oxford.

Hirnoven, K. 1968. "Matriarchal Survivals and Certain Trends in Homer's Female Characters," *Annales Academiae Scientiarum Fennicae,* Ser. B 152. Helsinki.

Hirschon, R. 1978. "Open Body / Closed Space: the Transformation of Greek Sexuality." In Ardener 1978: 66-88.

Hoekstra, A., ed. 1989. *A Commentary on Homer's "Odyssey,"* bks. 13-16. 2nd ed. Oxford. Originally published 1984 in Italian under the title *Omero, Odissea, libri xiii-xvi: Introduzione, testo e commento.* Fondazione Lorenzo Valla, Rome. In Heubeck A. and A. Hoekstra, eds. 1989.

Jaeger, W. W. 1945. *Paedeia: The Ideals of Greek Culture.* Trans. by Gilbert Highet. New York.

Janni, P. 1964. "Agido e Agesichora," *RFIC* 92: 59-65.

Jones, A. H. M. 1957. *Athenian Democracy.* Oxford.

Jones, J. 1962. *On Aristotle and Greek Tragedy.* Oxford.

Kakridis, J. 1971. *Homer Revisited.* Publications of the New Society of Letters at Lund, 64: 68-75. Lund.

Kamerbeek, J. C., ed. 1970. *The Plays of Sophocles II: The Trachiniae.* Leiden.

Kennedy, G. A., ed. 1989. *The Cambridge History of Literary Criticism.* Vol. 1, Cambridge.

Kirkwood, G. 1941. "The Dramatic Unity of Sophocles' Trachiniae," *TAPA* 72: 203-211.

——. 1958. *A Study of Sophoclean Drama.* Ithaca.

Kitto, H. D. F. 1958. *Sophocles: Dramatist and Philosopher.* London.

——. 1961. *Greek Tragedy: A Literary Study.* 3d ed. London.

——. 1966. *Form and Meaning in Drama.* London.

Knox, B. M. W. 1952. "The Hippolytus of Euripides," *YCS* 13: 1-31.

——. 1977. "The *Medea* of Euripides," *YCS* 25: 193-225.

Knox, B. M. W. 1979. *Word and Action: Essays on the Ancient Theater*. Baltimore and London.

Kovacs, D. P. 1980. *The Andromache of Euripides: An Interpretation*. Chico.

—. 1980a. "Shame, Pleasure and Honor," *AJPh* 101: 287-303.

—. 1987. *The Heroic Muse*. Baltimore and London.

Lacey, W. K. 1968. *The Family in Classical Greece*. Ithaca.

Lattimore, R. 1958. *The Poetry of Greek Tragedy*. Baltimore.

—. 1964. *Story Patterns in Greek Tragedy*. Ann Arbor.

Lefkowitz, M. R. 1981. *Lives of the Greek Poets*. Baltimore.

Lefkowitz, M. R. and M. B. Fant. 1982. *Women's Life in Greece and Rome: A Source Book in Translation*. Baltimore.

Lesky, A. 1966. *A History of Greek Literature*. Trans. by J. Willis and C. deHeer. London.

—. 1968. *Die Griechische Tragödie*. 4th ed. Stuttgart.

—. 1983. *Greek Tragic Poetry*. Trans. M. Dillon. New Haven.

Lincoln, B. 1987. *Emerging from the Chrysalis: Studies in Rituals of Women's Initiation*. Cambridge, Mass.

Lloyd, M. 1992. *The Agon in Euripides*. Oxford.

Loraux N. 1979. "La gloire et la mort d'une femme," *Sorcières* 18: 51-7.

—. 1987. *Tragic Ways of Killing a Woman*. Cambridge, Mass., and London.

Lord, A. B. 1960. *The Singer of Tales*. Cambridge, Mass.

Luschnig, C. A. E. 1983. "The Value of Ignorance in the Hippolytus," *AJP* 104: 115-23.

—. 1988. *Time Holds the Mirror: a Study of Knowledge in Euripides' Hippolytus*. Leiden.

March, J. 1990. "Euripides the Misogynist?." In Powell 1990: 32-75.

Martin, R. P. 1989. *The Language of Heroes*. Ithaca.

Mastronarde, D. 1979. *Contact and Discontinuity: Some Conventions of Speech and Action on the Greek Tragic Stage*. Berkeley and Los Angeles.

McDermott, E. 1989. *Euripides' Medea: The Incarnation of Disorder*. London.

Mead, M. 1949, 1970. *Male and Female: A Study in the Sexes in a Changing World*. New York.

Merkelbach, R. 1957. "Sappho und ihr Kreis," *Philologus* 101: 1-29.

Michelini, A. N. 1987. *Euripides and the Tragic Tradition*. Madison, Wis.

—. 1989. "Neophron and Euripides' *Medeia* 1056-80," *TAPA* 119: 115-35.

Morrow, L. S. 1974. *Euripides' Treatment of Women*. Ph.D. diss., Ohio State Univ.

Murnaghan, S. 1985. "Penelope's Agnoia," *Helios*, New Series 13(2): 103-13.

———. 1987. *Disguise and Recognition in the Odyssey*. Princeton.

Murray, G. 1912. *The Medea of Euripides*. London.

———. 1940. *Aeschylus: The Creator of Tragedy*. Oxford.

Musurillo, H. 1966. "Euripides *Medea*: A Reconsideration," *AJP* 8: 52-7.

Nagy, G. 1974. *Comparative Studies in Greek and Indic Meter*. Cambridge.

———. 1979. *The Best of the Achaeans*. Baltimore.

———. 1983. "Sêma and Nóesis," *Arethusa* 16: 35-55.

———. 1989. "Early Greek Views on Poets and Poetry" *Cambridge History of Litterary Criticism*, ed. G. A. Kennedy, 1:1-77. Cambridge.

———. 1990a. *Pindar's Homer: The Lyric Possession of an Epic Past*. Baltimore.

———. 1990b. *Greek Mythology and Poetics*. Cornell.

———. 1992. "Homeric Questions," *TAPA*: 17-60.

Olson, S. D. 1992. "Servants' Suggestions in the *Odyssey*," *CJ* 87.3: 219-27.

Østerud, S. 1970. "Who sings the Monody 669-79 in Euripides' *Hippolytus*?," *GRBS* 11: 307-20.

Padel, R. 1983. "Women: Model for Possession by Greek Daemons." In Cameron and Kuhrt 1983: 3-19.

Page, D. L. 1938. *Euripides: Medea*. Oxford.

———. 1951a. *Alcman: The Partheneion*. Oxford.

———. 1951b. *Sappho and Alcaeus: An Introduction to the Study of Ancient Lesbian Poetry*. Oxford.

Parry, A., ed. 1971. *The Making of Homeric Verse: The collected Essays of Milman Parry*. Oxford.

Peradotto, J. 1990. *Man in the Middle Voice: Name and Narration in the Odyssey*. Princeton.

Peradotto, J. and J. P. Sullivan, eds. 1984. *Women in the Ancient World: The Arethusa Papers*. Albany, N.Y.

Pickard-Cambridge, A. 1962. *Dithyramb, Tragedy and Comedy*. Oxford.

———. 1968. *The Dramatic Festivals of Athens*. Oxford.

Podlecki, A. 1966. *The Political Background of Aeschylean Tragedy*. Ann Arbor.

Pomeroy, S. B. 1975. *Goddesses, Whores, Wives, and Slaves: Women in Classical Antiquity*. New York.

Powell A., ed. 1990. *Euripides, Women and Sexuality*. London.

Pucci, P. 1980. *The Violence of Pity in Euripides' Medea*. Ithaca and London.

———. 1987. *Odysseus Polutropos*. Ithaca.

Reckford, K. J. 1974. "Phaedra and Pasiphae: The Pull Backward," *TAPA* 104: 307-28.

Richter, D. C. 1971. "The Position of Women in Classical Athens," *CJ* 67: 1-8.

Riele, G. J. M. J. 1955. *Les Femmes chez Aeschyle*. Groningen.

Romilly, J. 1961. *L' évolution du pathétique d'Eschyle à Euripide*. Paris.

Rosenmeyer, T. 1982. *The Art of Aeschylus*. Berkeley.

Russo, J. A., ed. 1992. *A Commentary on Homer's "Odyssey,"* bks. 17-20. 2nd ed. Oxford. Originally published 1985 in Italian under the title *Omero, Odissea, libri xvii-xx: Introduzione, testo e commento*. Fondazione Lorenzo Valla, Rome. In Russo, J. A., M. Fernández-Galiano, and A. Heubeck, eds. 1992.

Russo, J. A., M. Fernández-Galiano, and A. Heubeck, eds. 1992. *A Commentary on Homer's "Odyssey."* Vol. 3, bks. 17-24. Oxford.

Schmid, W., Stählin, O. 1934, 1940. *Geschichte der Griechischen Literatur*. Munich.

Schwinge, E. R. 1962. *Die Stellung der Trachinierinen im Werk des Sophocles*. Göttingen.

———. 1968. *Die Verwendung der Stichomythie in den Dramen des Euripides*. Bibl. d. klass. Altertumswiss. n.s. 2, 24. Heidelberg.

Scodel, R. 1984. *Sophocles*. Boston.

Scott, J. A. 1921. *The Unity of Homer*. Berkeley.

Seale, D. 1982. *Vision and Stagecraft in Sophocles*. Chicago.

Searle, J. R. 1976. "A Classification of Illocutionary Acts," *Language in Society* 5: 1-23.

Segal, C. P. 1967. "Transition and Ritual in Odysseus's Return," *La Parola del' Passato*: 40: 331-342.

———. 1970. "Shame and Purity in Euripides' *Hippolytos*," *Hermes* 98: 278-99.

———. 1977. "Sophocles' *Trachiniae*: myth, poetry, and heroic values," *YCS* 25: 99-158.

———. 1981. *Tragedy and Civilization: An Interpretation of Sophocles*. Cambridge Mass.

———. 1986. *Interpreting Greek Tragedy: Myth, Poetry, Text*. Ithaca and London.

———. 1988. "Confusion and Concealment in Euripides' *Hippolytus*," *Metis*, 3: 263-282.

Segal, C. P. 1992. "Signs, Magic, and Letters in Euripides' *Hippolytus.*" In *Innovations of Antiquity*, ed. Ralph Hexter and Daniel Selden. New York and London: 429-455.

——. 1993. *Euripides and the Poetics of Sorrow*. Durham and London.

——.1994. *Singers, Heroes, and Gods in the* Odyssey. Ithaca and London.

Segal, E., ed. 1968. *Euripides: A Collection of Critical Essays*. Engelwood Cliffs, N.J.

Shaw, M. 1975. "The Female Intruder: Women in Fifth-century Drama," *CP* LXX: 255-66.

Smith, W. D. 1960. "Staging in the Central Scene in the *Hippolytos*," *TAPA* 91: 162-78.

Solmsen, F. 1973. "'Bad Shame' and Related Problems in Phaedra's Speech," *Hermes* 101: 420-5.

Sommerstein, A. 1988. "Notes on Euripides' *Hippolytos*," *BICS* 35: 23-41.

Spatz, L. 1982. *Aeschylus*. Boston.

Stanford, W. B., ed. 1965. *The Odyssey of Homer*. 2nd rev. ed. Vols. I, II, London.

Stevens, P. T. 1971. *Euripides: Andromache*. Oxford.

Strohm, H. 1957. *Euripides: Interpretationen zur dramatischen Form*. Munich.

Taplin, O. 1977. *The Stagecraft of Aeschylus*. Oxford.

——. 1978. *Greek Tragedy in Action*. Berkely and Los Angeles.

Thomson, G. D. 1954-1961. *Studies in Ancient Greek Society*. London.

——. 1966a. *Aeschylus and Athens: A Study in the Social Origins of Drama*, 3rd ed. London.

——. 1966b. *The Oresteia of Aeschylus*, rev. ed. Amsterdam.

Vellacott, P. 1975. *Ironic Drama: A Study of Euripides' Method and Meaning*. Cambridge.

——. 1984. *The Logic of Tragedy*. Durham, N.C.

Wace, A. J. B. and F. H. Stubbings., eds. 1962. *A Companion to Homer*. London.

Webster, T. B. L. 1936. *An Introduction to Sophocles*. Oxford.

——. 1962a. "Polity and Society: A Historical Commentary." In Wace and Stubbings 1962.

——. 1962b. "Preparation and Motivation in Greek Tragedy," *Classical Studies Bulletin Supplement* 14.

——. 1968. "Greek Tragedy." In *Fifty Years (and Twelve) of Classical Scholarship*. 2d ed. Oxford.

Webster, T. B. L. 1970. *The Greek Chorus*. London.

West, S. 1988., ed. *A Commentary on Homer's "Odyssey,"* bks. 1-4. 2nd ed. Oxford. Originally published 1981 in Italian under the title *Omero, Odissea, libri i-iv: Introduzione, testo e commento*. Fondazione Lorenzo Valla, Rome. In Heubeck, A., S. West, and J. B. Hainsworth, eds. 1988.

Whitman, C. H. 1951. *Sophocles: A Study of Heroic Humanism*. Cambridge, Mass.

———. 1958. *Homer and the Heroic Tradition*. Cambridge, Mass.

Williamson, M. 1990. "A Woman's Place in Euripides' *Medea*." In Powell 1990: 16-31.

Wilamowitz-Moellendorff, U. von 1875 *Analecta Euripedia*. Berlin.

Winnington-Ingram, R. P. 1960. "Hippolytus: a Study in Causation." In Entretiens sur l'antiquité classique, *Euripide*, Vol VI. Geneva.

———. 1980. *Sophocles: An Interpretation*. Cambridge.

Young, F. W. 1965. *Initiation Ceremonies: A Cross-Cultural Study of Status Dramatization*. Indianapolis, New York.

Young, S. P. 1953. *The Women of Greek Drama*. New York.

Zeitlin, F. 1985. "The Power of Aphrodite: Eros and the Boundaries of the Self in the Hippolytus." In Burian 1985: 52-111.

Zuntz, G. 1963. *The Political Plays of Euripides*. Manchester.

Zürcher, W. 1947. *Die Darstellung des Menschen im Drama des Euripides*. Schweiz. Beitr. z. Altertumswiss. 2. Basel.

Index

Achilles, 2, 10, 37n79, 48n119
action, 4-7, 9, 51, 55, 60, 64, 75-79, 82, 112, 115-118, 121-122, 130-131, 142-144, 148, 156, 158-163, 165, 168, 171-174 176-177, 179
actor, 4, 6, 37, 111-112, 116n6, 118, 174-175, 179
advice, 1, 3, 5, 8, 13, 15n26,16, 20, 22, 40- 42, 49, 51-56, 58, 73-74, 77-79, 81-82, 86, 106, 118, 122, 125, 130, 151n111, 159, 171-174
advisor, 2, 10, 74, 82, 179
advisory role, 6, 48, 58, 79n52, 163
Aeschylus, 1, 4, 5, 64, 69, 76, 122n26
Agamemnon, 48n144, 69n15, 97, 144n93, 145n95
Agamemnon, by Aeschylus, 69-70, 97
Agido, 4n7, 6, 48, 53, 83, 92, 136, 146, 153, 177
agonistic, 4-6, 10, 30-31, 48, 53, 58, 147, 154
agôn 'debate', 48, 53, 105, 113, 118, 133, 140-141, 144-147, 153-155, 160, 176, 178
agora 'assembly', 25
agoreuein 'speak in public', 5, 40, 45-46
aidôs 'shame', 141
Aigeus, 112

Aigisthos, 65-67, 69-73, 76, 86n81
ainos 'praise', 147n101, 153-154, 177-178. *See also* praise
Alcestis, 34n86, 57, 61
Alcman PMG 1, 4, 6, 35, 48, 53, 75n34, 83, 92, 114, 116, 136, 140, 144, 146; 43-45: 153, 177
Andromache, 5, 64, 76, 83-89, 90n93, 92-93, 99n112, 102n122, 109n143, 142n88, 145, 151n112
Andromache, by Euripides, 1, 2, 5, 64, 76, 83-92 *passim*; 802-819: 87; 866-880: 90; 93, 99n112, 101, 102n121, 109n143, 112, 121nn23-24, 124n32, 125nn35-36, 127n42, 132n60, 139n81, 140n83, 142n88, 143n89, 145, 151n112
Antikleia, 12
Aphrodite, 2, 17, 93, 98, 112, 116n6, 117, 119-121, 122n29, 125n36, 136n72, 139-140, 143n90, 148n104,149-150, 151n111, 152, 154, 160-161, 165n149, 166, 168n158, 169n161, 172-175, 177, 179
Apollo, 74, 93n100,128
approval, 1, 3, 5, 8, 21, 25, 41, 45, 52, 54, 86, 89, 118, 127, 157, 160, 178
Arete, 23n44, 33n72, 57, 61
Argo, 94

Index

Artemis, 109, 120, 121n23, 125, 129n52, 172-173, 179
Athena, 13, 16, 18, 19, 20n35, 29, 30n66, 46n112, 49, 52, 54, 60, 79
Athenian drama, 4, 6, 75, 116n4, 142n88, 146, 179
Austin, J. L., 9
authority: definition, 3; hierarchical, 8; institutional, 19; language/speech of, 3, 5; manifestations, 5; Nurse's, 1, 3, 5-6, 8, 10, 16, 18- 19, 22, 30, 33-38, 40, 42-43, 48, 53-54, 56, 58, 75-76, 78, 80, 82-83, 85, 92, 106, 108, 115-118, 126-128, 130, 138, 147, 160-162, 165, 174, 177-179; and old age, 3; and *paideia*, 8
Autolykos, 26-27

beggar (Odysseus desguised), 10, 24, 33, 42, 47-48, 52, 56, 58. *See also* Odysseus
blame, 1, 3, 10, 24, 33, 53-54, 56, 58, 82, 85, 89, 97, 115, 118, 137, 139, 147, 153-155, 163, 167, 169, 170. *See also* disapproval

Calame, Claude, 4, 75, 116, 146
captatio benevolentiae, 79, 91, 147, 152
chambermaid, 50, 51. *See also* maid/maids
children, 2, 3, 17, 77, 79-80, 87, 133, 142, 166, 172; of Medea, 93-108, 110, 113; of Phaedra, 133, 142-143, 173
Chilon, 128

Choephoroi. *See Libation-Bearers*
choral: aggregate, 4n6, 83, 136, 139; performances, 3-4, 35, 136, 179. *See also* performance/performances
Colchis, 94, 97, 100
common sense, 1, 76n36, 90, 126, 150n110
Conacher, D. J., 69
'contest of words'. *See agôn*
Corinth, 93-95, 111, 113
Corinthian women, 113,140n83
criticism, 65, 72, 76, 77, 78, 79, 86, 97, 103, 105, 139

Daulis, 65
debate. *See agôn*
Deianeira, 5, 64, 76-83, 86, 91, 112
Delphi, 84, 128
Demeter, 2, 15n25,16-17, 120
dia gunaikôn 'noblest of women', 34, 57, 61
didaskein 'teach/instruct', 38
directions, 3, 5, 8, 20-21, 36, 56, 58-59, 65, 75, 80-81, 105, 115, 118, 122, 173, 175, 179
director, 116n6, 118, 174-176
disapproval, 1, 3, 5, 8, 24, 33n73, 41, 54, 65, 67n8, 72, 79, 85n76, 86, 89, 91-92, 96n104, 97, 105, 118, 127, 154, 165, 171, 172n168
dmôiê 'handmaid', 9, 13, 30
Dolios, 18
draein/drân 'do/act', 122

education, 2-3, 19, 34, 38n85, 56n135. *See also paideia*

Electra, 65, 66n4, 69n15, 74-75, 76, 102n123, 146
Electra, by Euripides, 76n36, 78n46, 102n123, 146, 172n168
Eos, 149
epic, 1-3, 8-9, 10n9, 20n31, 48, 53, 78, 110n148, 179
epithet/epithets of Eurykleia, 3, 9, 12n16, 13n18, 14n22, 17, 33, 36n23, 56-57
ergon 'deed/act', 142
ethical formation, 2, 56
eukleês/ eukleeis 'with good reputation', 119-120, 143, 154, 169
eukleia 'good reputation', 125n36, 143n90, 148, 152-154, 176
Eumaios, 6, 11n14, 15n26, 20n37, 22, 27n53, 33n72, 36, 40, 42, 47n116, 55, 57, 59, 61
Eumenides, by Aeschylus, 74
Euripides, 1, 4-7, 64, 71n21, 76, 78n46, 83, 93n100, 94n102, 97n108, 98nn110-111, 99n113n115, 101n117, 105n131, 111, 115, 119nn14-16, 120n18,122n26, 127n41, 130n54, 133, 141n85, 142n88, 145, 150n109, 158, 159, 174n171
Eurykleia, 1-6, 8-61, 73n27, 80n55, 88, 106n132, 116, 128n49, 129-130, 166n151, 179
Eurynome, 10, 14n21, 15n25, 20n34, 32-33, 49, 50, 51-53
exemplum/exempla a fortiori, 149n108, 150, 152

experience, 3, 18, 19, 27, 35, 48, 53, 58, 83, 97, 100n116, 124, 127n45, 177

formula/formulaic, 9, 14, 20, 27n55, 33n72, 46n113, 52n130, 57n138

Garvie, A. F., 69
gnômês hodos 'course of thought' 132, 141, 144, 146
Goff, Barbara,115, 116, 179

Hagesikhora, 4n7, 6, 48, 53, 83, 92, 136, 146, 153, 177
hamartia, 134-135
Handmaid, 5, 64, 76, 83-86, 92-93, 99n112, 101, 102n121
handmaids, 12-13, 20, 66, 166. *See also* maids
Hekate, 121
Helen, 23n43, 28n58, 34n74, 57, 61, 93n100, 130n54, 144n93, 149n108, 151n111
Herington, 116, 146
Hermes, 66, 93n100
Hermione, 5, 64, 76n36, 83-92, 121n23, 125n35, 127n42, 132n60, 139n81, 145-146
hetairai 'companions', 161
hierarchy, 3-4, 6, 35, 75, 136, 146, 178-179
Hippolytus, 4, 30n64, 85n78, 116-120, 121n22, 122n25, 125n37, 126, 127n46, 129n52, 133, 134nn64-65, 136n12, 137-138, 140-142, 145, 147n102, 148, 150, 153, 155, 157-159, 160n131, 161-163, 164n145, 165-169, 170n163,

171, 172n166, 173-176, 178-179
Hippolytus, by Euripides, 1-6, 30n64, 48n119, 64, 77n42, 82n66, 83nn67-68, 84n70n73, 85n78, 87n84, 88nn85-87, 89nn88-89, 93, 96n106, 98n110, 99n113, 100n115, 102n121, 107nn134-137, 108, 110n148, 112-113; 115-180 *passim*; 176-177: 122; 186-188: 123; 189-197: 123; 207: 125; 236-238: 126; 252: 127; 261-266: 128; 267-270: 129; 284-287: 130; 288-300: 131; 301-303: 133; 336: 136; 344-352: 137; 358-361: 139; 391-402: 142; 431-432: 144; 433-436: 147; 473-481: 152; 482-485: 153; 490-497: 155; 501-502: 156; 507-515: 158; 521-524: 160; 601-615: 164; 656-660: 167; 695-701: 170; 702-703: 171; 704-705: 171; 706-709: 172; 725-731: 173
Homer, 1-10, 20n36, 23n43, 30, 34, 58, 61, 116
Homeric heroes, 10
housekeeper, 2, 13, 14, 16, 19, 34, 52n129, 61. *See also tamiê*
hubris, 151, 152
Hyllos, 76-79, 81-82
Hymn to Demeter, 2, 15n25, 16-17, 35, 37n79, 38n85, 50n125, 61

Iliad, 2, 9, 10, 23n42, 34n74, 37n79, 48n119, 61, 96n106

influence: of the Nurse, 2, 3, 6, 8, 16, 20, 30n64, 36, 40, 52-53, 58, 76, 92, 112, 146, 151, 174
Iolkos, 93-94
Ithaca, 5-6, 20n37, 26-27, 28n58, 36, 53

Jason, 93-97, 98n110, 100-109, 110n145, 111-113, 142n88
judgement: of the chorus, 153-154; of the Nurse, 16, 38, 56, 58, 60, 78, 104, 108, 113, 175

Kamerbeek, J. C., 81
kedna iduia 'devoted', 11, 22, 57, 60
khorêgos ' leader of the *khoros* (song and dance)', 4, 6, 8, 35, 75, 116, 118, 153, 179
khoros 'song and dance', 4, 8, 35, 48, 53, 75n34, 146, 153, 176, 177
Kilissa, 5, 64-75, 86n81, 87n84, 123, 130
Klytaimnestra, 64, 65-66, 67n8, 68n11, 69n15, 71-74, 76, 85n77, 86n81, 130
Knox, Bernard, 115, 117, 148, 156,
Korybantes, 121
Kreon, 95, 96, 98, 99n114, 101, 103, 107n136, 109, 111 154n114
kurios 'master', 6, 130

Laertes, 11, 12, 18, 19, 42, 55, 60
Libation-Bearers, by Aeschylus, 1, 2, 5, 23n43, 64-76 *passim*; 731-733: 66; 734-743: 67; 743-765: 68; 766-782: 71; 86n81,

Index 195

87n84, 120n21, 122n26, 123n30, 130, 172n168
logos 'speech', 69n16, 78, 111n148, 117, 118, 148n104

maia 'nurse', 15-16, 21, 29-30, 33n71, 37, 43, 47, 52, 57-58, 63, 88, 127
maid/maids, 5, 8-10, 12, 18, 21-22, 24, 29n63, 30n65, 31n67, 32-38, 40-42, 52-56, 58-61, 74n28, 84n70, 88n86, 99n112, 106n131, 124, 162, 166,169
mantis 'seer', 72n26, 126, 137-138, 147n101, 161, 178
Martin, Richard, 9-10, 20, 25, 31
maxim, 81n63, 107, 127, 128, 149n108, 150-151, 163, 178
Medea, 5, 64, 76n36, 85n77, 93-113, 122n28, 129n53, 138n79, 140n83, 151n112, 159n130
Medea, by Euripides, 1, 2, 5, 64, 76n36n40, 83n66n69, 84n70n73, 85n77, 86, 93-114 *passim*; 1-15: 94; 16-35: 95; 36-48: 99; 115-130: 108; 139-143: 109; 820-823: 111; 89-95: 104; 98-110: 106; 120n21, 121n23n25, 122n28, 124n32, 128n47, 129n53, 140n83, 142n88, 151n112, 154n114, 159n130, 166n151, 172n168
mêdea 'thoughts' 17, 18n31
mêkhanai 'devices', 84, 151-152, 169n159
Menelaos, 37n79, 83, 84n72, 86n80, 91, 130n54, 144n93, 145
menos 'strength', 16n28, 30-31, 40, 120

mental skills, 33, 61
Mentes, 13, 16n28, 30n66, 79n52
Mentor, 16n28, 30n66, 79n52
Messenger in *Medea*, 104
mêtis 'wisdom, craft', 27, 55
Murnaghan, Sheila, 26, 27, 55
muthos 'story, speech', 67, 78, 175.

Nagy, Gregory, 4, 27, 55, 75, 118, 146, 179
Neoptolemos, 84, 86n80, 91
nêpios 'infant', 21
noos 'mind', 27, 55
noou poluïdreiêisin 'with a mind that knows many things', 14, 57, 61
nosos 'sickness', 119, 142
Nurse/nurse: in *Andromache*, 83-92; in general, 1-7; in *Hippolytus*, 115-180; in *Libation-Bearers*, 64-76; in *Medea*, 93-114; in the *Odyssey*, 8-58; in *Women of Trachis*, 76-83

Odysseus, 2-3, 5-6, 8-10, 11n11, 12n17, 13-14, 15n25, 18, 21-33, 35-46, 47n116, 48-63, 73n27, 88n85, 129-130
Odyssey, 1, 2, 5-6, 8-63 *passim*; i 428-429: 11; i 430-435: 12; ii 345-347: 14; iv 750-753: 19; iv 754-757: 19; xix 22-25: 21; xix 353-356: 23; xix 378-381: 24; xix 386-393: 25; xix 399-404: 26; xix 467-475: 28; xix 482-490: 29; xix 492-498: 31; xix 500-502: 32; xx 147-156: 34; xxii 395-397: 37; xxii 417-418:

38; xxii 420-427: 39; xxii 428-429: 39; xxii 431-432: 39; xxii 481-484: 41; xxii 486-489: 41; xxii 491: 42; xxiii 115-116: 49; xxiii 289-296: 51; xxiii 52-57: 46; xxiii 5-9: 44; xxiii 70-79: 47; xxiii 9-14: 44; 73n27, 74n28, 79, 80n55, 88, 96n106, 106n132, 127n41, 128n49, 129, 179
oikos 'house', 116, 126
old age, 2, 37, 44, 48, 57, 61, 80, 82, 104n128, 107n137, 108, 127-128, 165, 178
old woman, 2, 9-10, 12-13, 15-17, 22-23, 25, 27-28, 32, 37-38, 40-41, 43, 45, 51-52, 57-58, 61-62, 80, 108, 128- 129
Ops, 11, 14, 34
orders, 1, 3, 5, 8-10, 13, 22, 34-36, 39, 41n93, 52-54, 56, 60, 65, 67n8, 72-73, 75-76, 106n152, 130, 173
Orestes, 65-76, 78n46, 91-92, 102n123, 121

Page, D. L., 104, 113
pai 'child', 86, 88-90, 124n34, 125-126, 131, 132n60, 165, 170
Paidagogos/paidagogos, 2, 56n135, 93, 98, 105n131
paideia 'education', 2, 3, 6, 8, 20n34, 34-36, 48, 52-53, 58, 82
Pan, 121
Parry, Milman, 9
Peisenor, 11, 14, 34
Peleus, 84, 85n78, 92n99, 145
Pelias, 94-95, 98

Penelope, 2, 5, 6, 8-10, 11n12, 15n25n27, 16, 18-25, 29, 30n65, 32-36, 38-61, 63, 79, 88, 96n106
performance/performances, 3, 5-6, 9-10, 25, 31, 35, 48, 53, 111, 136, 146, 176, 178
peripeteia 'reversal', 65, 76, 82, 91
periphrôn 'wise', 23, 33, 36, 57, 61
persuasion, 5, 7, 48, 58, 66n4, 73, 79, 82, 88-89, 90n95, 116-118, 132-133, 135n67, 146, 149, 157, 161-162, 165, 166n150, 177
Phaeacians, 24
Phaedra, 1, 4, 6, 48n119, 80, 82, 84n73, 87n84, 88n85, 89n88, 92, 96n106, 107n134, 108, 110n148, 115-180
pharmakon 'drug', 111n148, 141, 151-152, 159, 170
philai 'friends', 87, 124, 139, 143, 160n132, 169
philê 'dear, friend', 14n22, 33n71, 47, 52, 57, 58n138, 88, 131, 132n60
philoi 'friends', 65, 84, 103, 161, 177-178
Philoitios, 42, 55
Phoenix, 2, 37n79
Pickard-Cambridge, A, 112
Plato, 2, 18, 56; *Laws*, 2; *Protagoras*, 2, 18, 56
playwright, 116 n6, 174-175
poetics, 1, 3, 8, 19, 92, 114
polis 'city', 116
Poluarêtos 'the much prayed for', 27

poluidris 'knowing much', 47n117, 57, 61
praise, 1, 3, 10, 25, 45n108, 53, 54, 56, 58, 89n92, 115, 118, 128, 153-154, 177, 178. *See also* approval
Prometheus, 57, 61
Pucci, P., 97
pukimêdês 'with dense thoughts', 13, 14, 17, 22-23, 57, 61
pukina phresi mêde' ekhousa 'having dense thoughts in her mind', 17, 22-23, 57, 61
Pylos, 13, 14, 59

Racine, 1
reputation. *See eukleia*
respect, 2-3, 19, 22-23, 36, 38-39, 52-53, 72, 92, 120, 127-128, 136, 166, 178
rhesis, 76-77, 80, 83, 93, 101, 109
rhetorical skill, 79, 89, 152, 154, 174
role of the Nurse, 1, 2, 5, 64, 77, 126

Sappho, 4n8, 121n22, 138; fr.1 27-28:161; fr.130: 137n76; fr.160 :161; 177-178
scar, 25-28, 30, 46-47, 48n118, 54-55, 129
scenario, 174. *See also muthos*
Searle, J. R., 9
Segal, Charles, 28n58,115
sêma, 27, 46, 50, 55, 80, 128-129, 142
Seneca, 1, 120

sententia/sententiae, 87, 89, 93-95, 98, 103-104, 107, 124-125, 128
servant/servants, 2, 5, 9, 11, 13, 15n26, 18-19, 20n37, 24, 25n48, 27n53, 28n58, 29-30, 33, 34n74, 36-39, 40n89, 41-42, 49n121, 52-53, 66-67, 73-74, 76-77, 85-86, 88, 91, 102, 103n124, 105n131, 110-111, 113, 120n20, 121n25, 124, 136n72, 149nn106-107, 160n132, 167. *See also* maids
Seven Sages, 128
Shakespeare, 1
slave/slaves/slavery, 2, 12n15, 18n33, 19, 39, 65, 77-79, 83nn67-68, 84-85, 90, 103, 104n128
sophê 'clever', 128n48, 159, 166, 177
sophia 'cleverness, wisdom', 7, 112, 118, 160-161, 177-178
Sophocles, 1, 2, 4-5, 64, 70n20, 76, 78, 81, 102n123, 120n18, 122n26, 146, 172n168
sophoi, 'wise', 119, 128, 131, 150, 170-171, 178
sôphrôn/sôphrones 'moderate', 126n38, 139,143, 155, 171, 173
sôphrosunê 'moderation', 121n23, 138n79,139, 144, 156, 167, 173n170, 174
Sparta, 13-14, 24, 59
Spartan, 4n7, 75n34, 153, 177
speech: effective/effectiveness of 3, 5, 79- 80, 82, 92, 113, 117, 156; power of, 73, 116
'speech-act', 5, 9-10, 24-25, 53

198 *Index*

steward/stewardess, 2, 13-14, 17, 51, 110
stranger (Odysseus), 21- 24, 45, 54, 67, 91
suggestions, 5, 15n26, 20n34, 22, 32n68, 39n86, 40, 42, 49n121, 54-56, 130, 132, 152, 156
suicide, 80-82, 86n82, 89n88, 91-92, 101, 119-121, 140, 143, 166n150, 173, 175
suitors, 10, 15-18, 21, 29, 31, 35-38, 40, 44- 46, 48, 52, 54, 58n138, 59
sunergos 'ally', 161, 175
supplication, 29n62, 30n64, 103, 118n11, 130, 134-136, 157n123, 158-159, 163, 165, 172

tamiê 'steward', 2, 13, 14, 51, 61. See also steward/stewardess
teacher/Teacher, 2, 6, 18, 22-23, 33, 36, 56
tekhnai 'devices', 169. See also *mekhanai*
teknon 'child', 16, 21, 38, 40, 86, 88-91, 124, 125n36, 132, 165n148, 170-171
Telemakhos, 2, 5-6, 8-22, 24, 27, 29n63, 30n66, 32-34, 36-40, 42-43, 45, 47n116, 49-51, 53-56, 58-60, 62-63, 73n27, 79, 88n85
thalamêpolos 'chambermaid', 51
Theogony, by Hesiod, 56, 61, 161
therapaina 'handmaid', 76n37, 83, 85, 175
Theseus, 6, 117, 119-121, 129-130, 134-135, 145, 147-148, 150, 159, 167, 173, 175

Trachiniai. See Women of Trachis
tragedy, 1-5, 64, 67n8, 69, 71n21, 79, 81n63, 82, 83n68, 86n82, 88, 90n93, 92, 96n105, 112, 114, 119, 123n31, 124, 127n41, 129n52, 133n61, 145-146, 147n100, 168n158, 172n168, 179
Triptolemos, 57, 61
Troizen, 179
Troizenian women, 120, 140, 172, 177
Trophos/trophos 'nurse', 1-2, 4-5, 13, 23, 29, 37, 51, 56n135, 57, 63, 65, 74, 76n37, 83, 85-86, 121, 175n172. See also Nurse/nurse
'typical scene', 20
Tutor/tutor, 37n79, 79n52, 85n70, 93, 98, 101-105, 112-113

Vellacott, P., 104

wisdom, 1, 3, 7, 23, 25, 27, 33n72, 47, 57-58, 78, 91n97, 102n122, 113, 127-128, 131, 137, 141, 178
Women of Trachis, by Sophocles, 1, 2, 5, 64, 76-83 *passim*; 1-3: 81; 49-60: 77; 61-66: 78; 61-66: 78; 943-946: 82; 87n84, 91, 92, 112, 120n21, 121n25, 124n32

young girls, 3

Zeus, 17n31, 19, 20, 72, 110, 149

About the Author

Helen Pournara Karydas holds a B.A. in History and Archaeology and and a B.A. in English and American Studies from the University of Athens, a M.A. in English from Washington State University, and a M.A. and Ph.D. in Classics from the University of Washington. She has taught English, Latin, Greek, and Modern Greek at Washington State University and at the University of Washington, and she currently teaches Greek and Latin at the Boston Latin School. She has given lectures and presentations on Roman poetry, Greek epic and tragedy, and she has received many grants and fellowships from the National Endowment for the Humanities and also a Post Doctoral Fellowship from Harvard University.